Publicity's
Secret

How
Technoculture
Capitalizes on
Democracy

Jodi Dean

Cornell University Press

Ithaca & London

First published 2002 by Cornell University Press
First printing, Cornell Paperbacks, 2002

Printed in the United States of America

Library of Congress Cataloging-in-Publication Data

Dean, Jodi, 1962-
    Publicity's secret : how technoculture capitalizes on democracy / Jodi Dean.
        p. cm.
Includes bibliographical references and index.
    ISBN 0-8014-3814-4 (cloth : alk. paper)—ISBN 0-8104-8678-5 (pbk : alk. paper)
    1. Publicity. 2. Political science. 3. Culture. I. Title.
    HM1226 .D4 2002
    659—dc21

                                2002003715

Cornell University Press strives to use environmentally responsible suppliers and materials to the fullest extent possible in the publishing of its books. Such materials include vegetable-based, low-VOC inks and acid-free papers that are recycled, totally chlorine-free, or partly composed of nonwood fibers. For further information, visit our website at www.cornellpress.cornell.edu.

Cloth printing   10 9 8 7 6 5 4 3 2 1

Paperback printing   10 9 8 7 6 5 4 3 2 1

For my aunt, Anna Dean Johnson,
in love and gratitude

Contents

Acknowledgments   ix
Introduction
    Communicative Capitalism: The Ideological Matrix   1
1. Publicity's Secret   15
2. Conspiracy's Desire   47
3. Little Brothers   79
4. Celebrity's Drive   114
Conclusion
    Neo-Democracy   151
Notes   177
Index   205

Acknowledgments

As I began reflecting on all the people, places, and practices that established the conditions that enabled *Publicity's Secret* to be written, I was struck by the way that acknowledgments serve as a sort of academic prayer. More than a list of sponsors or funding agencies, that is to say, more than a commercial, acknowledgments are a way of giving thanks. They are not simply direct "thank you's," as in the increasingly lost art of the thank-you note. Rather, acknowledgments are givings of thanks in the presence of others, ways to let others know for what and for whom one is thankful. And no doubt because these are academic acknowledgments, and the others are expected for the most part to be academic others of some sort, the list is partial, specific to its context, not a broad, inclusive enactment of thankfulness. (I'm thinking here of my grandfather's Thanksgiving prayers. A good Southern Baptist, he could thank and thank until the children were crying and the gravy was lumpy. That may explain why my grandmother moved dinner time closer to the beginning of the day's first football game—the game provided the necessary closure of the prayer.) In any case, I now give thanks.

The Institute for Human Sciences in Vienna, Austria, is wonderful. Its support, generosity, good food, and encouragement provided the ideal environment for finishing *Publicity's Secret*. I am especially indebted to Cornelia Klinger, Klaus Nellen, and Anita Traninger for how they enriched my stay in Vienna.

I also thank Kjell Soleim and Haldis Haukanes of the Centre for Women's and Gender Research at the University of Bergen, Norway. Their invitations to speak at the conferences *Feminism 2000* (April 2000) and *Sexual Difference: Beyond Constructivism* (October 2000) instigated the reflections that became chapter 4.

Noortje Marres and Richard Rogers invited, criticized, inspired, taught, and entertained me in Budapest (July 2001, at a workshop on the social life of issues, "Competing Realities: The Social Lives of Issues on and off the Web") and Amsterdam (August 2001, at Maastricht Summer University, *Better Than Fantasy: Reality Engineering and the Computer*). Their work on issue networks on the Web helped me begin thinking more clearly about democratic alternatives to the public sphere. I hope to continue learning from and thinking with them.

Faculty research grants from Hobart and William Smith Colleges provided much needed financial support for this project. Challenges from HWS's political science students in the senior seminar on the public sphere provoked and sharpened some of the initial thinking that went into the book. Particularly helpful were Turk Johnson, Melissa Miller, and Aaron Trenor. I am also grateful to Andrew Heitman, Colleen McDonough, and Brian Whelan for their diligent and creative research assistance. Thanks as well to Paula Durbin-Westby for her careful work on the index and to manuscript editor Ange Romeo-Hall.

As is typical of academic work, many of the arguments in the book have benefited from comments, conversations, and criticisms that have taken place during panel discussions at meetings or during the question-and-answer period of seminars and talks. All too often some of the most helpful insights have come from someone whose name I don't know or who rushed out for coffee before I had a chance to catch them. At other times, the ideas emerged through the exchange itself, rather than coming from a specific remark. Nevertheless, I want to acknowledge the gift of these engagements. I also thank the following friends and colleagues for taking the time to read and comment on various chapters: Bill Chaloupka, Tom Dumm, Lee Quinby, Patchen Markell, Catherine Rice (my editor at Cornell University Press), Mike Shapiro, Alison Shonkwiler, John Shovlin, and Stephen White.

Paul Passavant has read countless drafts of the book's chapters. Even when disagreeing with some of the book's major claims (for example, that democracy can do without a notion of the public), he answered emergency phone calls and e-mails to help shore up my arguments when they started to wobble and I started to doubt them. He also provided that extra encouragement and support that got me through the lonely uncertainties of theory and writing. Thanks, then, to Paul, for the challenges and wonder you incite.

Early versions of chapters 1 and 3 were previously published in *Political Theory and Theory and Event*, respectively. They appear here with permission.

JODI DEAN

Vienna
December 16, 2001

Communicative Capitalism
The Ideological Matrix

The intense circulation of information in the networks of contemporary technoculture is trapped in a weird matrix: at just that moment when everything seems fully public, the media pulses with invocations of the secret. Secrets appear as markers of vulnerability. They stand in for that which is threatened by new technologies, providing a file for our anxieties about the mysteries of digital life: just what can really be done these days? *Corporations trade in our secrets. Surveillance cameras capture them. The government accesses them.* Secrets appear as lures, enticing us as ever-present objects of desire. Television hails an audience with promises to reveal all. Tabloids tempt us with the secrets of celebrity diets. *We want to know.* Secrets appear in waves. The Net overflows with secrets that wash across newspapers, magazines, and television shows in what we can barely resist experiencing as a global infostream. And if we want more, we can check out *Secrecy News* at http://www.fas.org/sgp/news/secrecy/index.html. *Somebody out there knows.*

Although we can no longer have secrets—they are already exposed on the Net—we can at least be them. When we are the content of databases, when our numericized and digitalized identities provide the content that circulates, the content that might momentarily interest or stimulate a stranger thousands of miles away, we become secrets. So we worry that secrets will be—and are—revealed, that in some way who we are as subjects, those precious dimensions of ourselves that we hold most dear, will be stained and tarnished by circulating as so much Net drivel. Yet, at the same time, we worry that our secrets won't be revealed, that who we are isn't significant enough to merit a byte of attention.

This excess of secrets is accompanied by its opposite, the presumed value of publicity. That is to say, technoculture materializes aspirations long associated with the public sphere. Indeed, it sometimes seems a machinery produced by the very ideals inspiring democracy. Advances in computer-mediated interaction provide ever-greater numbers of people with access to information. No longer a privilege of the elite, information is available to anyone with a computer. Similarly, more people have opportunities to register their thoughts and opinions on political topics than ever before. Chat rooms, cybersalons, and e-zines are just some of the new electronic spaces in which people can participate as equals in processes of collective will formation.[1] Describing the early nineties ecstasy over the possibilities of computer democracy, Hubertus Buchstein writes,

> If one accepts the claims of the optimists, the new technology seems to match all the basic requirements of Habermas's normative theory of the democratic public sphere: it is a universal, anti-hierarchical, complex, and demanding mode of interaction. Because it offers universal access, uncoerced communication, freedom of expression, an unrestricted agenda, participation outside of traditional political institutions and generates public opinion through processes of discussion, the Internet looks like the most ideal speech situation.[2]

As Buchstein makes clear, the ideal of a public links together a whole complex of norms.[3] Of course the meanings of these norms change with respect to time and place. They combine with each other in different ways. Particular valences move to the fore, only to be supplanted by another set of emphases. The shifts and ambiguities within notions of the public facilitate the invocation of the public as a critical referent, as a force to which an appeal is made in the name of democratic modes of governance. Some of the primary normative elements linked together through publicity include ideals of openness, inclusivity, visibility, equality, accessibility, and rationality.

Technoculture is thus often heralded for the ways it enhances democracy by realizing norms of publicity. From virtual town halls to the chat and opining of apparently already politicized netizens, computer-mediated interaction has been proffered as democracy's salvation (as if all we ever lacked was information or access). Indeed, new technologies seem to solve the old republican worry about whether deliberative democracy can work in societies too big for face-to-face discussion. In technoculture we can have the privilege and convenience of democracy without the unsightly mess, as millions and millions of people participate in a great big public sphere.

Or at least that's the fantasy. New media present themselves for and as a democratic public. They present themselves *for* a democratic public in their eager offering of information, access, and opportunity. They present themselves *as* a democratic public when the very fact of networked communications comes to mean democratization, when expansions in the infrastructure of the information society are assumed to be enactments of a demos. As the surfeit of secrets attests, however, the expansion and intensification of communication and entertainment networks yield not democracy but something else entirely—communicative capitalism.[4]

In communicative capitalism, what has been heralded as central to enlightenment ideals of democracy takes material form in new technologies.[5] Access, information, and communication as well as open networks of discussion and opinion formation are conditions for rule by the public that seem to have been realized through global telecommunications. But instead of leading to more equitable distributions of wealth and influence, instead of enabling the emergence of a richer variety in modes of living and practices of freedom, the deluge of screens and spectacles undermines political opportunity and efficacy for most of the world's peoples. As Saskia Sassen's research on the impact of economic globalization on sovereignty and territoriality makes clear, the speed, simultaneity, and interconnectivity of electronic telecommunications networks produce massive distortions and concentrations of wealth.[6] Not only does the possibility of superprofits in the finance and services complex lead to hypermobility in capital and the devalorization of manufacturing, but financial markets themselves acquire the capacity to discipline national governments. In the United States, moreover, the proliferation of media has been accompanied by a shift in political participation. Rather than actively organized in parties and unions, politics has become a domain of financially mediated and professionalized practices centered on advertising, public relations, and the means of mass communication. Indeed, with the commodification of communication, more and more domains of life seem to have been reformatted in terms of market and spectacle, as if valuation itself had been rewritten in binary code. Bluntly put, the standards of a finance- and consumption-driven entertainment culture set the very terms of democratic governance today. In effect, changing the system—organizing against and challenging communicative capitalism—seems to require strengthening the system: how else to get out the message than to raise the money, buy the television time, register the domain names, build the websites, and craft the accessible, user-friendly, spectacular message? Democracy demands publicity.

This book considers the impasse in an ideal of publicity that works simultaneously to encode democratic practice and market global technoculture: precisely those technologies that materialize a promise of full political access and inclusion drive an economic formation whose brutalities render democracy worthless for the majority of people.[7] In consideration of this impasse, I focus on the ways in which publicity and secrecy provide the matrix through which we think about democracy and within which technoculture is materialized. Publicity, I argue, is the ideology of technoculture. The meme: publicity is to technoculture what liberalism is to capitalism. It is the ideology that constitutes the truth conditions of global, information-age capital. Publicity is what makes today's communicative capitalism seem perfectly natural.

It may seem strange to use a notion like ideology in connection with contemporary technoculture. For one, ideology seems to reduce the problem of domination to the idea that "people don't know what they're doing." Insofar as it highlights "false consciousness," the concept suggests that people are naive and ignorant, duped into mindless compliance with oppressive structures of power. For another, ideology appears especially ill chosen as a concept for today. The present has already been characterized as post-ideological, as plagued by the collapse of overarching worldviews and the crass triumph of a pervasive cynicism. And finally, doesn't a notion of ideology posit a totality that flies in the face of the proliferation of competing conceptions of the real that marks the familiar strangeness of an alien age?[8]

Responding to these problems as they appear in traditional Marxist accounts of ideology, Slavoj Žižek has upgraded the concept, making it particularly productive for critical engagement with communicative capitalism.[9] He uses Lacanian psychoanalysis in a reconfiguration of ideology that theorizes the ways our deepest commitments bind us to practices of domination. Žižek agrees that ideology critique today must do more than simply "unmask" the lie. In fact, his reconfiguration of ideology builds from this point as it finds ideology in the pervasive cynicism of contemporary technoculture: precisely because cynicism already incorporates an ironic distance from official culture and everyday social reality, unmasking is clearly pointless. People know very well what they are doing, but they do it nevertheless.

The grocery store where I shop, for example, supplies customers with a discount card. When customers "swipe" their cards, the store gets information about our buying habits, product preferences, and so forth. I willingly let the store track me and my purchases, facilitate its edging out of smaller, local markets, and help it tighten its hold on my consumption—and often for savings of only about thirty cents. I'm neither coerced into using my shopper's card nor deceived about its function. I'm not deluded into thinking that the store really wants to save me money. I cynically accept that it is trying to make money, and I actually help it do so by shopping there. I don't need a critique of ideology to expose my false consciousness. I have a critical distance from my actions, from what I'm doing, but still I do it.

The Žižekian concept of ideology draws attention to the persistence of these actions that fly in the face of what one knows. If we know that we are "just going through the motions" or "just doing something for the sake of appearances," we are still acting. This acting, moreover, materializes a set of beliefs. It reproduces not only the belief that appearances matter, say, but also the very appearances that matter, the appearances in which we believe. This materialized set of beliefs is ideology. So, in Žižek's account of ideology, actions and belief go together. They stand apart from knowledge. Actions manifest an underlying belief that persists, regardless of what one knows.

Michael Wolff's book *Burn Rate*, an account of the gold rush years of the Internet, clarifies the way acting persists in the face of seemingly contrary knowledge. In the book, Wolff describes his generally futile efforts to attract high-level investment to his Internet company. No one was interested in talking with him until he was mentioned in an article on the front page of the *Wall Street Journal*. Wolff writes:

> Because publicity is the currency of our time, it is not unreasonable to assume that there is a Darwinistic capitalistic earning process to such riches. Even people who should know better (even those for whom manipulations of the press are a daily accomplishment) are almost always impressed, or rankled, by someone else's publicity. Even though nine times out of ten that fix is in, we somehow can't help regarding rich people as having earned their money, or publicity hounds as deserving their fame.[10]

We know that publicity, like money, has no intrinsic worth or merit, that it is easily manipulated and has no connection with some kind of value inhering in its object; nevertheless, we act as if we did not have this knowledge—*we can't help it*. We tend to be impressed by publicity, even when we know that it is generated by press agents. In fact, this is what makes the practice persist, it's why press agents are employed—it makes no sense to try to get publicity if one doesn't believe that others believe in its value. Our actions therefore suggest that we believe publicity is a sign of something more, something real—the belief of others, an amorphous public, perhaps, that something is impressive, worth remarking on. Even when we know that a huge campaign and massive amounts of money enabled something to garner a great deal of media attention, we tend to act as if the fact of this attention resulted from the item's meriting attention.

Žižek emphasizes that belief is much more than an individual's internal mental or emotional state. Belief is "radically exterior, embodied in the practical, effective procedure of people."[11] So, on one level, belief refers to what we do even when we know better—like crossing our fingers for good luck or laughing at a joke that isn't funny. On another level, however, belief involves more than one's own actions; as the example from *Burn Rate* demonstrates, belief is exteriorized in larger cultural practices and technologies. In effect, no one today *really* has to believe; our institutions do it for us. In going through the motions, we uphold these institutions, again materializing a belief through our actions even if we don't think we believe it. As materialized belief, the practices imbricated in institutions and technologies relieve of us of our duty to believe. They do it for us, freeing us up to think other things, providing us with a distance that enables us to think ourselves detached from ideology even as we act in accordance with it.

I've argued thus far that Žižek's notion of ideology is useful for theorizing contemporary technoculture. Unlike accounts that view ideology as that false consciousness that dupes people into participating in their own oppression, Žižek's version shifts the effects of ideology from what we *know* to what we *do*, especially when we know better. Indeed, he emphasizes that the basic formula for fetishism in general is "I know, but nevertheless . . ."[12] With his emphasis on the way that doing persists in a fetishistic disavowal of what we know, Žižek avoids the elitist and condescending positing of a theoretical position outside of ideology; indeed, he frequently observes that such a positing is the ideological move par excellence. And even better, this shift to an account of ideology in terms of practices of belief highlights a particularly pressing paradox of contemporary cynicism—the way cynical reason resists "unmasking" because it never claims to believe; rather, it materializes belief through actions that continue regardless of what we know.

But what about the third problem of ideology that I mentioned, the problem of presuming totality in the face of competing conceptions of the real? There are two answers. First, ideology in no way implies a consistent and unified set of beliefs and practices. Second, the clashes of ideas and identities exacerbated by contemporary technoculture should nevertheless be considered as situated within the larger networks of communicative capitalism. Žižek's notion of ideology doesn't require a conception of a totalized social field. But recognizing the new configurations of power brought about by the technocultural materialization of publicity and struggling within and against them may well entail a political choice to view communicative capitalism as the hegemonic formation to be resisted today.

The very strangeness of competing conceptions of the real sometimes hinders organized resistance to global corporate control and opposition to the commercialization of ever more domains of life. The plurality of worldviews deflects our attention from the materialized effects of technocultural practices that ultimately limit freedom for many as they produce a commodified vision of diverse freedoms readily open for consumption by the few. The problem today, in other words, is the opposite of that assumed in critical rejections of the notion of totality: how does the valorization of fragmentation and contingency benefit global capital by preventing it from being understood as a totalizing modality of power? How does the emphasis on multiplicity and plurality naturalize communicative capitalism to such an extent that a fresh, transformed, and invigorated democratic life is nearly unimaginable?

As I've said, Žižek emphasizes that actions produce social reality (the beliefs and appearances that matter). This social reality is in turn sustained by the "as if," an underlying fantasy of what things are like. For example, a key technocultural fantasy is that "the truth is out there." Such a fantasy informs desires to click, link, search, and surf cyberia's networks. We fantasize that we'll find the truth, even when we know that we won't, that any specific truth or answer is but a momentary fragment. Still, the fantasy keeps us looking. Fantasy, then, covers over the gaps, antagonisms, inconsistencies, and lacks that pervade the social field. Another way of understanding ideology is thus as a bunch of inconsistencies held together by a fantasy and materialized through everyday actions, practices, technologies, and institutions.

Consequently, Žižek's corresponding notion of ideology critique operates not at the level of knowledge but at the level of the fantasy that sustains belief, that informs action. Its basic procedure involves identifying what fantasy holds belief together and analyzing the way it enables us to escape a certain problem, trauma, or deadlock. For example, some theories of postmodernity read cyberculture in terms of fluid, fragmented, and multiple subjectivities. These theories emphasize identity play, experimentation, and varieties of forms of life made available in virtual communities. On the one hand, these diverse subjectivities seem a conglomeration of gaps and contingencies held together by nothing at all. On the other hand, they may be better understood in terms of the beliefs materialized through their practical enactment, beliefs that circulate within a matrix of publicity and secrecy and reinforce the compulsions, restrictions, and inequalities of communicative capitalism.[13] This idea links back to my point regarding the political choice for a theory of ideology insofar as it considers the contemporary in terms of a hegemonic field. Of course, postmodernity has ushered in new modes of subjectivization, but we may miss their inscription within and reproduction of communicative capitalism if we fail to read them in terms of ideology.

So, using ideology critique to consider the notion of the public, we can ask: why is there a belief in something like a public? Clearly, the public is not reducible to the set of opinions gathered by pollsters. Nor is it the same as those who vote or even register to vote (if it were, no one would worry about low voter turnout). And given the widespread differences of culture, practice, language, information, race, class, gender, sexuality, ability, opportunity, status, religion, education, and so forth, it doesn't make sense to understand "the public" as referring to all of us; the very terms of such a universal "we" have been heavily criticized and rightly rejected for well over a hundred years. Why, then, does the idea of the public persist?

Ideology critique begins to answer the question by considering the fantasy that holds the belief in the public together. By recognizing the indeterminacy and polysemy of "the public," the critique does not assume that the norms of publicity are in any way fixed but presumes that a variety of conflicting meanings will infuse the concept, as they do any ideological formation. Yet it asks what links these conflicting norms, what enables them to cohere into some kind of norm-complex. I contend that the fantasy of social unity animates belief in the public.[14] The public sphere provides democratic theory with the reassuring fantasy of a unitary site and subject of democratic governance. Democracy appears convincing, in other words, because of the fantasy that we are all part of the same thing, members of the same public. We don't have to worry about violence and factionalism tearing us apart, nor do we need to concern ourselves with racial, sexual, or class conflict, because none of these matters is fundamental; the public is a unity, the collective subject capable of self-governance.

With this underlying fantasy of unity, the ideal of a public displaces antagonism from politics. This antagonism reappears, however, in the form of the secret. Protecting the fantasy of a unitary public, a political "all," from its own impossibility, the secret renders as a contingent gap what is really the fact of the fundamental split, antagonism, and rupture of politics. In her definitive account of secrecy, Sisela Bok explains that the secret "presupposes separation, a setting apart of the secret from the non-secret, and of keepers of a secret from those excluded. . . . The separation between insider and outsider is inherent in secrecy; and to think something secret is already to envisage potential conflict between what insiders conceal and outsiders want to inspect or lay bare."[15] As the other of publicity, secrecy suggests a world of relationships that have been withheld. Yet it marks a division even as it invokes the possibility that this division can be repaired once what is hidden has been revealed. The actual contents of any secret are therefore immaterial. The secret is a form that can be filled in by all sorts of contents and fantasies—economic secrets, military secrets, sexual secrets, secrets to power, wealth, and immortality.[16] Thus what is at stake is not content but connection, the relationship within and between communities held together and apart within a matrix of secrecy and publicity. The secret promises that a democratic public is within reach—as soon as everything is known. All that is necessary to realize the ideal of the public is to uncover these secrets, to bring them to light.

Under norms of publicity, the secret appears exceptional, an exception to the rule that everything should be out in the open. This exceptional dimension, moreover, imbues the secret with mystery and importance. *Why must it remain hidden? What is so vital or wonderful or horrific that it can't be revealed?* Georg Simmel writes, "the secret produces an immense enlargement of life: numerous contents of life cannot even emerge in the presence of full publicity. The secret offers, so to speak, the possibility of a second world alongside the manifest world; and the latter is decisively influenced by the former."[17] This mystical possibility of a hidden world, this capacity to produce a realm beyond the given in which anything might happen, gives the secret an irresistible aura. What makes the exception produced by secrecy so attractive is the possibility of a hidden power, a power that can make new worlds as well as shape the old one. Those who share in the secret seem to have this kind of power, and they seem to have it by virtue of sharing in the secret—this is what sets them apart.

At the same time that it promises the realization of democracy once nothing is hidden, secrecy generates the very sense of a public that it presupposes. The secret designates that which is desired to be known, that which impels its own discovery but which hasn't yet been disclosed.[18] In so doing, it presupposes a subject that desires, discovers, and knows, a subject from whom nothing should be withheld. The public as that subject with a right to know is thus an effect of the injunction to reveal. A public isn't exactly called into being through publicity, through revelation or exposure; rather, publicity as a system or set of belief-materializing practices produces the sense of the public. The public is symbolic; it doesn't exist, but it still has effects.

Each chapter of this book sets out a different exploration of the matrix of publicity and secrecy. The first two chapters consider the ways in which democracy has been configured within this matrix. The third and fourth focus on how the matrix of publicity and secrecy is materialized in communication technologies. I won't reproduce the division between these chapters by summarizing them here. Instead, I address some of the ideas that traverse and link the chapters.

Žižek argues that the "democratic attitude is always based upon a certain fetishistic split: *I know very well* (that the democratic form is just a form spoiled by stains of 'pathological' imbalance), *but just the same* (I act as if democracy were possible)."[19] For Žižek, this split is the source of democracy's strength; it is an internal limit to democracy, a limit that enables democracy to acknowledge that its failures result not from an external enemy but from something unavoidable within itself. In chapter 1, I show how Jeremy Bentham's defense of publicity is structured as such a fetishistic disavowal, the disavowal of a constitutive split in the public held in place by the secret.

My argument differs from Žižek's position in two respects, however. First, insofar as the split constituting democracy is held in place by the secret, insofar as the secret incites publicity as a "system of distrust," to use Bentham's term, democratic possibility is undermined. A fundamental compulsion to know generates suspicions that displace that element of belief in the belief of the other which is necessary to sustain social institutions. When everyone is supposed to know, when everyone has a right to know, no one has to—or should—believe. Informed citizens find out for themselves. The democratic split, then, insofar as it is held in place by the secret, is not the source of democratic strength. Conceived in terms of publicity, democracy turns on its internal failures in order to expose them. I draw out these effects of suspicion in chapter 2.

Second, the concrete materialization of publicity in contemporary technoculture, a materialization incited by the lure of the secret and the fantasy of its revelation, replaces the fetishistic split with the conviction that democracy is possible; in other words, the knowledge that democracy is not possible is eliminated, replaced by the sense that new technologies enable full access, full inclusion, full exchange of opinions, and so forth. This new sense is expressed in some theories of deliberative democracy, specifically those that follow Habermas in emphasizing large-scale societal rationalization processes. It also provides the ideological support for the networked communications of the new global economy. I take up this theme in chapter 3 by juxtaposing a brief history of computing with Habermas's attempt to introduce communicative rationality as an alternative to instrumental rationality. In technoculture, I argue, there's no difference.

One of the ways communicative capitalism naturalizes itself as "just the way things are" in the most heavily networked technocultural domains is through the production of new subjectivities oriented around conspiracy and celebrity. The circulating practices of mediatized technocultural experience interpellate these subjects via an ideology of publicity. Thus an additional argument in this book is that the democratic subject today is interpellated as a conspiring subject, on the one hand, and as a celebrity, on the other. These two different accounts of technocultural subjectivization rely on two different relations to the secret. The conspiratorial injunction that we search for information invokes the secret as a hidden object of desire. In celebrity, the secret becomes the "scoop," a bit of forgettable dreck circulating in entertainment culture's networks of drive.

The promise that answers are out there, that all we have to do is find the evidence and make the links and then we will know, animates efforts to extend the reach of communication networks and intensify mediatization of various domains of life. As I explain in chapter 2, this reduction of freedom to a freedom of information makes technocultural practices look a lot like those of conspiracy theorists. Conspiracy theorists search for the truth, doubting everything they find, always suspecting that something else remains to be revealed. This impulse, this suspicion, is materialized in technoculture's cameras and screens. The subject of democracy wants to know—and this very desire to know drives the new information economy. In this respect, then, the technocultural subject is a conspiring subject

At the same time, a drive to be known, and the presumption

that what matters is what is known, provides a different economy of subjectivization, one in which the technocultural subject is configured as a celebrity. This is my argument in chapter 4. The continued configuring of publicity as the ideology of technoculture operates through the production of publicized subjects: in recognizing themselves as known, celebrity subjects posit a public that knows them. And what makes people think they are known? It is an effect of multiply-integrated communication technologies: people experience themselves as informationalized, their secrets already compiled in databases, their sins and successes already circulating on the Internet. Indeed, popular culture frequently invokes the contemporary ubiquity of celebrity. Ads from Hewlett Packard that poke fun at celebrity chefs while lamenting the little-knownness of inventors and television programs that worry about hidden cameras in high school women's bathrooms are but two examples. Much ink has been spilled lamenting the effects of the surveillance society but relatively little on the enjoyments that may accompany the sense that one is known, *that people know who we are, that we are somebody*. An inquiry into these pleasures, it seems to me, is crucial for any analysis of the contemporary production of the democratic subject as the consuming subject of communicative capitalism.

An ideal of the public sphere, a veneration of publicity, has been central to democratic theory. Such an ideal now functions ideologically, protecting the circulation of global capital in its assumption that communicative expansion enhances democracy. Put more strongly, the realization of publicity turns into its opposite. Instead of public deliberation, we have private acts of consumption. Instead of public governance, we have the privatized control of corporations. Instead of rule through thoughtful deliberation, we have the compulsive forces of markets. In effect, the notion of the public sphere has become the weakest link in what we might imagine as the networks of democracy today.

I can't resolve this paradox (although this would be a good place for a commercial for a follow-up book that provides a fabulous, practical, and all around socially beneficial alternative). My inquiry, in other words, doesn't amend its critique of the public with a reassuring model for new possibilities. In fact, it's clear to me that such a model, such a reassurance, cannot and should not precede critique; instead, it follows from it. The demand for a reassuring alternative threatens to cut off critique before it starts, thus protecting some generally dominant forms of thinking before asking why, exactly, such thinking should be protected.[20] Rather than offering a model, then, I conclude by reflecting on different practices and configurations of democratic politics. I imagine these configurations as "neo-democracies" that simultaneously work through and challenge the power of the matrix. But these imaginings are incitements, not sustained arguments, because again my primary purpose is to unsettle the taken-for-grantedness of the link between publicity and democracy. No one today should accept a model of political life that would work just as well as a motto for Microsoft or AT&T. This book shows why.

CHAPTER ONE

Publicity's Secret

Critical democratic theory and capitalist technoculture converge today around a single point—the necessity of publicity. Publicity is the organizing element of democratic politics and the golden ring of infotainment society.

Few on the Left are willing to theorize democracy without some notion of publicity. No matter how entangled politics becomes in networks of sentiment and spectacle, many continue to think that rule by "the public" is enhanced by practices that enable the production and dissemination of public opinion, practices generally implicated in technologies of surveillance and expectations of entertainment. So they emphasize public spheres, oppositional counterpublics, and subaltern counterpublics as if these concepts referred to more than media productions, interest groups, or rhetorical categories invoked to mobilize a particular point of view. They underscore the public's right to know, positing, as it were, a secret, the knowledge of which would solve the problems preventing the public from being all that it can be. In short, many critical democratic theorists assume the democratic potential of an ideal of publicity even as they avoid explaining what, today, that potential might be.

Publicity is also the governing concept of the information age. Contemporary technoculture relies on the conviction that the solution to any problem is publicity. More information, greater (faster, better, cheaper!) access seems the only answer. It doesn't even matter what the question is. People are supposed to find out for themselves, to search for the truth, to form their own opinions—and the way to do that is through new communication technologies. Conversely, in matters as disparate as science, violence, economic success, and personal career advancement, the key concern is with publicity, getting the finding before the public, alerting the public to a potential danger, gaining mindshare or brand identity, again by taking advantage of networked communications. These days, for example, subcultural success is depicted less in terms of the risk of "selling out" than it is in the promise of "making it," that is, of gaining larger cultural recognition. If something isn't public(ized), it doesn't seem to exist at all.

It would be stupid to claim that technologies, practices, and norms of publicity never make valuable contributions to democratic politics. Suspicious inquiries into potential wrongdoing often uncover real crimes and produce significant reforms. That an event is spectacularized, we might say, doesn't mean that it won't have positive political effects.[1] It is nevertheless also clear that the vast networks of news and entertainment that enable contemporary practices of democracy also threaten democratic forms of life—especially as they produce searching, suspicious subjects ever clicking for more information, ever drawn to uncover the secret and find out for themselves.

To call into question the obviousness of publicity as a norm of contemporary democracy, to unsettle its taken-for-grantedness in the hope of opening up possibilities for alternate understandings and practices of democratic politics, I look at publicity's limit—the secret. My concern is not with the contents of secrets or the proper determination of what should be made public. Rather, my concern involves what this "making public" means with respect to the function of the secret within a logic of publicity. I argue that democratic politics has been formatted through a dynamic of concealment and disclosure, through a primary opposition between what is hidden and what is revealed. The ideal of a public typically posited in Enlightenment-based theories of democracy relies on the secret as its disavowed basis. The secret, in other words, is the fundamental limit point of democratic validity. Publicity requires the secret.

This requirement can be understood in at least three different ways. First, publicity requires the secret constitutively, as that point of exclusion through which the public becomes intelligible. Using Jeremy Bentham's *Essay on Political Tactics*, I consider this aspect of the conceptual link between publicity and secrecy. I show how Bentham structures a notion of the public by splitting it and then by disavowing this split. The secret holds open this dis-avowed split in the public.

Second, the public requires the secret in a concrete, historical way. During the Enlightenment, a democratic ideal of publicity emerged through encounters with the sovereign privilege of se-crecy, with the aura of mystery and exception provided by the hid-den.[2] In the course of these encounters, publicity linked up with ideas of the reasonable and the moral. I make this point through a reading of Jürgen Habermas's and Reinhart Koselleck's accounts of Freemasonry. My interest is in the paradox of publicity as a prin-ciple of reason that is realized in the mystical practices of exclu-sive secret societies.

Third, the public requires the secret in a sense that I understand as ideological. As theorized by Slavoj Žižek, ideology refers to the "generative matrix that regulates the relationship between the vis-ible and the non-visible, between imaginable and non-imaginable, as well as changes in this relationship."[3] Publicity and secrecy, I argue, provide the matrix establishing the parameters of what can be seen, imagined, practiced, and understood as democracy. Put somewhat differently, publicity is the organizing concept of the ideology pushing us to make the links and discover the secrets.

Although this ideological dimension of the secret as that which protects the public from its own impossibility is present in Ben-tham's notion of publicity as a system of distrust and in the En-lightenment practices analyzed by Habermas and Koselleck, it is most readily apparent today. Indeed, it is central to the dynamic of a mediatized technoculture glutted with screens and celebrity, scandal and indignation. Within publicity as technocultural ideol-ogy, the secret sustains the fantasy that disparate audiences are a collectivity capable of being represented as a unitary actor or polit-ical site. Such a fantasy, I argue, damages possibilities for democ-racy as it becomes materialized in practices of spectacle and suspi-cion. This third way of conceptualizing the link between secrecy and publicity, then, considers the ideological aspect of publicity as a merging of the first two aspects: publicity in its ideological form is not an *unrealized* ideal, a mask or a fiction. Rather, publicity as ideology *realizes* the ideal and in so doing renders it a nightmare.

As I show three different relations between secrecy and public-ity—constitutive exclusion, concrete historical, and ideological—I am also presenting a dynamic of conceptual change. The localization of democratic potential in the public is inevitably accompanied by perceptions of conflict, failure, and weakness in the public. Differently put, the more publicity is idealized as the key to democracy, the greater the pressure to materialize a public that can live up to or instantiate an ideal of public reason. Yet precisely this concrete materialization of an ideal of publicity unleashes and multiplies those suspicions that undermine the public sphere. Publicity, in realizing or materializing itself in the practices of contemporary technoculture, negates itself. The materialization of publicity makes explicit the antagonisms within the ideology of the public sphere.

A System of Distrust

What fantasy underpins the practices that materialize belief in the public? Bentham's account of the law of publicity points to the secret. The secret fills out the gap between two competing notions of the public, compensating in advance for the public's failure to serve as the unitary subject of democracy. It points to the fantasy of unity, to the inclusive social body to come after the hidden barrier to its realization has been disclosed. Practices of concealment and revelation materialize belief in this fantasy, making the public appear as precisely that subject from whom secrets are kept and in whom a right to know is embedded.

Two notions of the public inform Bentham's attack on government by secrecy.[4] First, Bentham supports the idea of a powerful, incorruptible, undeniably certain, public tribunal that unites "all the wisdom and justice of the nation" and "decides the destiny of public men."[5] I refer to this universal public tribunal as the public-supposed-to-know.[6] What it knows is less important than this public's fundamental claim *to know*, its constant, active *knowing*. Second, Bentham defends the public-supposed-to-know against a different notion of the public, the public-supposed-to-believe. With a flux of conflicting opinions, this public is easily seduced and unable to judge its true interests. Its judgments stem from trust ("belief in the belief of the other") rather than knowledge.

Bentham introduces this split in the public when he addresses objections to the principle of publicity. He explains that some defend government by secrecy with the argument that the public lacks a capacity for judgment. But this view, he argues, mistakenly unifies what is in fact divided: the public is actually split into three classes—the many who have no time for public affairs, the middle who believe through the judgments of others, and the few who judge for themselves on the basis of the available information. Bentham is clear that the many and the middle can't *really* judge. Guided by their needs and desires, they are inconstant and likely to err. The third class, however, is certain and constant. It has the ability needed to judge but not the information it needs to judge well: "if this class judge ill, it is because it is ignorant of the facts—because it does not possess the necessary particulars for forming a good judgment."[7] So rather than trumping the public-supposed-to-believe with the public-supposed-to-know, Bentham builds both concepts into a system of publicity.[8] Publicity will supply the information, the facts, that will stabilize and guide the judgment of the public-supposed-to-know.

Interestingly, Bentham allows that the benefits that information provides to the judging portion of the public don't directly impact the mass of people at the bottom. Instead, there is a trickle-down effect that leads to the betterment of those in the middle class because they adopt for themselves the opinions of the small, well-informed, judging class. The way the middle class forms its opinions doesn't change through enlightenment; it still believes. It becomes enlightened not because its beliefs are replaced by knowledge directly but because it believes through the more certain knowledge of others, that is, through the few who judge well. It believes that others believe; its opinion is that others have an opinion that is valid, knowledgeable, well informed. The law of publicity doesn't transform the public-supposed-to-believe into the public-supposed-to-know; it affirms the split within the public, giving some the certainty of knowledge necessary for judgment while positing others who believe in them.

That part of the public believes but doesn't know should not be read as a failure of publicity or an exclusionary limiting of the public. On the contrary, that not everybody knows is necessary to sustain the fantasy of the public. It reassures Bentham as well as his audience that they need not worry about the middle and the many making all sorts of horrible decisions, sticking their noses into political matters that they don't understand, and generally disrupting the order of things. The split public secures in advance precisely that barrier to a tribunal of the many that enables Bentham to appeal to a principle of publicity. He can argue for a public tribunal because he can be sure that the whole public won't *really* judge.

The public is constant and inconstant, informed and ignorant, knowing and believing. The limits of each notion are deferred, displaced through the invocation of the opposing concept. Of course, this deferral is asymmetrical. For even as the belief of the two lower classes operates at a distance, always as a belief in the public-supposed-to-know, their belief has to stop somewhere; it has to rely on the sense that *someone* in fact knows. This is where publicity as a principle comes in. Publicity provides the information that enables the public-supposed-to-believe to believe that someone knows.

Recall that Bentham's argument against those who oppose publicity on the grounds that the public is ruled by passion and ignorance emphasizes the competence and certainty of the judging class. The institutional conditions of government by secrecy hinder this class from judging well; they prevent the public-supposed-to-know from knowing. This judging portion of the public is constant and certain, but its certainty is suspended, held out as the possibility that the public will judge well so long as it has the proper information. What publicity as a system provides is the possibility of informed judgment, the guarantee that someone will know, even though no one can say precisely who. Publicity holds out the possibility of good judgment to the public-supposed-to-believe. From this angle, the public-supposed-to-know seems only that presupposition necessary for the public-supposed-to-believe. It provides the guarantee of knowledge that stabilizes belief. The public-supposed-to-believe, then, should not be reduced to a failure of enlightenment or seen in mass culture terms as a bunch of pleasure-seeking dupes. Nor should the public-supposed-to-believe be interpreted as Bentham's cynical rejection of the ideal of a constant and universal public tribunal, a reductive acceptance of the way things are instead of a utopian embrace of the way things might be. On the contrary, the public-supposed-to-believe installs that element of believing through the other necessary for publicity to function as a system of democratic governance. It marks the important place of social ties rooted in trust.

That the judging class acts for the lower two classes frees up the lower classes to amuse themselves.[9] Because they are not involved in finding information and making judgments, they can enjoy publicity's pleasures, *"the amusement which results from it."*[10] For them, publication of the goings-on in the assembly is entertainment. Bentham thus sees added value in freeing some in the public from the duty to judge—a measurably happier nation. So the pleasures of publicity enable the multitude of "all classes in society" to become more attached to and confident in government.[11] Just as the lower classes act and judge through the third class, so does the judging class enjoy through the lower classes. Again, what sustains the fantasy of the public is the barrier to its realization, the unlikelihood that everyone will be burdened by having to dig around for information, weigh it, evaluate it, and really make a judgment.

In Bentham's discussion, certainty is held out as a promise, a possibility. It is never simply grounded in a particular set of facts. Indeed, the very certainty of the public precedes and justifies its right to know the facts. The information that proves the truth of public judgment is out there, although it may be (and is always) withheld, out of reach. To this extent, the authority of the public-supposed-to-know carries with it an aura, a sense of mystery. *How do they know?*

The answer is the secret, or more precisely, the secret is the answer. The secret fills out the gap and conceals the inconsistency between the public-supposed-to-know and the public-supposed-to-believe. It holds open the reassuring possibility that the judging public will judge correctly, the possibility in which the believing public needs to believe. The secret marks the absence necessary to sustain belief in the public-supposed-to-know. It's that missing information warranting the rightness of the opinion of the public tribunal. Once they have the information, the truth, their judgment will embody the certainty they already have.

For example, Bentham presents the enemies of publicity—the malefactor, the tyrant, and the indolent man—as benefiting from secrecy. These three have good reason to flee from the judgments of public opinion: they have already forfeited their reputations. They are already guilty. Their very preference for secrecy is a sign of their guilt: "Suspicion always attaches to mystery. It thinks it sees a crime where it beholds an affectation of secrecy; and it is rarely deceived. For why should we hide ourselves if we do not dread being seen?"[12] The certainty with which the public knows in these cases indicates in advance that there is something for it to know. Suspicion is justified. Someone is guilty. The innocent, the good, and the wise have nothing to fear. The public tribunal knows the secret guilt of the malefactor, tyrant, and indolent man, and this is why they hide. Ultimately, the mysterious power of the public-supposed-to-know, its certainty, its fundamental, underlying rightness, is secured by the secret—that key to representational power that had been reserved to the king. The secret is the gap linking together knowledge and belief, the basis upon which some believe in the certain knowledge of others.

The public sutured together through the secret thus incorporates a certain ambivalence.[13] On the one hand, its certainty is reassuring. One can take confidence that it will judge rightly, that given the right information, it will provide a retroactive interpretation of what has been revealed such that the meaning of whatever is uncovered will be clear. On the other hand, this public is overwhelmingly suspicious, even paranoid. In Bentham's words, the regime of publicity is a "system of *distrust*."[14] Publicity operates through the threat of publication, through the motivating force that accompanies risk of exposure and desire for attention. Without that risk, there can be no public. In fact, we might even say that the enjoyment that publicity promises to the many and the middle provides the energy driving its suspicions: its threat to reveal only exerts a pressure insofar as it can transform the transgressive secret enjoyment of some (the malefactor, the tyrant, the indolent) into the spectacular public enjoyment of others. The suspicion that something has been withheld, that the information needed for judging properly is hidden and needs to be exposed, sustains this system. Nothing can or should escape its gaze.

As I mentioned, the law of publicity does not simply provide information that will stabilize the judgment of the public tribunal; that judgment is already there. No, this law is a practice-generating program installed into the social for the very production of the public. Demanding that nothing be concealed, this law posits and in so doing interpellates the public tribunal. It provides the objects of judgment, the issues to try. Publicity holds out the promise of revelation, the lure of the secret. Its pervasive mistrust drives the will to seek out and expose. At the same time, the certainty of the public-supposed-to-know becomes materialized in practices of revelation and disclosure as the guarantee that its search is justified, right, and universally valid.

Freemasons Rule the World!

If the public depends on a prior command to reveal, how is the validity of this command established? My answer is that it is not established. Rather, it is simply the condition for the possibility of the invocation of the public. As such a condition, it is presumed as a principle of reason. I make this argument by looking at secrecy as the historical context for the emergence of publicity as a normative ideal in the Enlightenment. How did the public come to be imbued with an authority to know? Through what process did a form of power based on uncovering the secret and a politics of suspicion, surveillance, and unmasking install itself in the name of democracy, as the very meaning of popular sovereignty?[15]

For answers to these questions, I take up work by Jürgen Habermas and Reinhart Koselleck. Each provides a compelling analysis of the social materialization of "the public" in seventeenth-and eighteenth-century Europe as that which can be invoked as a critical authority. Both Habermas and Koselleck describe the appearance of the critical invocation of the public in the increasingly autonomous sphere of letters: critics, first of art and literature and later of absolutist governments, spoke in the name of public opinion. Both link as well this critical invocation to the reconstitution of political authority under the bourgeoisie: they agree that the materialization of the public depends on the protections provided by secrecy and that the materialization proceeds through the production of suspicious subjectivities. In effect, both answer the question regarding the validity of the command to reveal in the same way: in the course of the political changes in seventeenth-and eighteenth-century Europe, the political was reconstituted such that publicity came to carry with it an irreducible claim to reason.

Yet the differences in Habermas's and Koselleck's accounts of the practices through which the political was reconfigured lead them to opposing assessments of public power. Habermas describes publicity as a "principle of control" that attempts to change the terms and conditions of political authority even as it "renounce[s] the form of a claim to rule."[16] Publicity is a new form of control that, wrapped in the universality, accessibility, and *in-*

escapableness of reason, presents itself as the guarantor of legitimacy by remaking the political terrain in its own terms. In contrast, what Habermas understands as the rationalization of authority, Koselleck interprets as ideology.[17] For Koselleck, the emergence of the public as the warrant for a claim to rule is less the triumph of reason than the mystical transfer of the aura of power from the monarch to society via the conjurations of the critics (and indeed, Koselleck's repeated use of "conjure" presents a stark contrast with Habermas's language of reason, rationality, and law). So, despite the fact that Koselleck is the theorist who emphasizes the rituals and arcana of Freemasonry, Habermas is the one whose failure to maintain the split between the public-supposed-to-know and the public-supposed-to-believe makes uncovering the secrets the key to democracy. For him, the command to reveal really is rational; it isn't simply a taking over of reason's function, as it is for Koselleck. In other words, Habermas's account of the concrete realization of publicity as a norm of reason should be read as its own inversion, that is, as an account of the processes through which popular sovereignty is configured as a politics of suspicion.

I begin with Koselleck, whose *Critique and Crisis* preceded and influenced Habermas's *Structural Transformation of the Public Sphere*. Koselleck views the Enlightenment as a triumph of hypocrisy and dogmatism that reiterates the structure of the absolutist state. Just as the Hobbesian sovereign appears as a command of reason outside political conflict, so is the authority of the public justified via a separation from politics effected through a claim to reason.

Koselleck's argument proceeds from the rise of absolutism out of religious civil war. Drawing from Hobbes, Koselleck reads absolutism in terms of a constitutive split between politics and morality, a split held in place by the sovereign decision as the imposition of reason. To end the wars of religion and find a political solution capable of preventing moral convictions from destroying political order, Hobbes posits reason as a third authority. Reason, in this case a rational decision for security, can provide the fundament that will keep morality and politics separate. For Hobbes, the result and instantiation of this reason is the sovereign. Beyond politics and morality, his decision grounds law in an act of pure will."[18]

The Hobbesian subject, Koselleck argues, is also split. It exists in two domains—the exterior political sphere of acts subject to law and the interior moral sphere of conscience. Here Koselleck emphasizes Hobbes's formulation that man is "in secret free." By separating internal conscience from external acts, the absolutist state allows for a space of free will, belief, and conscience that is neutralized in the political domain. In effect, this space is the secret at the heart of the absolutist state, the secret that man as a human being has been eliminated from the structure of the state.

Indeed, the state's claim to neutrality depends on this omission: the formal legality of laws renders them rational, not their content. Law derives from the exceptional will of the sovereign. It can rationally protect its subjects only to the extent that it is immunized from the turmoil of their moral and political disputes. Before the law, then, subjects are the same, bound to obedience. In themselves, however, they are free to believe what they like.

Koselleck reads Locke's account of "The Law of Opinion or Reputation" as a broadening of Hobbes's interior conscience into a secret morality. For Locke, citizens' views about virtue and vice are more than private opinions; they are judgments with the character of moral laws. They matter. So in Locke's view, as in that of Hobbes, these judgments remain secret from the state, but Locke expands their scope. Instead of confined to the individual, these judgments receive "their universally obligatory character from an unspoken accord of the citizens, 'by a secret and tacite consent.' " Instead of confined to matters of conscience, the judgments of this secret bourgeois morality now "determine the moral value of human actions."[19] Actions that were once subject only to the laws of the sovereign are now subject to the praise and blame of one's fellow citizens, to the law of reputation. And as Bentham would come to argue, this public opinion would inevitably be right.

Freemasonry institutionalized Locke's law of reputation and censure.[20] Koselleck explains that the lodges were secret inner spaces within the absolutist state, spaces that were separated from the political by the very mysteries whose protections enabled the lodges to serve indirectly as a counter to the state. "Freedom in secret," Koselleck writes, "became the secret of freedom."[21] The lodges were ritualized enactments of nonfamilial, nonmarket relations outside of the state; they provided forms of association and experiences of connection beyond those delimited by absolutism. On the one hand, this freedom was established by the new bonds of belief created by shared initiation into Freemasonry's arcana—the organization's ritual and hierarchy demanded that some believe in others' arcane knowledge. Members were thus bound together through the secret as well as through their exceptional position in relation to the absolutist state. On the other hand, the mysteries of Freemasonry imbued it with the aura of the unknown. This aura competed with the aura of the crown, countering the representational power of the sovereign with its own mysterious authority. Being free in secret was externalized in Freemasonry.

More specifically, secrecy enabled the interior space of the conscience to expand into larger social connections. "Joint participation in the same arcanum" linked initiates from various classes and estates, establishing a secret mutuality that "separated the brethren from the rest of the outside world." It attached members to the lodge by making them suspicious of outsiders: "A ceaselessly evoked fear of 'betrayal' contributed to an increasing consciousness of one's own new world, and of one's duty to serve it."[22] Secrecy also functioned as a disciplinary mechanism, providing an incentive for initiates to practice the obedience necessary for advancement into the higher ranks of the lodge. To achieve enlightenment, initiates had to submit themselves to the authority of the Masonic leaders, a leadership that, in some versions, remained invisible to those in the lower orders. Those who believed, in other words, had simply to believe that there were some above them who knew. Koselleck notes that lodge practice materialized this belief: the Bavarian Order of Illuminati instituted an elaborate secret reporting system, requiring brethren to write extensive monthly reports on themselves and each other. Application to and promotion within the Illuminati included the filling out of a thirty-two-page questionnaire consisting of several hundred questions aimed at revealing the various dimensions of the candidate. Koselleck writes: "Here the secret was initially considered a vehicle of moral education, as 'man's leaning toward the hidden and mysterious is used in a way so advantageous to morality,' but at the same it delivered the neophyte to the 'moral regimen,' to that 'directorate of tolerance' which on the strength of the secret was already terrorizing brethren in the name of morality."[23] At each stage of initiation, ritual practices enabled adepts to believe that others believed. Functionally, then, the secret enabled equality *and* hierarchy; it replaced the distinctions characteristic of the old regime with a new elitism of rank, knowledge, and enlightenment.

Of course, Masons could not guarantee that members would keep the secret. Consequently, they had to substitute moral force for coercive force. They had to produce their own law, to obey a law they gave themselves. Because of their position outside the state, therefore, Masons judged themselves in accordance with their own moral standards. In practice, this meant that the lodges trained their members to judge, to invoke and follow the law of reputation and censure. The need for secrecy thus installed trust, duty, and self-control at the basis of Freemasonry's social order. The sense of being entitled to judge, an entitlement Bentham invests in the public, emerges in Freemasonry out of the ritualized transmission of rites and arcana. As the process of initiation works on the wills, actions, and bodies of lodge members, they interiorize a set of beliefs and habits of judgment. They believe in their order even as they must increasingly distrust the world outside.

Koselleck emphasizes that this new form of social pressure, this new moral force that had to forego direct coercion, "was always simultaneously an act of passing moral judgment on the State."[24] As he explains:

> What the secret made possible was one's seclusion from the outside world, which in turn led to a form of social existence which included the moral qualification to sit in judgment on that outside world. The medium of the secret widened the private conscience into a society; the society came to be a large conscience, a conscience of the world from which the society voluntarily excluded itself by way of the secret.[25]

The secret rituals of Freemasonry allowed this moral interior to expand and, in so doing, to emerge as a counter to a politically, and increasingly morally, unworthy state. Because it distinguished itself from the absolutist state as deliberately nonpolitical and avowedly moral, Freemasonry threatened state sovereignty. As Koselleck writes: "political absence in the name of morality turned out to be an indirect political presence."[26] The system of values circulated secretly, linking lodges in a shared spirit, a con-

spiracy, of judgment. Extracted from the political field of the absolutist state, the morality nourished in secret could claim a new dominion, a sovereignty of reason apart from, and above, politics.
Like absolutist sovereignty itself, this morality was exceptional.
Like absolutist sovereignty, it too made a claim to reason.

For Koselleck, Masonic secrecy is the key to enlightenment:
Freemasonry's mysteries and arcana established a network within
the state, indeed, a network that traversed and transgressed the
boundaries of the European states, a network that occupied the
same location of exception claimed for the sovereign. Concealment protected practices of freedom and new forms of alliance as it
produced a unity by sustaining a division between those supposed
to know and those supposed to believe. The sense of an entitlement to judge grew out of practices of belief in the context of suspicion. Because Koselleck anchors this judging in secrecy, moreover, he can theorize bourgeois morality as a trump, a power play, a
dogmatism that rejects as tyranny any power that it itself does not
accept or justify. The lodges did not engage politically. In this refusal, they replaced action with moralizing judgment.

Koselleck does not ignore the influence of the republic of letters. In fact, he observes that criticism's rise to prominence took
the same course as Freemasonry's: its initial separation from the
absolutist state became the basis of an authoritative right to judgment. Moreover, as the influence of the bourgeoisie enabled them
increasingly to challenge the state's legitimacy, criticism "assumed the role Locke had at one time assigned to moral censorship; it became the spokesman of public opinion."[27] Claiming a capacity to argue both for and against a position, critics represented
themselves in terms of the triumph of reason. That is to say, they
grounded their claim to a right and capacity to judge in their claim
to reason. They could judge because they were reasonable. And
their reason was the same as public reason.

Accordingly, anything or anyone unwilling to be subjected to
their critical gaze, the gaze of the public, was automatically suspect. The invisible authority circulating secretly throughout the
lodges thereby extended its reach, representing itself to itself as
"public" as it became oriented to a reading audience and more directly political in its criticism of the state. The opinion of this new
public, its assessment of the rightness or legitimacy of that which
it judged, established the terrain and terms of the political—pre

cisely because the public sphere was beyond, above, politics. At the same time, the invisible authority of Enlightenment morality continued to present itself as universal, rational, and above politics.

Although Jürgen Habermas's theory of the bourgeois public sphere is widely read for its account of publicity as the rational achievement of Enlightenment universality, it also, and perhaps surprisingly, acknowledges the constitutive place of the secret. Habermas considers two links between publicity and secrecy. The first involves Hobbes. Habermas reverses Koselleck's reading of Hobbes, emphasizing not the publicity of the sovereign and the secrecy of the subject but the emergence of rational legal norms. Habermas writes: "Historically, the polemical claim of this kind of rationality was developed, in conjunction with the critical public debate among private people, against the reliance of princely authority on secrets of state. Just as secrecy was supposed to serve the maintenance of sovereignty based on *voluntas*, so publicity was supposed to serve the promotion of legislation based on *ratio*."[28] The secret, in other words, was crucial to sovereign power. It protected decisions based on will, ensuring that they were the prerogative of the king and that they were not subject to any competing authority. In this context, publicity was appealed to as a new kind of rationality. Publicity provided a way to counter, to rationalize, arbitrary sovereign power by subjecting it to the scrutiny of reason.

But Habermas's next argument is the one I want to emphasize. Taking up the practices out of which the sense of a public sphere emerged, Habermas includes in his account of salons and coffeehouses the secret societies typical of Freemasonry. He writes:

> The decisive element was not so much the political equality of the members but their exclusiveness in relation to the political realm of absolutism as such: social equality was possible at first only as an equality outside the state. The coming together of private people into a public was therefore anticipated in secret, as a public sphere still existing largely behind closed doors. . . . Reason, which through public use of the rational faculty was to be realized in the rational communication of a public consisting of rational human beings, itself needed to be protected from becoming public because

it was a threat to any and all relations of domination. As long as publicity had its seat in the secret chanceries of the prince, reason could not reveal itself directly. Its sphere of publicity had still to rely on secrecy; its public, even as a public, remained internal. . . . This recalls Lessing's famous statement about Freemasonry, which at that time was a broader European phenomenon: it was just as old as bourgeois society—"if indeed bourgeois society is not merely the offspring of Freemasonry."[29]

Here Habermas complicates the equation of reason and publicity, secrecy and will, that he employs in his discussion of Hobbes. For Habermas, secret societies were proto-publics. Secrecy was a condition for the publicity of reason. Outside the state, Freemasonry's claim to reason transforms it into something "more public" than the state or government. Precisely because secret societies endeavored to cultivate reason in their adepts, they better represent the public sphere than do nonsecret associations based in custom and tradition. Masonic brothers, as they transmitted their principles for enlightenment, their rational measures for moral discipline and self-cultivation, were, for all their esoterica, vehicles for the reconstitution of political society in terms of a public sphere.[30]

Habermas combines this reading of secret societies as rational proto-publics with an interpretation of the publicity of the sovereign as mere spectacle. The sovereign's publicity was an irrational aura of power that was fashioned through practices of display before an audience. Unlike the audience-oriented publicity of the king, real publicity, in Habermas's view, has nothing to do with spectacle and display. In fact, it may well be secret. So again, Habermas's point is that in the historical context of the absolutist state, the norms of reason thought to underlie an expansion of the rights and liberties of the people had to be protected from prying eyes. They depended on remaining hidden.[31]

The usual emphasis on Habermas's discussion of the family and the literary public thus needs to be complicated by attention to Habermas's account of the emergence of a public sphere against and through secrecy. Private people came together as a public *in secret*. Practiced secretly within the lodges, publicity as a set of claims to reason countered the secrecy at the core of the absolutist state. Masonic principles of reason had to remain secret because they challenged this state's sovereignty.

The secrecy of the public, then, is not as paradoxical as it first seems: what matters for Habermas is the claim to reason, not the claim to inclusivity. Associations that judge, that reflect, on the basis of reason are for Habermas by definition public. They are the tribunal that inevitably and inevitably rightly judges. What is interesting is that despite the fact that Habermas seems to reiterate Koselleck's account of Freemasonry as a vehicle for the cultivation and circulation of the law of censure and reputation, Habermas ends up accepting Freemasonry's claims. Whereas Koselleck finds the Masons and Illuminati ultimately hypocritical in their subversion of the absolutist state through moral trumping, Habermas treats them as part of a general Enlightenment process of the rationalization of power. Emphasizing the rationality of Freemasonry, Habermas positions them as a public-supposed-to-know, a public whose absolute certainty is a product of practices of critical reflection. In contrast, Freemasonry in Koselleck's account works as a split public. As a public-supposed-to-believe, it is an affiliation conjured up through rituals, arcana, conspiracy, and mystery. As a public-supposed-to-know, it relies on certainty, knowledge, and unerring judgment. What holds it together is its secrecy, its position beyond the boundary of the state, as well as its fantasy of a powerful, unifying knowledge.

Of course, Habermas's account of the emergence of the bourgeois public sphere is more than a discussion of changes in the logic and terms of governance. It also includes a theorization of the ways in which these changes are linked to a reconfiguration of subjectivity. The lodges do not play much of a role in this theorization. Instead, Habermas emphasizes the domestic sphere and the literary public. With respect to the former, he focuses on the autonomy of the bourgeois subject. With respect to the latter, he considers the importance of self-clarity or transparency. Paradoxically, these emphases lead to precisely that "system of distrust" or suspicious subjectivity that Koselleck associates with secret societies.

Habermas depicts the self-understanding of the bourgeois family in terms of private autonomy. The family, he writes, "seemed to be established voluntarily and by free individuals and to be maintained without coercion; it seemed to rest on the lasting community of love on the part of two spouses; it seemed to permit the non-instrumental development of all faculties that mark cultivated personality."[32] Ideally (and Habermas acknowledges the real existing gender inequities in the bourgeois family), each spouse entered into the marriage consensually. Ideally, each spouse freely remained a family member, choosing to do so because of the fulfillment family life enabled. The ideal of the family, then, was the ideal of an emancipated inner world, a world of purely human relations in contrast to the competition and commodification within the market.

The novel provided a vehicle for the exploration of the personality cultivated within the family. Not only did structural changes in literary genres introduce new forms of psychological identification and experimentation, but the rise of reading circles extended the practices of exploration and reflection from the immediacy of the family to a larger social audience. In the literary public sphere, Habermas writes, "the subjectivity originating in the interiority of the conjugal family, by communicating with itself, attained clarity about itself."[33] Rather than irrevocably opaque and unspeakable, the subjectivity Habermas theorizes strives for transparency. It is fundamentally open and ready for discussion. Interiority is to be communicated; it is not simply the condition of communication but its content.

For Habermas, interiority designates a field of conscience that comes under the domain of the moral law, a field that is autonomous in the Kantian sense. To understand and realize itself as free, the subject needs self-clarity; it needs to reflect—and to be able to reflect—on its motivations and affections. To understand and realize itself as moral, as in keeping with the law, the subject orients itself toward publicity, toward a larger audience of which it is a part, one, and toward universally knowable and valid principles, two. Interiority emerges through practices of self-clarification and public presentation.

The problem with Habermas's account appears in his acceptance of Rousseau's and Kant's notion that one can be forced to be free. This force underlies the necessity of transparency: freedom depends on attaining clarity about the pure will.[34] The autonomy that depends on clarity is always in need of revelation, mistrustful of what is hidden from it, what could secretly be enslaving it. Precisely because freedom depends on this information, belief is dangerous. It opens up the possibility that the will is not free but determined by something outside itself. Without critical reflection, then, there can be no freedom. As Kant explains in the preface to the *Critique of Pure Reason*: "Religion through its sanctity and law-giving through its majesty may seek to exempt themselves from it [criticism]. But they then awaken just suspicion, and cannot claim the sincere respect which reason accords only to that which has been able to sustain the test of free and open examination."[35] So the autonomous subject in need of clarity is also the suspicious subject. Habermas cannot account for the invasive character of the demands of publicity because for him they are the same as the demands of reason.

The seriousness of Habermas's omission becomes evident in those instances when he acknowledges that the subjectivity emerging in the family was oriented toward an audience. Recall that the orientation to an audience was an aspect of the publicity of the king. In connecting this orientation to the family, Habermas enables, first, the conceptual transfer of the monarch's aura to the public. Now the public is imbued with that extra element that compels compliance just because it is there. More specifically, when attached to the sovereign, audience orientation connotes the force of display, the ineluctable mystery or "Thing" that gives the king his "kingness." Yet, whereas the sovereign's aura was linked to his exceptional position, to his secrecy or power of concealment, the aura of the public functions differently. When Habermas brings audience orientation together with the subjectivity emerging in the bourgeois family, he connects it to the command to reveal, to publicity as a system of distrust. The aura, the irreducible element of authority, now gives a presumption of rationality to the injunction that nothing be concealed. This presumption complicates publicity's link to the privilege of display: now publicity serves as a norm embodying the rightness of the demand to disclose, a norm premised on suspicion of the hidden.

Second, Habermas's account of the subject's orientation to an audience suggests less a reasoning subject than one deeply bound to the opinions of others (although this may well be the same thing). The subject in need of transparency is compelled (by reason and freedom) to create and present itself before a judging and normalizing audience of others. This normalizing and judging role was already present in Locke's account of the public tribunal in terms of the law of reputation and censure. In Habermas, however, this impact of publicity on behavior is dissolved into publicity's equation with reason, an equation that assumes publicity's rationality and uses this assumption to increase publicity's compulsive force.

Habermas's bourgeois public sphere relies on a fantasy of unity. Just as the autonomy of the bourgeois subject is the result of reflective self-clarification, so does critical debate lead to a free, enlightened public. Indeed, for Habermas, critical debate *is* the very process of transforming the public-supposed-to-believe into the public-supposed-to-know. Discussion is a kind of purification through which what is revealed is held up to the scrutiny of reflection. With consensus as the anchor, the ultimate outcome of the critical exchange of reasons in the public sphere, there is never any doubt about the rightness of public judgment. All it needs is information.

Habermasochism

Although radical in the Enlightenment, the certainty of reflection pervades contemporary technoculture. From an affiliation born of arcane contents, of reason, ritual, and abstracted knowledge, the public has emerged as the model for reasonable, democratic, political attachment. The suspicious demands of a public-supposed-to-know have escaped the salon's small discussion groups and Freemasonry's secret societies and taken material form as the basis of science, law, politics, and media. New technologies have virtually eliminated the barrier to the realization of the public sphere. In the networks of mediated technoculture, there seems to be no difference between the judging public, the many, and the middle. The demand to know goes all the way down. It extends throughout the social as, on the one hand, the compulsion to search, find, and link exteriorizes belief in technologies of dissemination and surveillance and as, on the other, the idea that each person is entitled to an opinion changes the terms of inclusivity.

That the public has a right to know is one of the most prominent political clichés.[36] It's the mantra, the meme, the ideology of the information age. It's the presumption that powers the new networked economy of nonstop media and seamless interconnection. Why did we need an "information superhighway" (the now quaint term for the Internet that politicians such as Al Gore and Newt

Gingrich used to generate publicity for networked communications in the early nineties)? Because we needed to be informed. Information makes us strong, makes us "us." It justifies our certainty in our convictions. In a statement taking for granted the link between publicity and suspicion, Joseph Nye and William Owens write,

> Knowledge, more than ever before, is power. The one country that can best lead the information revolution will be more powerful than any other. . . . This advantage stems from Cold War investments and America's open society, thanks to which it dominates important communications and information processing technologies—space-based surveillance, direct broadcasting, high-speed computers—and has an unparalleled ability to integrate complex information systems.[37]

The society of complex telecommunications, for Nye and Owens, is the society of suspicion. It presumes that all should be revealed. It knows that it has the power to compel this revelation. And it has technologies that can make it happen.

Fax, voice mail, e-mail, website, pager, cell, answering service, satellite, television, telephone, magazine, newspaper, instant paperback—what links them is the way they mediate the relations of the connected to one another, integrating the wired into a web that acts as if the facts, the information, the secrets are but a link away. Encoding information through the binary of secrecy and publicity, contemporary technoculture formats the networks of influence, opportunity, access, and desire. It sets the terms and conditions for affiliation and resistance, regulation and compliance. Notice, for example, how information published in the past in major news forums becomes a scoop, something new and significant: "Timothy Leary Cooperated with the FBI." Notice the way that public knowledge becomes condensed as what *you* know. If the information age is the new political hegemony, its ideology is the public sphere. The presumed value of information—the public must know—morphs political action into compliant practices of consumption: good citizens must have magazines, televisions, Internet access. Without *USA Today*'s colorful polls and info-bites, how would we know what we think? How would we represent ourselves to ourselves as citizens? How would we know what and how to opine, to judge, as a public?

It's odd that, in a society of spectacle and simulacra, publicity has continued purchase as a critical political and moral ideal, that it refers to more than celebrity, PR, and the fears of superstars. It's odder still that theorists such as Nancy Fraser can presume that today publicity needs no defense: "I am going to take as a basic premise for this chapter that something like Habermas's idea of the public sphere is indispensable to critical social theory and to democratic political practice."[38] As I see it, the new configuration of technology, publicity, and secrecy in the information age pushes us to challenge the premise of the public sphere, indeed, to think about the ways publicity functions as technocultural ideology.

Adding an "s" to the theorization of the public in no way suffices as a response to this challenge.[39] Habermas, in work I discuss more thoroughly in chapter 4, follows Fraser in appealing to multiple, differentiated publics as a solution to the problem of a unitary public sphere.[40] But the multiple publics argument is more confusing than it is convincing. The "s" gives a sameness and equality to radically different networks and spaces. It creates the illusion of options in some sort of marketplace of ideas and opportunities. And despite its best intentions, the multiple public spheres approach reinforces the priority of an official public sphere as the goal, arbiter, and ideal of inclusion. This appears in Habermas's account in his language of "center" and "periphery," in his emphasis on the porosity of publics to each other, and in his notion of the "final authority" of the public. In short, with Habermas's references to "the" public and his notion of the public as an audience before which "actors" appear, appeal to "the rules" of communication, and claim that the public must be "informed" and "convinced," it is hard to find any different(iated) public spheres at all.

In his initial account of the public sphere, Habermas opposes two versions of publicity, one oriented toward critique and one oriented toward consumption.[41] He links critical publicity to reason, with the requirement that everything included in public discussion be open to critique. He connects consumer-oriented publicity with staging and manipulation. Here public opinion does not arise out of critical debate; it is engineered through advertising or "pub-

lic relations." This engineering, for Habermas, distorts the normative force of publicity. Public relations treats the public sphere as a
political space, a space of conflict, power, and engagement, rather
than as a space for critical-rational judgment. Habermas acknowledges that public relations may very well effect desirable changes,
but he argues that it comes at the cost of the public sphere's transparency: once the image and event-making strategies of public relations start to establish the terms of public discussion, we start
questioning the motives and worrying about the styles used in critical debate.

In this early argument, Habermas is more pessimistic than in
his later work, finding politics hopelessly imbricated in public relations because of the importance of media in bringing matters to
public attention. Politicians need exposure, TV time. Media enable
a competition for political—as well as cultural and economic—
mindshare. But media opportunity has its price: the consumerist
reconfiguration of the public sphere. Habermas writes, "Because
private enterprises evoke in their customers the idea that in their
consumption decisions they act in their capacity of citizens, the
state has to 'address' its citizens like consumers. As a result, public authority too competes for publicity."[42] Habermas nevertheless
concludes that the contest between critical-rational and con-
sumerist-manipulative publicity is far from decided. Indeed, he
urges that the success of democracy in social welfare states depends on reorganizing the public sphere so as to enable publicity to
fulfill its critical potential.

Habermas does not provide the details of such a reorganization,
but he suggests that it involves more publicity. Why? Because the
problem with consumer-oriented publicity lies in its continued reliance on secrecy. Habermas explains: "At one time publicity had
to be gained in opposition to the secret politics of the monarchs; it
sought to subject person or issue to rational-critical public debate
and to render political decisions subject to review before the court
of public opinion. Today, on the contrary, publicity is achieved
with the help of secret politics of interest groups."[43] So, for Habermas, the continued impact of these secrets means that publicity
doesn't go far enough; it stops too soon. Publicity needs to extend
all the way down, to all the institutions and practices that have
"lived off the publicity of other institutions rather than being
themselves subject to the public's supervision."[44] The very means

of public discussion must become matters for public inquiry and discussion.

Habermas's call for more publicity seems to have been answered by and in contemporary technoculture. But the result has not been a new rational public sphere. Instead, permanent media, interconnected television, newspaper, radio, and Internet use their own "critical" self-reflection to strengthen their hold on popular imaginations. Trying to distinguish between consumer-oriented and critical publicity makes no sense in the networks of the information age. Clearly, media engage in both at once. Media repeatedly criticize themselves and use this self-criticism to sell copy and generate audience. Talking heads attack the polarizing emotion and spectacle of television shows featuring talking heads. They talk and criticize for us even as they implore us to watch, to be in the know. In an eight-hundred-channel satellite TV universe, it's necessary to feed the pundit, to provide fast, cheap commentary dished up as content. What's easier than reversing the cameras, taping the taping? Reflecting on the process of production is now more appealing than focusing on what's produced. In the face of this materialization of belief, critical publicity seems a norm out of control, a kind of habermasochism of media self-cannibalization.

Critical reflection is more than a selling point or a way to generate audience by claiming a rationality and objectivity superior to one's media competitors. It's the very hallmark of the ideology of the public sphere. Žižek notes that "an ideological identification exerts a hold on us precisely when we maintain an awareness that we are not fully identical to it."[45] The ideological hold of an ideal public with the right to know is strengthened by the observation of the manipulative effects of consumer-oriented publicity. The critique of consumer-oriented publicity, a critique that generations inculcated in media grow up making, attaches us all the more firmly to the media of publicity: now we know. We are distant and ironic enough not to be seduced. Materializing practices of concealment and disclosure, engagement and debate, media believe, so that we don't have to. Advertisers are learning these tricks; so are television programmers, the suppliers of news magazines, and the producers of new media. Douglass Rushkoff brings the point home in his analysis of "wink" marketing, the use of irony to hail sophisticated consumers. He writes, "Advertisers know that their viewship prides itself on being able to deconstruct and understand the coercive tactics of television commercials. By winking at the audience, the advertiser is acknowledging that there's someone special out there. . . . If you are smart enough to get the joke, then you're smart enough to know to buy our product."[46]

Media sensationalize their reports, reduce complex statements to sound bites, and depend on corporate goodwill for advertising revenue. But they nevertheless continue to proclaim that the public has a right to know and that media will and should provide us with information. The possibility of escape from bad consumerist publicity drives a call for more publicity, even though the result will simply be more bad publicity. And it installs over political life a screen of cynicism that directs our attention away from the often positive effects of media spectacle.[47] Just as in contemporary theories of democratic discourse that reduce democracy to procedures and discussion and substitute the means of political power for its exercise, so in the public sphere does publicity become the end of politics. Getting at the secret, uncovering the truth behind the scenes of publicity's staging, supports media culture's drive for information.

When we think about the public-supposed-to-know and the public-supposed-to-believe posited in the critical and consumerist orientations to publicity, the ideological function of the distinction between "critical" and "consumerist" appears in stark relief. The critical account of the public sphere presumes a public of citizens who debate matters of common concern. These debating citizens need to be up to date, informed about political issues. They are supposed to know. In this view, democracy is threatened when the critical public is left in the dark, when instead of "debating the issues" it is playing Doom or yakking in chat rooms. The audience before the staged public sphere, moreover, is said to be filled with naive, gullible, consumers who either identify with emotionally laden figures and representations or cynically dismiss that which is raised in the public sphere as raised merely for the sake of publicity. Are these two publics, these debating and consuming publics, simply the two halves of the same old public that appears in Bentham?

No. Although the consuming public looks like the public-supposed-to-believe, the problem rests not with what it believes but with what it doesn't. In a nutshell, it doesn't believe that the public-supposed-to-know knows, and it doesn't need to; mediated technologies materialize this belief as if there were some believing public. Let me explain.

Habermas's argument presumes that the problem with publicity comes from the consumer orientation of the public, but his solution misses its target. The consuming public's relationship to information is the same as that of the many and the middle in Bentham's account. We know this because to be manipulated by media presupposes that one believes the media in some form or another. The habermasochistic solution to the problem of consumerist publicity does not affect this belief. Rather, it supplies more information, more criticism, more reflection, targeting, as it were, the public-supposed-to-know. But they aren't the problem—in either Habermas's or Bentham's account. Recall that the system of publicity is supposed to convince the public-supposed-to-believe to believe in the public-supposed-to-know. Information can't solve the problem because the problem is one of belief, not knowledge. And the collapse of this belief is what's at stake in contemporary technoculture and displaced from the analysis through Habermas's equating of publicity and reason. The endless exposure of ever more secrets, the continued circulation of critical reflection, hails each as an expert entitled to know even as it undermines any sense that anyone knows anything at all. Precisely because each is an expert, no one believes in the expert opinion of anyone else. Everybody has to find out for him or herself.

In this context, the technologies believe for us, accessing information even if we cannot. Permanent media bring us closer to the secret but continue to hold it just out of reach. The secret thus no longer sutures together the split public. Installed in new technologies, it now functions as the stimulus and currency of the information economy.

Might not the critique of consumerist publicity be a way to repress publicity's pleasures, to deny our enjoyment of publicity? For example, by now it is a commonplace of the media event that media will comment on and condemn their own excesses. On talk radio, in the letters section of editorial pages, and on the Internet, the audience is addressed in its critical outrage, given ample opportunity to rage against the media machine that yet again has gone too far. At the same time, media report their increased ratings, the multitudes sharing the collective experience, the poll numbers confirming the publicness of it all. The excess is what makes the event, what produces the pleasures of publicity. Enjoyment makes it/the public. Those who hold on to the ideal of a rational public sphere of course respond to this enjoyment reproachfully: there is too much media, too little rationality; there is too much consumerism, too little critical reflection. So we can't win: if we continue to engage in the event, we are entrapped by the "too much," and if we dismiss it we are guilty of "too little."[48]

The critical mantra that there is too much media but too little (real) information may often be effective in making the audience feel guilty. I felt a little guilty during the impeachment of Clinton, for example, because I knew that I was following a story of illicit sex, that I had enjoyed Monica Lewinsky's interview with Barbara Walters, and that I paid much more attention to the whole Lewinsky affair than I ever had to the boring Whitewater investigations. Does this mean that I—or any among us who feels guilty for failing to live up to the ideals of critical reason claimed for the public sphere, for failing to be an informed member of the judging public—really think that there is a rational public sphere or that one would emerge should the correct media practices somehow start to govern our political lives? No—the guilty feelings conceal the fact that the public doesn't exist at all.

As Žižek explains, when subjects act *as if* they believe, they maintain an order of appearances, a set of practices carried out for the sake of the "big Other." This "big Other" of the sociosymbolic order stands outside the subject as a hidden agency pulling the strings. It's a kind of meta-subject, like "divine Providence" or "the public."[49] With respect to ideology, the big Other operates in various modes. It can function as the subject-supposed-to-believe. It can also and at the same time serve as the subject-supposed-to-know and the subject-supposed-*not*-to-know.[50] If we treat this as a third notion of the public, the public-supposed-*not*-to-know, we recognize that the claim that the public has a right to know can be supplemented by a sense of what the public should not know. Most importantly, it should not know that it isn't there. It should not know that the polls that register its opinions give rise to the belief that it is there. It should not know that critical invocations of it are nothing more than buttresses for already particular claims. And it should not know that the social is already fundamentally split, torn apart by conflicts, antagonisms, and contradictions that simply cannot be fantasized away. The public should not know that the secret functions to hold open the formal space of the fantasy that screens out the failure of the public as a category of political society.

Žižek emphasizes that ultimately the big Other is not supposed to know that it doesn't exist. To protect the big Other from this knowledge, the subject "escapes into guilt." It's better to feel guilty than it is to acknowledge that American politics, say, really has become reduced to boring, sentimental, spectacles like the Lewinsky affair. It's easier to feel guilty—as if all democratic governance really required was for us to read detailed budgetary reports and follow news about pesticide regulations—than it is to reconceive the political in terms of fundamental struggles over the distribution of wealth, health, and freedom. It's easier for us to feel guilty about enjoying publicity's excess than to acknowledge the nonexistence of the public sphere. We assume guilt because we have to keep up appearances, and this compulsion is an ideological effect of the big Other. We feel it even when, *precisely when*, we don't believe the big Other is there at all.[51]

But You Don't Lose Anything

In the preceding section, I addressed three aspects of publicity as ideology: our distance from it, our enjoyment in it, and our sacrificial guilt before it. These topics return me, then, to the role of the secret in securing the public sphere as an ideological construction. Žižek gives "one of the most elementary definitions of ideology" as "a symbolic field which contains . . . a filler holding the place of some structural impossibility, while simultaneously disavowing this possibility."[52] If we apply this definition to the public sphere, we see that the secret marks the constitutive limit of the public, a limit that the public sphere cannot acknowledge. That this limit cannot be acknowledged, that it in fact stimulates not simply the continued imposition of the public but the explosion of networked media, points to the ideological function of the ideal of publicity in the information age. How do we know when we have enough information, when the ultimate secret has been revealed? We don't. We can't—the secret is a matter of form, not content, so it can never fully or finally be revealed. Similarly, the gaps and failures pervading democracy are problems of neither knowledge nor information. They are problems of practice, most particularly of practices that materialize democracy within the matrix of publicity and secrecy. The striking paradox we encounter today, then, is that the more information we have, the less we think we have.[53] This inability to know if and when we are satisfied undermines the normative claim for publicity as it reminds us of power's decisive intervention, of the point of decision. The public sphere rests on the constitutive impossibility of a politics without, outside of, beyond, power, a politics in which decision is postponed in favor of a consensus that has always been already achieved.[54]

So what might appear as the technocultural loss of the public isn't the loss of anything at all—the public was never there. The public is a fiction, a wish that "fantasizes a unified 'people' where there is, in reality, a heterogeneous citizenry," in Lisa Disch's helpful formulation.[55] The emphasis on making public, whether through the rules and procedures of the rational public sphere or the networked intensities of publicity in global technoculture, provides a fetish screening the fact that there is no public that can act. Fascinated by publicity in its normative, technological, and celebrity formats, we disavow the fact that the public isn't there.

Of course the hold of the ideology of the public sphere is strong. Because technoculture materializes the belief that the public has a right to know, that which the public doesn't know strikes us as something withheld or denied, a kind of contrary malevolence: if there is nothing to hide, then why not come out, go public, tell all? But this injunction to reveal misreads the sense that something is withheld as the public's missing authorization. The secret can't be told. It can't be filled in. It's simply the form through which the fantasy of the public takes account of its failure in advance. No inclusion, whether of groups or information, people or issues, will provide enough legitimacy to justify what is claimed in the name of the public.

For Bentham, the secret marked the gap holding together the split public. The ultimate secret was not the missing information warranting the rightness of public judgment. No, the secret was that there wasn't really a judging public at all; there was just a different elite. The whole solution depended on not having everyone judge and on disavowing that this was a constitutive exclusion within the public. In contemporary technoculture, the function of the secret has changed. The barrier that sustained Bentham's fan-

tasy of the public has been removed in the information age promise of universal access. And this makes it possible not only to recognize publicity as ideology (the idea that the public has the right
to know drives the infotainment culture even as it deflects attention from fundamental antagonisms or turns them into the disposable contents of entertainment culture), but also to acknowledge
the secret as both the generative limit of publicity and its currency. (Technoculture materializes the belief that the key to democracy can be found in uncovering the secrets. Even if no one really believes, satellites, the Internet, and surveillance cameras
believe for us.)

Similarly, in the absolutist state, secrecy protected the sovereign decision's political interventions. It also protected Freemasonry's moral opinion, enabling its certainty in judgment to
emerge in practices of belief. In the contemporary ideology of the
public sphere, the secret reappears in the sense that something is
always missing, hidden. But what is hidden is the guarantor of the
legitimacy of any decision backed by the name of the public; what
is missing is the rule that can compel obedience without coercion,
the supplement that will make everything just, okay, fair. As an
externalization of publicity's constitutive gap, the secret motivates
continued effort in publicity's behalf. Something or someone
stands right outside us, our knowledge and our visibility, with-
holding our legitimacy from us, preventing us from realizing the
rightness that we claim, that should be ours. Include just a few
more people, a few more facts; uncover those denied details, those
repressed desires; do this and there will be justice. These injunctions attest to publicity's secret, to the structural impossibility
that generates the public sphere. From the perspective of the public, the secret always withholds just what we need from us. At the
same time, any revelation calls us together, addressing the audience who receives it as the public and continuing to reproduce suspicious subjects in a system of distrust.

Few contemporary accounts of publicity acknowledge the secret. Instead, they adopt a spatial model of a social world divided
between public and private spheres. For the most part, these accounts claim either the priority of the one or the other, ignoring
the system of distrust, the circuit of concealment and revelation,
that actively generates the public. To this extent, they seem unable
to theorize the power of publicity, the compulsion to disclose and

the drive to surveil that so pervade the contemporary. Recent expansion in technologies of surveillance and publicity reminds us, however, that networked communications impact our everyday lives in often unsuspected ways. Media publicize the private: they produce audiences and collectivities, interpellating a citizenry, a tribunal, through the use of individuated screens and targeted invitations to consume. This mediatization accompanies a reconfiguration of the political: few contemporary Americans would disagree with the claim that the personal is political. Taking up the political claim that what was once hidden should be revealed, Reagan conservatives, for example, redirected the countercultural message of the 1960s to wage their own wars around sexuality, race, and gender. These wars were often fought through the dynamic of concealment and revelation—a particularly effective tactic in the context of an entertainment culture desperate for the sensations that will boost ratings and the "stickiness" of websites. Hidden behaviors and desires were exposed, forced out of the closet and into the light of a judging public. In this setting, it makes sense to reconsider in terms of secrecy some issues currently formatted as "private." How does this internalized limit continue to generate precisely that public and affirm precisely that ideology that drives contemporary technoculture?

Indeed, in light of the importance of the secret as a generator of the public, it seems clear that the notion of the public hinders more than it helps democratic efforts. The desire to uncover the hidden deflects attention from the system of distrust, from the seemingly inescapable oscillations between the public as constant and universal and the public as uncertain and in flux, between the public-supposed-to-know and the public-supposed-to-believe. At the same time, it displaces attention from the belief materialized in the mediated networks of the information age, the way suspicious subjects are produced who act as if they believed in a unified public and the truth that is out there. When conceived within and confined to the public sphere, democratic politics concentrates on access, on questions of inclusion and exclusion within this imaginary space—as if the public were constant and the failure to redeem its claim to universality were simply a contingent numerical issue of ensuring that each and every voice "count." Ostensibly democratic polities justify themselves and their actions by invoking a public with beliefs, tastes, and preferences that all too often confirm the interests of whomever is doing the invoking. And precisely because public opinion is always displaced as the opinion of someone who isn't there, these invocations themselves have political effects: If a big-city mayor justifies efforts to increase the presence of the police and decrease the presence of the homeless on the basis of public opinion, is it not possible that some will believe that others have this opinion? And hence might this mayor then actually produce the opinion to which he claims to be responding?

When based on the notion of the public, democratic political theory is likely to focus mistakenly on revealing, outing, and uncovering what has been concealed or withheld from the public. Practically, these restrictions narrow the range of thinking about politics, distracting us from fundamental social and economic antagonisms and deflecting attention from questions of biopolitics, transnational alliance, and the place of fantasy, to mention just a few. Theoretically, this restrictive focus renders democracy a failure in advance: because the public can never live up to its promise (a failure marked by the secret), a dynamic of suspicion and surveillance (now materialized in technoculture) is installed as the next best thing. In this respect, what passes as democratic politics seems to depend on not telling the biggest secret of all: that despite the rhetoric of publicity, there is no public.

CHAPTER TWO

Conspiracy's Desire

As the global networks of the information age become increasingly entangled, they ever more successfully reproduce the suspicious subjectivities posited by publicity as a system of distrust. Many of us are overwhelmed and undermined by an all-pervasive uncertainty. Wars in one place seem diversions from the *real* wars going on elsewhere. Disclosures may really be concealments. Far from passively consuming the virtually entertaining spectacles of integrated media, we come to suspect that something is going on behind the screens. What we see is not what we get. The truth may not be out there, but something, or someone, is. Accompanying our increasing suspicions are seemingly bottomless vats of information, endless paths of evidence. As Kathleen Stewart writes, "Events and phenomena call to us as haunting specters lodged somewhere within the endless proliferation of images and reports . . . the more you know, the less you know."[1] When everything is linked, there may be more information than we can bear. And what about that which isn't linked, which eludes the Web? Is that more or less bearable?

Having it all, bringing every relevant and available fact into the conversation, as the Habermasians like to say, may well entangle us in a clouded, occluded nightmare of obfuscation. I'm thinking here of my childcare provider's efforts to understand the legalities of her divorce or my mundane and consumerist attempts to choose an affordable cell phone company. We're linked into a world of uncertainties, a world in which more information is always available, and hence, a world in which we face daily the fact that our truths, diagnoses, and understandings are incomplete—click on one more link, check out one more newscast, get just one more expert opinion (and then, perhaps, venture into the fringe; after all, some HMOs cover alternative remedies).

These two ideas—that things are not as they seem and everything is connected—are primary components of how we think about and experience the information age. They are also the guiding impulses of conspiracy theory. Are the lawyers and judges in our small town colluding against my nanny? Are telecoms, like some Windowed-monster, engaging in monopolistic practices that will enrich their stockholders? Or might the fantasy that conspiratorial machinations are afoot displace our attention from the fact that nothing is hidden behind the screens at all: the legal system *is* working against my nanny in its failure to provide her with assistance, and the telecoms *are* obviously out to increase the value of their stock by any means necessary.

The previous chapter considered the secret at the heart of the public, arguing that the notion of the public is held together by a secret. The secret plays the formal role of a container for the fantasy of unity that covers over the constitutive split in the public. In this chapter, I'm interested in the public at the heart of the secret, the paradoxical sense that everything we need to know is right in front of us, but still we don't know. This paradox highlights the changed function of the secret in technoculture, the persistence of its tantalizing effects (the way we continue to want to know), one, and its connotative shift from fact to technique, from knowledge to know-how, two. To access this paradox, I click on various conspiracy cites from the Declaration of Independence, to mainstream political science, to Hillary Rodham Clinton. My interest is in the workings of the matrix of publicity and secrecy, in how the matrix structures political engagements even as those empowered through concealment or revelation shift and change. Looking at evocations of conspiracy as they have appeared in U.S. politics, I highlight the obscene underpinnings of publicity in the ways that the production of a public has relied on conspiracy. Moreover, I emphasize how the practices of searching, clicking, and linking in technoculture turn us all into conspiracy theorists, producing, as it were, suspicious subjects who trust no one because the technologies believe for us. Even though the secret no longer sutures together a split public, it remains the object-cause of the desire to know materialized in contemporary technoculture, luring us down the uncanny pathways of cyberia. Configured as the suspicious subjects of publicity as a system of distrust, we end up conspiracy theorists. In technoculture, as in conspiracy theory, we make the connections.

Literally Public

Conspiracy theory takes disclosure seriously. As with publicity, so in conspiracy thinking, something important is always hidden. Whatever it is that keeps the system, the government, from being/doing right, is a secret that must be revealed. So conspiracy theory runs the same program as does the principle of publicity. Indeed, we might say that it literalizes the claims of publicity as a system of distrust.

Conventional academic accounts of conspiracy theory look at it rather differently. They want to distinguish conspiracy thinking from rational or Enlightenment thought. The first, and indeed primary, task of these accounts is to figure out what exactly makes something a conspiracy theory (*I'm not a conspiracy theorist, but . . .*). In identifying conspiracy theory, they generally focus on its style, its preoccupation with plot, or its pathological motivations.[2] None of these approaches is satisfying.

First, the emphasis on style oscillates between accusations that conspiracy thinking is excessively rational, overinterpretive, and too preoccupied with evidence, on the one hand, and that it is irrational, locked into a rigid interpretive framework, and pays little attention to the facts, on the other hand. Conspiracy theories are viewed as either too complicated or too simple. They are never "just right." As Slavoj Žižek observes, this oscillation suggests that we are dealing here with *jouissance*.[3] Critics of the paranoid style are troubled by the *pleasures* that conspiracy theorists take in interpretation, by their leaps in imagination and willingness to deviate from common sense, by their excessive delight in documenting all sorts of horrible, unimaginable crimes and violations. (An example of such excess might be Cathy O'Brien's *Trance Formation in America*, which includes stories of George W. Bush using heroin and participating in elaborate orgies with Richard "Dick" Cheney and his sex slaves.) Richard Hofstadter points to style in his influential essay "The Paranoid Style in American Politics." His criticism of conspiracy theory highlights its distance from "conventional political reasoning," from "the normal political process of bargain and compromise."[4] Robert S. Robins and Jerrold M. Post agree. For them, conspiracy thinking is a distortion, caricature, exaggeration, or parody of the useful, prudent, and sound practices of normal political behavior.[5]

The style critics have a point. After reading theories that connect prominent members of the Church of Satan with U.S. Army intelligence, the executive officer of the 306th Psychological Operations Battalion at Fort MacArthur, and "a string of abuse investigations of military daycare centers," I even find myself agreeing.[6] But might not the very excesses of conspiracy theory click on the surpluses, the libidinal supports, of political and economic power? Žižek argues that "public state apparatuses are always supplemented by their shadowy double, by a network of publicly disavowed rituals, unwritten rules, institutions, practices, and so on."[7] Conspiracy theory, through its amassed details, focuses on these unwritten rules and shadow institutions. Understanding state and corporate authority as always stained by excess, it highlights the surplus integral to the maintenance of power (even as what it actually designates as a particular surplus, say, robotic implants in half the state of California or LSD in the Baltimore water supply, may seem idiotic).

Power exceeds the conditions that authorize its use. This excess is a crucial aspect of the way we experience political power, of subjectivation. The shadowy network provides the excess, the violence, which functionalizes the system. The film *Boys Don't Cry* concentrates on this obscene supplement to power in its depiction of the violence through which sexual difference is inscribed and maintained: although identified as a female at birth, the protagonist lived as a male and was killed for not conforming. On a different, although still unsettling, level, many of us when faced with complex bureaucratic procedures, unhelpful clerks, and vague recollections of innocent people locked on death row find ourselves acting as if we believed we were caught in a Kafkaesque trial, even though we know law doesn't really work that way. Conversely, many of us may also find our exercise of authority tainted—and enhanced—by similar excesses, demanding that others not simply comply but that they comply *and like it.* (I do this with my kids. They are supposed to mind me *and smile.*)[8]

Second, interpreters of conspiracy theory who emphasize plot are not convincing because most conspiracy theories fail to provide a complete or intelligible mapping or narrative of anything.

Conspiracy theories—like most theories—are always disrupted by gaps and uncertainties. Most of us know *that* there are conspiratorial explanations for the JFK assassination, the origins of the AIDS virus, the crash in Roswell, N.M., and the eye and pyramid images on American currency. But we don't know *what* these explanations are—what sorts of plots and shadowy figures are involved and how they fit together. All we know are bits and pieces without a plot. This is the way conspiracy theories work. Most fail to delineate any conspiracy at all. They simply counter conventionally available narratives with questions, suspicions, and allegations that, more often than not, resist coherent emplotment or satisfying narrative resolution (*did MK ULTRA involve CIA mind-control experiments, and what about those sex slaves, anyway?*). Fear and unease are always conspiracy theory's residue. We might say, then, that conspiracy theories are critical theories, critical theories generally misread as empirical theories (exposés).

In conspiracy theories, the possibilities of malevolent plays of power link facts, speculations, and questions. Was the mass suicide in Jonestown, Guyana, part of a CIA mind-control experiment?[9] What explains the fact that the CIA was the first to report the massacre and the presence of CIA agent Richard Dwyer? Was it a plot to kill hundreds of African Americans? Rather than mapping totality, conspiracy's questions and insinuations disrupt the presumption that there is a coherent, knowable reality that could be mapped.

Finally, the emphases on pathological motivation either employ an indefensible diagnosis or discount the embeddedness of conspiracy thinking within what they understand as mainstream history and elite groups. They explain conspiracy thinking as a symptom of outsider status. In trying to demonstrate the abnormality of political paranoia, however, those who view conspiracy as pathology have to concede that sometimes there really are conspiracies afoot and sometimes paranoia in politics makes good sense.[10] Paradoxically, were they to follow through with this concession, their diagnoses would be premised on establishing whether or not a conspiracy exists, thereby transforming the critics themselves into conspiracy theorists. Similarly, efforts to render conspiracy thinking as some kind of "status-deficit disorder" have to confront the conspiracy mindedness of elected politicians (Senators Joseph McCarthy and Barry Goldwater, for example) and official governmental policies (those carried out in the United States during the Cold War).

Of course, there are more sophisticated critiques of conspiracy. Since the work of Paul Ricoeur, a strand of critical social theory has voiced its suspicions of a hermeneutic of suspicion. In a recent version of this argument, Eve Kosofsky Sedgwick criticizes paranoia in queer theory, asking how it happened that paranoia (as an illumination not of how homosexuality works but of how homophobia works) moved from an object of antihomophobic theory to its methodology.[11] She observes that the paranoid style is marked by a "faith in exposure" and by a sense of a naive audience that will be outraged and motivated by the unveiling of the scandalous secret. Sedgwick writes: "What is the basis for assuming that it will surprise or disturb—never mind motivate—anyone to learn that a given social manifestation is artificial, self-contradictory, imitative, phantasmatic, or even violent?"[12]

Sedgwick's question regarding the assumptions of a hermeneutic of suspicion suggests an answer to her question regarding the shift from object to method in queer theory, an answer important for thinking about conspiracy theory. The belief in exposure marks the fundamental fantasy of publicity as a system of distrust. Suspicion as method practices this belief, searching for and uncovering the truth, bringing it to light, making it available for reflection. When queer theory and conspiracy theory adopt a methodological paranoia, they are reiterating, adopting, but not without revision, the desire for truth at the heart of the ideal of public reason. Indeed, this method not only presumes an illegitimate nonconsensuality within the secret and private, but it also links publicity to consensuality—what is public is what is accepted by the "public." The assumption of surprise Sedgwick finds characteristic of the impulse to uncover thus points to an underlying fantasy of a public in which some know with certainty and constancy, in which others believe that there are some who know, and in which apparatuses of publicity materialize the fantasy that revelation and discussion will lead to justice. Critiques based on this assumption exhibit a confidence in their own significance.

Conspiracy thinking is a method for thinking critically when caught within the governing assumptions of a public sphere. So the problem with conspiracy thinking is not its failure to comply with public reason *but its very compliance,* a compliance that re-iterates some of these assumptions even as it contests others, a compliance that demonstrates all too clearly the paranoia, surveillance, and compulsive will to know within the ideal of publicity. We might say that by reiterating the compulsions of publicity, conspiracy's attempts to uncover the secret assemble information regarding the contexts, terms, and conditions of surveillance, discovery, and visibility in a culture in which democracy is embedded in a system of distrust. The facts it uncovers, then, are not so revealing. But conspiracy theory's practices of revelation are of interest insofar as they express the ideology of technoculture. When publicity feeds the mediated networks of the information age, conspiracy theory challenges the presumption that what we see on the screens, what is made visible in traditional networks and by traditional authorities, is not itself invested in specific lines of authorization and subjection. It rejects the fantasy that the secret has been revealed even as it reinscribes the secret as an object-cause of desire.

Thus, in contrast to thinking about conspiracy theory in terms of style, plot, or pathology, I find it makes better critical sense to emphasize the way conspiracy theory *takes the system at its word.* This does not mean that conspiracy theory believes the rhetoric of publicity—that democracy is a system through which free and equal citizens rationally discuss and decide matters of public concern. Rather, it believes through the practices of publicity, that is, conspiracy theory operates within a system of distrust, acting as if discovery of the secret were the key to democratic legitimacy. Conspiracy theory literalizes the claims of publicity.

For the most part, this literalization is accompanied by an inversion: conspiracy theory tends to make public information the content of the secret. Contemporary American conspiracy theory, for example, usually operates by making connections between political figures and powerful corporate bigwigs (*they went to the same schools, are members of the same clubs, sit on the boards of the same corporations; they all know each other!*). It rereads available information to demonstrate that *it's right before our eyes.* Challenging conventional interpretations of the way things are, conspiracy theory brings out the obscene stain of power to show how conspiratorial networks of privilege work through law, that they are law, they are governance. With its emphasis on massive amounts of detail, conspiracy theory occupies itself with the excess that always accompanies and supplements authority.

Make links, search for truth: within these injunctions one is free insofar as one gathers information. More powerful, more persuasive, than market and consumerist conceptions of freedom, freedom as information gathering confirms a conception of democratic engagement long part of the ideal of the public sphere: the public has a right to know. Citizens are free, so long as nothing is hidden from them. They must watch, surveil, expose, and reveal. Conspiracy theory or publicity as technocultural ideology?

Obsessive Fears

Conspiracy theory has a long, rich history in America. In fact, it helps produce the very public proclaimed in the Declaration of Independence. Pauline Maier observes that most modern discussions of the Declaration concentrate on the first two paragraphs, devoting little serious attention to the charges against the king.[13] But she argues that the charges were "essential to the Declaration's central purpose," which was "to demonstrate that the King had inflicted on the colonists 'unremitting injuries and usurpations,' all of which had as a 'direct object the establishment of an absolute tyranny.' "[14] The recounting of this history, the charges leveled at the king, includes claims that he refused to pass laws, dissolved representative houses, obstructed the administration of justice, "plundered our seas," "ravaged our coasts," "burnt our towns," excited domestic insurrections, and endeavored to bring on the "inhabitants of our frontiers the merciless Indian savages." The grievances were not just statements of fact introduced to identify specific crimes and injuries. They were part of a political strategy. They were evidence of a conspiracy.

Maier notes that today even professional historians would have trouble identifying the precise sources of some of the accusations leveled against the king; in fact, the sources likely were also unclear to many in the eighteenth century. Some events were referred to only obliquely. Others were expressed so ambiguously as to provide only the barest clues as to what Jefferson had in mind. Indeed, a writer at the time thought the American effort to find reasons for separating from Britain "suffered for lack of 'truth and sense.' "[15] "The grievances in the Declaration were not meant to identify,"

Maier explains, "precisely which event had reconciled Americans to separate nationhood. The grievances in the Declaration served a different purpose—not to explain the Americans' change of heart but to justify revolution by proving that George III was a tyrant."[16] The grievances, for all their imprecision and ambiguity, were strategically disclosed as information, as revelations that could call a public into being. Maier points out that the most common method of proclaiming the Declaration was to read it before large audiences. These readings presented audiences with of a pattern of actions indicative of tyranny, a pattern that today we might think of as a conspiracy.[17]

According to Bernard Bailyn, that there was a conspiratorial pattern to British actions was a common idea at the time. Bailyn argues that the political pamphlets appearing in the years immediately preceding the revolution reflect the conviction that nothing less was afoot than "a deliberate assault launched surreptitiously by plotters against liberty both in England and America."[18] Similarly, Gordon Wood finds "internal decay" to be a predominant image in prerevolutionary writing: "A poison had entered the nation and was turning the people and the government into 'one mass of corruption.' "[19] Wood notes that by the 1770s, most every piece of Whig writing—pamphlet, newspaper, essay, or letter—dwelt on an obsessive fear of conspiracy.[20]

For Bailyn and Wood, conspiracy thinking is central to the founding of the United States. Bailyn claims that the dominant elements of revolutionary ideology were fears of corruption and of a ministerial conspiracy.[21] Wood goes even further, arguing that the belief in a ministerial conspiracy against the colonists' liberties was "the only frame of mind with which they could justify and explain their revolution."[22] Conspiracy thinking, far from the paranoid irrationality it would become associated with in pluralist theory, was part of a new science of human affairs, the application of rational principles, the tracing, disclosing, and connecting of motives and events to an ulterior plan. Wood writes:

the tendency to see events as the result of a calculated plot . . . appears particularly strong in the eighteenth century, a product, it seems, not only of the political realities and assumptions of the age, but of its very enlightenment, a consequence of the popularization of politics and the secu-

larization of knowledge. . . . Enlightened rationalists as well
as Calvinist clergy were obsessed with the motives that lay
hidden by deceiving, even self-deceiving statements, and
they continually sought to penetrate beneath the surface of
events in order to find their real significance in the inner
hearts of men. Yet in replacing Providence with human motivation as a source of historical explanation, men still felt
the need to discover the design, "the grand *plan*" that lay beneath the otherwise incomprehensible jumble of events.
Now it seemed possible to men of this enlightened age that
they would be able . . . to disclose at last what had always
been in darker days "the hidden and . . . uncertain connection of events."[23]

According to this early version of what became known as the Whig
conception of history, events were caused by human actions, actions that were understood in terms of motives and intentions, actions that had meaning, especially when placed in connection
with one another.

That events could be scientifically analyzed in terms of patterns
of meaningful, intentional actions gave a logic to the colonists' demands. It made them, in a word, rational. This was particularly
important given that the Americans were hardly an oppressed
people. As Wood points out, "they had no crushing imperial shack-
les to throw off."[24] Nonetheless, armed with a theory of action, the
colonists could use the threat of conspiracy to produce a new political space. Bailyn writes: "The fact that the ministerial conspiracy against liberty had risen from corruption was of the utmost
importance to the colonists. It gave radical new meaning to their
claims: it transformed them from constitutional argument to expressions of a world regenerative creed."[25]

François Furet makes a similar argument in his account of the
French Revolution. He finds that the idea of an aristocratic plot
worked as a "relay" to provide the ideal of equality with revolutionary energy. As an opposing principle to the democratic equality, the aristocratic plot "created conflict and justified the use of
violence."[26] Evocations of a plot mobilized belief into action as
they provided explanation for failures and justification for events.
Fouret's words apply equally well to the role of conspiracy in the
American Revolution. He writes:

The idea appealed not only to a religiously oriented moral sensibility that had always seen evil as the work of hidden forces, but also to the new democratic conviction that the general, or national, will could not be publicly opposed by special interests. Above all, it was marvelously suited to the workings of revolutionary consciousness, for it produced the characteristic perversion of the causal schema by which every historical fact can be reduced to a specific intention and to a subjective act of will; thus the crime was sure to be heinous, since it was unavowable, and crushing the plot became a laudable and purifying act.[27]

Similarly, conspiratorial constructions of British power relied on a logic of publicity to produce the American public as a body that was threatened by devious political machinations. Bringing this shadowy network to light required a particular kind of know-how, a kind of scientific knowledge of making connections, showing how various acts were linked into a general system or pattern.

For the colonists, conspiracy theory—a theory that disclosed hidden links among a variety of political acts and concluded that such interconnections were evidence of tyrannical designs— helped produce an American public. Encoded through the dynamic of publicity and secrecy, the grievances relied on a knowledge of the excesses of power, a knowledge that made links among seemingly disparate and not strictly factual events. Distrust of British authority helped produce a new "we" of suspicious subjects. This "we" was constituted out of those who knew about corruption and ministerial conspiracy, those who used a new knowledge to ground the certainty of its judgment of British political actions, on the one hand, and those who were hailed in the Declaration as colonists who might believe that the king was plotting against their liberty, on the other. Like the secrecy that bound and dispersed the networks of Freemasonry in the early years of the Enlightenment, conspiracy theory enabled the colonists to act extralegally while claiming to act in the name of the law of reason.

Fears of Obsession

Conspiracy thinking has played a key role in the making of America. As the work of some major historians of the American Revolution demonstrates, conspiracy was installed from the outset in what would be known as the American public. Invoking conspiracy helped produce new, suspicious, political subjects. It called into being a "public" united around the conviction that conspiracies are afoot. It did so through a knowledge of linked excesses, by knowing, in other words how the obscene excesses of power were connected. So despite the derision with which conspiracy thinking is treated in the academy, it is not just a sideline to a mainstream politics of reasonable discussion and rational exchange.

Conspiracy theory continues to function as a primary format of American politics, although how it functions has changed since the revolution. Much of the concern has shifted from the conspirators to the conspiracy theorists. The worry, in other words, is not that a conspiracy may be afoot but that those who think in terms of conspiracy constitute a danger to democracy. This is the way conspiracy theory functions in American pluralism. It plays an integral role in maintaining the fantasy of the reliable center, the public, the "we" recognized and accepted by mainstream American political science.[28] It does this in part by occupying the position of that which has to be excluded if the center is to hold. Conspiracy theory's obsessive preoccupation with power's obscene supplement is precisely what mainstream political thinking works to disavow.

American liberal pluralism sees politics as a balanced search for coalition and compromise. Within the safely sanitized sphere of the political, actions are predictable, rational. Diverse groups push their interests while nonetheless working to keep conflict to a minimum. They calmly introduce their claims, make their arguments. Although competitive, these interest groups do not aim for total victory. They are content with practical solutions capable of accommodating a variety of needs and demands.

Although pluralists premise politics on diversity, they do not include an endless variety of political positions. Pluralism is not about multiple networks of political struggle and multiple forms of political engagement. As William Connolly explains, "outside the warm, protected spaces of the normal individual and the territorial state, conventional pluralists project a lot of abnormality, anarchy, and cruelty in need of exclusion or regulation. . . . Stark definitions of the outside contain the range and reach of diversity on the inside, and vice versa."[29] Pluralism seems a strong account of a fair and legitimate process of political bargaining precisely because anything that can threaten it is blocked from the terrain of politics.

Consequently, extreme positions are disallowed. The very constitution of the political requires that antagonism, whatever is radical or extreme or a mark of the split in the public, be excluded in advance, before politics can get under way. We might think of this in terms of pluralist theory's fears of obsession. For example, Seymour Martin Lipset and Earl Raab view "pluralism" and "extremism" as mutually defining terms: "Extremism basically describes that impulse which is inimical to a pluralism of interests and groups, inimical to a system of many nonsubmissive centers of power and areas of privacy. Extremism *is* antipluralism or—to use an only slightly less awkward term—monism."[30] Politics depends on discerning extremism and setting up barriers against it. There are limits to what the public can tolerate, limits to what can count as reasonable. Eliminating conspiracy thinking, thinking that might challenge the very terms of politics, is necessary if there is to be a politics at all.

Lipset and Raab view American history as a struggle between pluralism and extremism or monism. They characterize monism as moralistic, simplistic (searching for historical explanations that rely on binary oppositions), and rooted in conspiracy theory. (In his recent study of conspiracy thinking, Daniel Pipes takes an opposing position. He claims that "common sense accepts simple explanations; in contrast, conspiracy theories add complicating elements."][31] As Lipset and Raab acknowledge the prominence of moralism in "mainstream" politics and point out the complexities of the various conspiracies alleged to have threatened American democracy, however, the way in which they determine exactly what counts as a monist position becomes unclear. Are they those movements that Lipset and Raab simply don't like? Michael Rogin hits the nail on the head: "Claiming to cover right-wing extremism as a whole, the authors actually attack movements of which they disapprove that were neither right-wing nor extremist, and they cover up a countersubversive tradition that cannot be reduced to religious prejudice, ethnic conflict, and status anxiety."[32] Lipset and Raab, in other words, are seriously invested in the fantasy of unity.

Not surprisingly, contesting the basic structure of American political proceduralism—the terms of inclusion and participation—is not allowed.[33] In the Lipset and Raab version, moreover, pluralism itself rests on a single "conceptual heart" and "article of faith," namely, the "properties of human reason."[34] Faith guarantees that there is a singular human reason that forms the basis of pluralism (although this faith is rational, whereas other kinds of faith may not be). The possibility of a variety of forms of reason, of what Connolly calls the pluralization of pluralism, is excluded in advance, in fact by the use of conspiracy thinking to demarcate the limits of inclusion within America as a public.

For the experts, then, what was considered a rational and scientific way of understanding political events at the time of the Declaration is now a sign of pathology: "In the paranoid's worldview, events do not simply occur; they are deliberately caused by someone. For the paranoid, coincidence does not exist. Everything happens by design."[35] Not only is there no difference between conspiracy thinking and paranoia, indeed, they are symptoms of each other, but the very search for a causal explanation is suspect. For Robins and Post, "One of the distinctive qualities of the paranoid appeal is its reliance on ideas, explanations, and arguments of causality."[36] This is not to say that Robins and Post don't supply causal explanations for conspiracy thinking. They do. And they don't think of their own explanations as one bit paranoid. These include a sociobiological theory that inscribes a will to paranoia as a natural outcome of evolution and as a basic factor of human psychology, a metaphorical account of paranoia in terms of infection (as bacillus and virus) that "distorts" healthy political responses, and an associative analysis of paranoid thinking with "the logic of the child or primitive people trying to make sense of the incomprehensible."[37] Robins and Post don't try to connect these explanations or make their metaphors consistent. This may be because they think connection itself is pathological.

In the vision of America produced by pluralist democratic theory, only some people are at liberty to think causally. Causal explanations are the currency of the few. If the uncredentialed attempt to use them, something must be wrong. They must be sick, childish, or attempting to spread infection. At the very least, those who think that there are patterns in politics and that intentional actions stand behind political events must not share in the common sense. What stands behind this critique of conspiracy thinking, then, is a conception of politics that relies on a separation between those who know, those with the know-how to make causal arguments properly, and those who are supposed to believe. When those who are supposed to believe start trying to know for themselves, they are pathologized, suspect. The only political actions they are entitled to, it seems, require knowing within the preestablished norms of reason, or believing in those who know. They are just supposed to watch, to bear witness to what happens in the sphere of politics as defined by elites, confirmed by the party system, paid for by lobbyists, and summarized in daily sound bites.

When pluralists attack conspiracy thinking, they are not aiming for more political involvement or increased political activity. Instead, they are trying to stabilize, to set boundaries around, the public produced by publicity as a system of distrust. They want to block the extreme and obsessive from the democratic public. But they encounter the problem of not knowing what to exclude: sometimes it is hard to tell the difference between conspiracy thinking and the nice, clean application of public sphere ideals. Put somewhat differently, critiques of conspiracy thinking do two things. They produce the normal by excluding conspiracy theory as pathological. At the same time, they normalize paranoia as a predominant logic of the public sphere. The fantasy of the public sphere supports the impossible demand that the secret be revealed and unity be secured.

Critics of conspiracy thinking often point out that those most likely to be "at risk of acquiring the virus" are the "politically disaffected," who have experienced exclusion, degradation, oppression, and marginalization.[38] Hofstadter finds that when people lack access to political processes of bargaining and decision-making, their "original conception of the world of power as omnipotent, sinister, and malicious" is confirmed.[39] He does not think, in other words, that people might turn to conspiracy theory to explain their exclusion. Instead, he presumes that people were paranoid originally, from the outset, before any exclusion. Robins and Post also begin from the idea that belief in conspiracy is misguided. They emphasize the harmfulness of conspiracy thinking, refusing the possibility that it might provide some people with a know-how that can enable them to engage in politics and to contest their exclusion from the nation's dominant political spheres.[40]

Like Robins and Post, Pipes points out the prevalence of conspiracy thinking among African Americans and similarly rejects those political views with "deeply unsettling implications about the existing order."[41] He dismisses communism, notions of imperialism, and Latin American studies as paranoid and "conspiracist"—his word for belief in conspiracies that are not real.[42] For Pipes, anything outside the mainstream is conspiracist; yet this very center is produced through the designation of some views as conspiracist. Challenging the status quo, then, is excluded as a political option. The only recourse for the marginalized and disaffected is simply to stop being marginalized, to enter the mainstream, to accept and legitimize the American political system.

Some attacks on conspiracy thinking seem to be attacks on independent or noninstitutionalized thinking altogether. In effect admitting to his delegitimation of the voices of the already excluded, Pipes emphasizes that conspiracy thinkers tend to be self-taught: "This is not the legitimate scholarship produced by academics with university training, membership in professional associations, and social esteem. It is, rather, the mirror world of conspiracism, with its amateur autodidacts who lack institutional affiliation and suffer exclusion from the established institutions."[43] Robins and Post observe that some who join conspiracy-oriented groups seek greater meaning in their lives. But none of these critics explains why one should disparage the efforts of another to find or create meaning. It seems, again, as though they are suspicious of any attempts to make sense of the world in ways not authorized in advance by major institutions and perspectives. Only some interpreters are authorized.

That the problem is the outsider status of conspiracy thinking becomes all the more clear when one recalls the contradictions in accounts of what, exactly, constitutes conspiracy thinking. Pipes claims that conspiracy theories are vague, illogical, and inconsistent. Hofstadter says that they are unambiguous, rationalistic, and consistent. Pipes finds conspiracy thinking in disreputable presses, unaccredited journals, and on the Internet. Yet he also acknowledges that reputable publishers and authors may think conspiratorially, especially if they are on the Left. He admits that discerning conspiracy thinking is a subjective process. It seems to me that finding the center, the mainstream, is even more subjective. Insofar as critics of conspiracy thinking aim to contain publicity as a system of distrust by excluding some forms of political thinking and knowing, they create precisely that sphere of predictable, rational, explicable political action, that space occupied by rational wheeler-dealers, that they condemn conspiracy theorists for presupposing. The critical accounts of conspiracy thinking prominent in American history and political science since the McCarthy era employ a notion of political reality that they produce through the demonization of some political movements, styles, and theories as extreme, radical, or paranoid.

The critics assume conspiracy thinkers are wrong, misguided, deceived, or deceiving. They attack conspiracy theorists for (mistakenly) believing something to be true that the critic knows is false. This is precisely how the critic is able to discern a distorted belief from an appropriate one. The critic knows that corporate, commercial, financial interests have no significant impact on American politics, say, and this knowledge enables him or her to discover the mistaken beliefs that mark a person as a conspiracy thinker.[44] Robins and Post claim that for the conspiracy thinker, "skepticism is treason" and "true belief does not permit question and doubt."[45] (This might mean that most ufologists don't count as conspiracy thinkers. The majority of those researching alien abduction and UFOs experience extreme doubt. They often don't believe even themselves. They pursue alternate explanations, test hypotheses, criticize each other rabidly, and so forth.)[46]

The practice of conspiracy theory suggests that conspiracy theorists are permanent (one could even say hysterical) questioners. They doubt everything. In fact, "doing" conspiracy thinking involves sifting through volumes of "evidence," debating what fits and what doesn't, and trying to discern how the events or plots at issue might have taken place. The instability of the facts, the uncertainty of the evidence, is the challenge facing the conspiracy thinker. Far from being treason, skepticism is part of conspiracy thinking.[47]

Finally, critics of conspiracy thinking reproduce precisely that element of conspiracy thinking they find most objectionable—the tendency toward moralism and judgmentalism. Conspiracy theorists are said to rely on a friends/enemies opposition, viewing world history in terms of an ultimate battle between two opposing forces.[48] They refuse to compromise, seeing not error but evil. For the critic, this refusal is grounds for excluding the conspiracy minded from the political process *in advance*. Because they cannot negotiate, they should not be party to the negotiations constitutive of politics. Hence the critics too, as they reduce the activities of conspiracy thinkers to questions of judgment, affect the same moralism and judgmentalism they condemn. The critics, having established that politics means compromise and negotiation, block those who might not believe it. In so doing, they reassert the absolute certainty of their own judgment, explicitly asserting the division in the public that Bentham had disavowed. In this respect, judging itself becomes the penultimate political act, the act that determines who is one of us and who can reasonably be excluded.

Perhaps I overstate my case. After all, isn't there a difference between believing in a New World Order and knowing that the tobacco industry has systematically deceived consumers? Isn't there a problem with linking these together? Sure. And the problem is that this is precisely what is done by those wishing to protect America and Americans from the infections, seductions, and distortions of conspiracy thinking. Those who dismiss conspiracy theory link together fears of the New World Order with fears of corporate political influence. They link together critical inquiry into the systematic workings of racism, critical exploration of imperialism, and complex stories of implants, surveillance, and international bankers. The critics turn issues of complaint and knowledge into questions of style, participating in the reduction of political actions to disclosure and judgment. In so doing, these pluralist theorists attempt to rein in the system of distrust and make sure that suspicious subjects don't suspect too much.

Ironically, even as critics of conspiracy thinking exclude possibilities for radical interrogation of basic political practices and institutions, they include within the political the policies and manipulations of the national security state. Thus, they rarely link Cold War mentalities, surveillance of populations, and experiments on civilians with the "virus" of conspiracy thinking. In their view, these are not distortions of the usual politics; hence they must be part of rational government, in keeping with the norms of the public sphere.

A Distrust of the System

Although an experienced politician, Hillary Rodham Clinton is obviously not a conventional pluralist. It is also clear that her loyalty to her husband during his frequent sex scandals did not demand that she turn to conspiracy theory. Thus, it was surprising when, on NBC's "Today" on January 27, 1998, she linked these scandals to a conservative plot to destroy his presidency: "For anybody willing to find it, and write about it, and explain it, is this vast right-wing conspiracy that has been conspiring against my husband since the day he announced for President. A few journalists have kind of caught onto it and explained it, but it has not yet been fully revealed to the American public. And actually, you know, in a bizarre sort of way, this [the Lewinsky scandal] may do it."[49]

Hillary Clinton's sweeping indictment fits with the broader politics of her husband's presidency. It evokes a politics of excess that reveled in Bill Clinton's transgressions and desires, in the big hair, lips, and stories of the women with whom he has been linked, and in the endless array of scandals around a special prosecutor, the White House, and a media out of control. Were her declaration simply another instance of these public excesses, it would not seem so audacious, so paranoid, so potentially crazy. For even as conspiracy is in the air, even as the *New York Times Magazine* can feature a cover story on those Clinton haters who weave conspiracy theories about Vincent Foster's suicide, obscure episodes in Arkansas politics, and schemes to make money and abuse power, the First Lady's embrace of conspiracy as an explanation for political events violates the rarely acknowledged norms of debate within what is presented as the national public sphere.[50] She dares to take conspiracy seriously. She dares to omit from her statement the all-too-common disavowal, "I'm not a conspiracy theorist, but . . ." In so doing, Hillary Clinton crosses the line dividing normalized political discussion from the "extremist" and "radical."

In taking conspiracy seriously, the First Lady stops keeping up appearances. No longer following the rules of the game inside the Beltway, she points to conspiracy as a secret that has not yet been "fully revealed to the American public." This secret is not the sexual secret that concerned the journalists and politicians of the official public sphere. Nor is it the secret enticing the public-supposed-to-know or suturing this public together with the public-supposed-to-believe. Rather, this secret, this conspiracy, has more to do with what the public-supposed-not-to-know is not supposed to know, namely, that political events are irretrievably entangled in power, privilege, connection, deal-making, and duplicity. It is a secret that challenges the disavowal of power and mediation that sustains politics as usual. Hillary Clinton's evocation of conspiracy refers to the way that what emerges as an event has little to do with our hopes for justice and the fairness of the American political system and a lot to do with publicity and who gets it and how. By making known what the public is supposed to not know, she exposes the illusion of the public. We might even say that she *tells the secret*. The impediment, the not known, is removed, and the illusion momentarily dissolves; for a while, at least, the rifts and fissures of political antagonism are perfectly clear. Hillary Clinton's appeal to conspiracy thus collapses the distinction between the public-supposed-to-know and the public-supposed-to-believe.

From the perspective of the knowing public inside the Beltway, her claims appeared outrageous. Internet writers made this point as they filled in the missing parts of her interview: "You know what I mean. Ken Starr is part of the New World order that's implanting chips in everybody and keeping the UFO's hidden at Area 51 and giving everybody cancer. I've seen him flying a black UN helicopter."[51] Such comments suggest that once mainstream political figures acknowledge conspiracy, anything goes. Any claim is as good as any other; there's no difference between the reasonable deliberations of the judging (who also know what not to know!) and the fears and fancies of the middle and many.

William F. Buckley invoked the threat to "normal politics" constituted by the blurring of the distinction between the public-supposed-to-know and the public-supposed-to-believe. In his judgment, conspiracy theory isn't *real* politics; it's kooky. Buckley associates "right-wing kookism" with the John Birch Society. He racializes "the kooky left" as those who claim "AIDS was an invention of the CIA to arrest the growth of the black population." Those on the Left who Buckley thinks actually were conspiratorial aren't kooky; they are "mischievous"—Buckley's odd, dismissive term for "American communists and their fellow travelers, who did everything from infiltrating government to stealing the secrets of the atomic bomb."[52]

The *Washington Post*, also anxious to restore the division between the knowing and believing publics, provided assurances that whereas the *American Spectator*, British tabloids, conspiracy theorists, and Jerry Falwell have indeed persistently attacked and denounced the Clintons, the Lewinsky matter is significantly different. According to the *Post*, "The news that Starr is investigating allegations that Clinton had a sexual relationship with the former White House intern and lied under oath about it was broken by mainstream news organizations—the *Washington Post*, ABC, *Los Angeles Times*, and *Newsweek*—not by the conservative press."[53] The public can believe because those who know have the right information. They know, and their judgments are as sure and certain as ever.

These responses to Hillary Clinton's declaration attempt to re-split the public that the First Lady's remark merges and, as a result, dissolves. They separate those who know from the strange and bizarre claims of those who should not be believed. They try to re-order the world, to reboot the political system. Hillary Clinton's appeal to that which has not yet been fully revealed opens up the possibility of a world enlarged to allow for power, conflict, and manipulated connections, a world in disarray, a world not only outside the system but the world in which the system is embedded. The voices of order respond to her evocation of mysterious possibilities with closure, as if to return to a time when Pandora's box had not yet been opened, as if this time could ensure an operational public even today.

Similarly confronting a democratic distrust of expertise and exclusivity, a number of politicians, pundits, and political theorists find themselves duty bound to ensure that the rest of us know the difference between responsible political thinking and crazed conspiracy theory. They think they know and that the rest of us should believe. Often these pundits and politicians inscribe their worries about conspiracy theory onto bodies. Some want to immunize the body politic from infection by conspiracy theories.[54] Others want to protect innocent citizens from the seductions of paranoia. The pundits warn us that we must avoid titillation as well as infection. Pipes, for example, finds conspiracy theory ripe with suggestive fantasies. He doesn't say why conspiracy seduces, but he invites readers to join him in his struggle against it.[55] It's as if these pundits view conspiracy thinking as political pornography, as a cognitive virus that stimulates not the mind but the body.

Nonetheless, Hillary Clinton's click on conspiracy opened up, at least momentarily, some sites beyond those of Beltway politics. Scrutiny immediately shifted from Bill Clinton to his critics, prosecutors, and enemies. The secret was no longer what happened between the president and a White House intern. It was now the possibility of a conspiracy. After Hillary Clinton's charge that not one person but "an entire operation" was behind the assault on her husband, mainstream news media such as the *New York Times*, the *Washington Post*, *Time*, and *Newsweek* provided detailed accounts of the links connecting key figures in the Lewinsky case.

The efficacy of the First Lady's click on conspiracy isn't surprising. Conspiracy thinking is deeply embedded in American history and is particularly resonant in the national present. It is clearly part of American politics, regardless of the admonitions and dismissals of elite experts. At least some people respond to it. These are the people and this is the politics Hillary Clinton was trying to access. Her effort to change a particular rendering of the secret did not hail television viewers as the public-supposed-to-know, as the rational subjects of an officially sanctioned public sphere. She was offering her audience access to a different discourse, one characterized not by norms of rational exchange but by suspicion and doubt. Or, better put, she was making explicit the fact that the politics of exposure is not rational debate and that there is something illusory, false, and limiting in treating as a fair and rational debate what is in fact a system of distrust.

It may be misleading to read Hillary Clinton's remarks as somehow resting outside the system of distrust, unsettling to link a reference to secrets and conspiracy on national television to an enlarged world outside of the usual politics. Doesn't it make more sense to admit that even in her efforts to expose the workings of the media-political complex, the First Lady remains trapped within it? The answer points to the changed function of the secret in contemporary technoculture. Of course the possibility of a secret, of something hidden, retains political currency. Secrecy is an issue that confronts the key intersections of state, capital, and information. But Hillary Clinton evokes the not-yet-revealed not as the missing information warranting judgment and belief but as a disavowal of the public's constitutive exclusion. Her response to the media move to expose (*the public has a right to know*) works not within the system of distrust, not on the level of the demands of publicity as the demands of the norm of reason, but outside it, at the level of the very command to reveal. Who can issue this command and under what terms? In what practices of revelation and concealment is the command embedded, and what fantasy do they materialize? By challenging the Beltway presumption of the public-supposed-to-know, the First Lady eliminates—if only momentarily—its aura, its presumption to know—and acts to disrupt the practices that materialize belief.

The cyberian context of Hillary Clinton's remarks, their embeddedness within contemporary technoculture's networks of televisual, print, and computer-mediated interactions, highlights an additional change at the level of the audience, of those who watch and consume politics. Žižek describes the West as fascinated by the gaze of the other.[56] America, it seems to me, likes to look at itself. It divides itself reflexively in terms of watchers and the watched. A program running within the system of distrust, this subroutine of publicity configures politics as a screen viewed by the governed. What counts as government is what is watched. The corresponding obligation of the governed is to watch, to stay informed (a point that, paradoxically, Habermas seems to agree with, as I explain in chapter 4). Anyone who doesn't watch is excluded— as are those who want to look behind the screens. These days, the screen may be more interactive than it was back in the sixties: it's no longer only a television screen like the one that broadcast the space program; now it relies more on polls, opinion, feedback, and response (*Choose one! Fill in! Click here!*). The materialization of watching in technoculture, then, brings about a twist: viewers don't believe something just because they see it on television. Practices of watching, clicking, and opining now materialize belief in a politics of encryption and disclosure such that technologies can believe for us even as we are interpellated as suspicious subjects wanting to know.

Webs of Conspiracy

More than two hundred years after the founding, Americans are still thinking conspiratorially. But conspiracy thinking doesn't mean the same thing. There are different modes of conspiracy, different conspiratorial codings and narratives in American history. Not all conspiracy theories concern themselves with the same enemies, the same fears. In a different time, a different context, the interconnected actions they invoke resonate with a different set of possibilities and fears.

At the time of the founding, worries over conspiracy expressed fears of tyranny and corruption. As a knowledge that produced as well as detailed political obscenities and events, making links throughout them, conspiracy suggested a kind of active political engagement, a way of producing a public through revelation. Conspiracy thinking, as well as the possibility of resistance, was embedded in the conviction that rational explanations of human behavior were possible, that events were caused by specific, intentional, interconnected actions. This conviction provided the reassurance of truth and rightness necessary to supplement the fragility of political connections produced in the context of a difficult-to-justify rebellion.

Today conspiracy suggests a more varied and complex set of anxieties around information, control, access, and credibility. When conspiracy theorists point to intentional actions and plots, to planned events and coordinated activities, many of us find them hard to believe. The world seems too complicated for planning, for resistance. People can't keep secrets. No group can coordinate its actions to the degree necessary to bring off something like the assassination of JFK or secret experimentation on civilian populations. Now explanations that emphasize pregnant or hanging chads, economies, markets, systems, population flow, or traffic patterns are more likely to be convincing. We don't attribute so much to individual agency. We know that "it's the system." To use a more specific example, with the shift to the permanent fund-raising, campaigning, and sound-biting spectacle of mediated politics, the terrain of legitimate political action for most people has been reduced to a set of practices that involve watching, filling out polls, and pulling little levers. So, again, with this change in how political action is understood, there has also been a change in the meaning of conspiracy.

Changes in information networks also affect the meaning of conspiracy. Media are fragmented and dispersed. We can get information from websites, newsgroups, chain letters, network news, public access TV, direct mail, magazines, newspapers, and radio. Various players are involved in the funding, production, and distribution of information. Pharmaceutical companies provide free information about new health hazards and the drugs necessary to combat them. Single corporations control numerous magazines. The dispersion of media makes it hard for us to know what to believe, whom to trust.

Even as we are inundated with information, moreover, there is still plenty that we don't know.[57] What kinds of loan programs are available for folks in my income bracket? How many downer cows in the United States have had mad cow disease? Was sarin gas used on Americans who allegedly had defected to Laos during the Vietnam War? There is a lot of information. But it doesn't completely eliminate the secret. The same explosion of information that makes conspiracy outrageous to some makes it necessary for others.

Representations of rationality have changed. Instead of linked into understandings presumed to be shared, rationality more often than not varies with its context. To be sure, there were different rationalities during the days of the Declaration. Some people worried about witches. Some practiced witchcraft. But for the most part, the homogeneity of the nation, of those white men who counted as part of the public, was supported by a set of beliefs in the unity of law and nature. Human actions had meaning within this specific context. Our world is too confusing, too unknowable, and too complex for design and causality to make sense.

Many of us are exposed to different ways of thinking. We saw the O. J. Simpson trial. We've heard the stories of satanic cults abusing children. And we've heard them from different sides, narrated from within different conceptions of rationality. Again, within conceptions of rationality accepted in and legitimated by the public sphere, conspiracy seems naive, a childish wish for meaning and connection in a complicated world. For those of us who do not try to subsume the conflicts, fragments, and doubts of the information age under a unitary reason, however, conspiracy thinking is simply another option, one with particular resonance given the confusions of late-capitalist technoculture.

This setting is important for understanding how Hillary Clinton's conspiratorial turn is more than a political gaff or a desperate attempt for some high-quantity air time. In fact, what gives her comment a particular robustness is its link to a more elaborate network of technocultural anxieties about knowledge production in the information age. On the one hand, interconnected media exacerbate the drive for content, for the scoop, for information, in their competition for audience. There must be some secret out there that has not yet been revealed. On the other hand, with the abundance of information available on the Internet, cable television, and radio come more personal concerns about the disintegration of privacy.[58] Many of us are monitored in our day-to-day activities. Hidden cameras observe nannies. Tape recorders track telemarketers, "to enable them to serve you better." We're accustomed to seeing video clips from ATMs and convenience stores on the evening news, especially when they feature black and brown faces. Anywhere at any time, anyone of us may be tracked, traced, observed. Websites can deposit a cookie or trace code onto my hard drive, making me readable, useable, tradeable.[59] We are all potential information. Hillary Clinton's outrage over the monitoring of her husband's activities, then, may well resonate with the frustration of some employees over their experience in the workplace. Not even the office of the president is safe from prying eyes. Inquiring minds want to know.

One might think that the possibility of limitless information would help realize the claims of a democratic public sphere. If those who participate in the "conversation" have an abundance of data at their disposal, shouldn't they be able to make more informed decisions? Some versions of public deliberation stipulate that nothing be omitted from consideration, that participants have access to all relevant information. Yet the conspiracy rhetoric pervading current assessments of the Internet links precisely this vision of an end to ignorance, secrecy, and the rule of expert knowledge that animates the ideal of a public sphere with gullibility, seduction, and widespread irrationality. The very prevalence of information and inclusion of multiple voices claimed on behalf of democratic discourse morphs into the undecideability of truth claims and the fear that "all kinds of people" will enter the conversation.

Computer industry analyst Esther Dyson announces, "The Net is a medium not for propaganda, but for conspiracy." She worries:

> The Net allows all kinds of people to enter the conversation. There are still reliable and unreliable sources, but for now, as people move onto the Net, they tend to lose their common sense and believe all kinds of crazy tales and theories.
>
> Unfortunately, we as a society haven't learned "Net literacy" yet. We take a story's appearance on-line, as well as in print, as proof that it has been subjected to rigorous journalistic standards, but there's so much stuff out there that no one has the time to contradict all the errors.[60]

Dyson doesn't specify which conversation she has in mind, so it's hard to be sure what she's trying to preserve and protect. Presumably, she's thinking about something like the public sphere, something in which "we as a society" participate, something that requires a "common" sense.

What might such an all-inclusive conversation look like? Dyson's horror at the thought of "all kinds of people" entering it tells us, one, that the reality of an inclusive public sphere, a sphere in which there is no difference between those who know and those who believe, conjures up anxieties around truth and trust; and, two, that what she defends as the public sphere relies on a conception of certainty and judgment excluded to all but the reasonable few. Who exactly loses her common sense and believes crazy theories because of a cruise on the World Wide Web? Presumably the ignorant, ill informed, and unsophisticated. Presumably those left unguided by reliable sources and entrenched authorities, those who don't believe in a public-supposed-to-know. Or perhaps just those who aren't really one of "us."

Dyson's "us" is remarkably small: who today shares her confidence in journalistic standards, especially amid the remarkable elisions between so-called respectable and tabloid journalism during the Simpson trial and the Lewinsky affair? In her anxiety around the inclusion and access the Web provides, Dyson returns to an eighteenth-century conception of truth and concomitantly a narrow assumption of trust. She posits a field of knowledge reliable precisely because of the credibility—to her—of a small group of authorized, trusted, speakers. Only a few can be believed. Only a few produce "real" knowledge. But should anyone think that, given the time, one could "contradict all the errors" threatening us out there on the Web? And even if one could contradict these errors, could one correct them? What would it mean even to recognize or identify something as an error?

As part of an increasing anxiety surrounding the relation between truth and trust in cyberia's mediated networks, links between conspiracy and the World Wide Web appear all over the place. Howard Fineman, in a 1997 *Newsweek* article on the Web's political impact, worries that "In a digital world, every unchecked 'fact' is all too available, every opinion equal. The nifty Web page of the Holocaust-denier can seem just as convincing as the rerun of *Schindler's List*. 'Now you can immediately link the obsessions

of a few like-minded folks in Tampa, Wichita, and Montana.' "[61]
On the Web, abundance, immediacy, and availability seem dangerous, fuel for suspicion and obsession. They threaten, exceed, a public sense of the bounds of truth and trust, and in so doing, they
hint at conspiracy. Anxiety about the World Wide Web tends to
center on its excesses, on the overabundance of information, the
overstimulation by graphics and gimmicks, the multiplicity of
links. In traditional media and political representations of the
Web, moreover, these excesses produce a flattening of distinctions
between authorized and unauthorized, official and covert, expert
and amateur, true and false that seems to threaten reason, democracy, and the proper gap between the public-supposed-to-know and
the public-supposed-to-believe.

The assumption that excess corrupts is an idea associated with
conspiracy. Like the Web, conspiracy theory is often derided for an
inability to distinguish fact from fiction, for illogic, and for ama-
teurism. The resemblance between the Web and conspiracy thinking is almost uncanny: each relies on odd, seemingly random,
links that have always already resisted a reconciling closure or coherence.[62] Each demonstrates a preoccupation with minutia, evidence, and documentation.[63] Each occupies and disrupts a popular,
populist political field. Attacks on the Web, again, like attacks on
conspiracy theory, attempt a reassuring delimitation of the known
even as they focus on hidden truths and secrets. Amy Harmon
writes: "The amorphous network often fosters the nagging hope
that if only all the data on it could adequately be sorted, truth
would finally emerge. This is coupled with the utter certainty that
such nirvana can never be attained, and thus the peculiarly com-
forting suspicion that something important is being hidden."[64]
Harmon doesn't tell us why the suspicion that something is being
hidden comforts. She doesn't tell us from whom this important
thing might be hidden or who might be doing the hiding. I suspect
that what animates her insight is both the fantasy of the public
and the relief, the comfort, that comes from the impossibility of
realizing it.

Conspiracy's haunting of media accounts of the Internet started
in the late nineties, about the time Pierre Salinger claimed that
TWA flight 800 had been shot down by a missile. This was also
when the World Wide Web replaced chat rooms, MUDs, and
usenet groups as (with e-mail) a primary way of thinking about the

challenges of cyberspace, virtuality, and computer-mediated inter-action. As the Web became the predominant understanding and experience of the Internet, the discourse on new media changed. No longer highlighting technology's and, by implication, our own progression toward truth and reason, toward ideally democratic publics, it began raising questions of filters, editors, belief, and credibility. These questions created a friendly environment for the conspiracy tropes already long part of publicity as a system of dis-trust.

The first change in the discourse on new media involved con-tent or data. From the old media perspective, the World Wide Web isn't the information superhighway promised by Al Gore and Newt Gingrich. Instead, it's a vast repository of drivel, pornography, con-sumption, and gambling. This lament is typically followed by sta-tistics on virtual casinos and amateur sex sites or moralizing over the fact that people use the Web to fawn over celebrities and docu-ment UFO sightings instead of, say, grappling with the constitu-tional implications of a recent Supreme Court decision. The com-plaint goes further: not only do few use the Web as a learning resource, but those who do can't find anything. The porn and drivel, the limited ability of the available search engines, and the likelihood that some corporation has bought its way to the top of a site list make serious work impossible. A search for information on the hazards of silicon breast implants, for example, results in promos for pharmaceutical companies and links to thousands of porn sites.

The second change in the discourse on new media involved the subject produced through networked interactions. Recent ob-servers have replaced earlier cyberwork's emphasis on the identity play that online interactions make possible with a conception of the Web subject as a gullible consumer in need of protection.[65] In-deed, in some accounts, the quintessential Web subject is a child threatened by porn and pedophiles, conspiracy and consumerism. One explanation for this refiguration may be that the Web opens up the Internet to vast numbers of new users. Like the PC, it brings the Net home. Web users are neither computer professionals nor devout hobbyists and hackers. They tend to be rendered in demo-graphic terms, part of an increase in Net use by members of cate-gory x, y, or z. Or they are those who sign on with AOL. Such Web cruisers are less likely to spend hours constructing their virtual identities than they are making links, jumping from site to site taking in ads, checking out new products, enjoying parodies and porn, and exposing themselves to the wild ideas of ufologists and conspiracy theorists.

Finally, the third change is in the characterization of computer-mediated politics. Instead of enabling participatory democracy through large-scale, real-time debates and candidate Q & A, Web politics is presented in terms of seduction, deception, and manipulation by conspiracy, neo-Nazi, and right-wing militia websites. Looking more for pleasure than information, casual users are thought to open themselves up to wily corporations, advertisers, and political bad guys. The assumption seems to be that the combination of drivel and inexperience lures and protects all those political and market forces heretofore barred from public debate by the standards of objective journalism and the containment provided by party politics.

That these particular changes in the discourse on new media have accompanied the rise of the Web was not inevitable. Other possibilities are out there now, even if they are not so readily available. One person's drivel may be another's delight. Some celebrate the fact that more people now have opportunities to put up websites. We don't have to watch reruns of *Baywatch* if we're bored. The consumer-oriented turn of the Web doesn't have to be a negative. A few small businesses may have a chance now that, say, Toys-R-Us can't monopolize toy sales. New bands and musicians can get their music out without having to go through industry record producers and exclusive forty-song play lists. Those of us in small towns aren't confined to shopping at Wal-Mart. Be that as it may, as I explore more thoroughly in the next chapter, the early rhetoric of free information, universal access, and virtual democracy implied that the Internet would realize the promise of the public sphere. The new discourse implies that it hasn't—and tries to explain why. With the coming to prominence of the World Wide Web, information has been formatted as porn and drivel, subjectivity as gullible consumerism, and political action as seduction, manipulation, and deception.

Conspiracy theory can be installed in depictions of the World Wide Web because of this new format. That is to say, the changes in the discourse on networked communications are particularly effective insofar as they citationally evoke anxieties around the corrosive illogic of conspiracy theory. The fear is less that the Web will be a vehicle for actual conspiracies than that it will enable conspiracy theorists to seduce gullible Web cruisers who happen upon their websites. Once voiced, this fear motivates calls for protective intervention. A dismissive attitude toward conspiracy theory is linked to critical assessments of the World Wide Web so as to make regulation seem natural, necessary. Indeed, the articulation with conspiracy establishes a moralizing agenda for intervention that relies on an idealized vision of politics and community. Save us from porn and drivel. Keep the market in its place. Reassert politics' proper borders. Give us (back) our public sphere.

That a language of conspiracy provides a compelling way to talk and think about the Web makes a certain sense. Even with the lure of the secret, the Web subverts a prominent experience of what has become mainstream politics, namely, generation of an already select audience through disclosure. Appealing to fragments and subsets, to small demographic units, and to curious, searching, individuals, the Web points to the dissolution of the fantasy of a universal and universalized public to which we all somehow belong. Instead of totality, it offers proliferation and dispersion. In so doing, it puts in stark relief the televisuality of what has served as the ideal of a public. If millions of websites are politically threatening, bringing with them risks of fragmentation, the legitimation of marginalized and extreme political positions, and the de-authorization of the traditional and mainstream information sources that gave weight to the public-supposed-to-know, then perhaps all along the public sphere was only *60 Minutes*, *Nightline*, and the evening news. Perhaps we were never more a public than when we gathered around our television sets watching a giant step for mankind or hearing about the state of the union. *When we sat there and believed*. By making the televisuality of the public visible, the Web unravels the narrowness operating in the name of the public. Conspiracy rhetoric clicks on this populist edge.

At the same time, however, the prevalence of conspiracy in the discourse on the technocultural impact of computer-mediated interaction suggests that the Web *is* the public; that it is an open, unending discussion by everyone. Such a suggestion, such a materialization, exposes the tensions previously hidden by the secret. What has been theorized as the public sphere is an exclusive conversation according to a set of norms designed to keep it exclusive even as they gesture to universality. The more open and dispersed the conversations, the more varying ideals and approaches proliferate, the greater the threat to those accustomed to authorizing truth, to determining the grounds of responsibility. Increased publicity challenges the systems and spaces that both drive and seek to contain it.

The Web is that place, that set of interactions, performances, and enjoyments, that realizes the fantasy of the public. There all secrets are told, all desires revealed. Everybody knows. On the Web, we get what we wish for—an inclusive public—and that's precisely the problem. The ideal of the public had relied on a gap between the public-supposed-to-know and the public-supposed-to-believe. It was premised on a disavowed limiting and closing off of the public. As I've shown, conspiracy theory takes this disavowal seriously, obsessively theorizing the limits of democracy via a literalization of the system of distrust: it continuously searches for what is going on behind the scenes, hysterically questioning and doubting that what we see is really the way things are—*what are politicians, media, and corporations really saying?* Through its practices of searching and linking, conspiracy theory acts out its fantasy of publicity. In contemporary technoculture, these practices materialize the fantasy of the public as they eliminate the gap between the public-supposed-to-know and the public-supposed-to-believe. Because everyone has the know-how to make the links and discover the secrets, there is no need to believe. The technologies believe for us.

CHAPTER THREE

Little Brothers

The year 1984 came and went and Big Brother is still not watching. Most obviously: no maniacal, authoritarian Big Brother is controlling things from the center of an all-powerful state. In fact, the opposite has occurred: the welfare state is withering away. Maniacal leaders in Britain and the United States have trimmed down government and let the market take over. Not only has this deregulation extended to television and radio, but advances in telecommunications and information technologies have led to a decentralization of production in numerous industries. Markets have expanded, and communication networks have extended.[1]

Big Brother may not be watching, but Little Brothers are. Surveilling our transactions and disseminating our secrets, a global network of Little Brothers trades in information.[2] They have access, data, Intranets, and billion-dollar capitalizations. They have global armies of programmers. They may lack Big Brother's state power, but the Little Brothers thrive in the excesses of the information economy. Radiating a sense of the new, the now, the bleeding edge, they promise freedom, prosperity, and democracy. With slogans like "we're all connected" and "information wants to be free," the Little Brothers represent themselves as all of us, for all of us.

Big Brother? Big Deal!

Big Brother's demise has ushered in a new power formation. I think of it in terms of the rule of Little Brothers, understanding that the flows and assemblages within which "rules" are given sense have changed. The practices of disseminating information and extending access to the means of communication, once lauded as the critical core of democratic governance, appear today in the service of communicative capitalism. As Michael Hardt and Antonio Negri argue, "The new communication technologies, which hold out the promise of a new democracy and a new social equality, have in fact created new lines of inequality and exclusion."[3] What is rapidly emerging as the central paradox of contemporary technoculture is the impoverishment of the demos as the price of democracy. The more decentralized, inclusive, and accessible the networks of communication are, the greater is the consolidation of wealth and power in corporations, on the one hand, and the lesser is the worth, impact, and authority of noncommercial voices and associations, on the other.[4]

Big Brother is an icon for technocracy; clicking on it runs a cybernetic system of centralized reason, efficiency, and control. In contrast, the Little Brothers are icons for technoculture, today's seemingly more fluid, anarchic, and individualistic—although nonetheless technologically mediated—field of interactions. Unlike technocracy, technoculture connotes flexible creativity, affective engagement, and the fugitivity of truth.[5] Computer technology is pervasive, even constitutive, but the accompanying techniques of power and arrangement are radically different from the technocratic vision of *1984*. The very ideals proclaimed as remedies to technocratic control configure today's regulatory matrix.

In this chapter, I look at this reconfiguring of technologically mediated communication from technocracy into technoculture. I begin with Apple's "1984" commercial. This announcement of the Macintosh is the media moment that marks the demise of Big Brother and the emergence of the Little Brothers. Second, I highlight the communicative ideal of publicity in the rhetoric of computer liberation and the information revolution. Some may be familiar with the utopian imagining of the personal computer—after all, it's what computer advertisements are all about. Nevertheless, I consider these early years in some detail in order to demonstrate how the creative and communicative potentials credited to new technologies reconfigure the assumptions of work and rule associated with technocracy and in so doing establish technoculture as a new political-cultural-economic formation. I argue that a shift in the locus of critique from systems to people enabled a move from worries about the programmed society to worries about the programmers themselves. So, third, with a focus on the suspicions of secrecy that accompany the rhetoric of publicity, I look at imaginings of programmers as a mysterious priesthood of the computer. Not only does this imagining of a priestly elite enable attacks on centralized computing to adopt a language and logic of democratic publicity, but it enables hackers to emerge as icons of democracy and play and thereby to supplant work as a key way of relating to computers. The language of democracy and the appeal to play derail the critique of technocracy by reconfiguring technology as the solution to technocratic rule.

With this genealogy in place, I turn, fourth, to the idea of technology as ideology in the critical theories of Herbert Marcuse and Jürgen Habermas. I do so in order to explore the ways a normative ideal of publicity, that is, an ideal of open communication and democratic debate, provides not an alternative to technocratic reason, as Habermas argues against the earlier generation of the Frankfurt school, but the very ideology of technoculture. In brief, Enlightenment-based accounts of democracy such as those of Habermas are committed to a view of democracy premised on an ideal of publicity. Not only does this ideal posit "the public" as democracy's site and subject, but its emphasis on reflective deliberation relies on a prior account of encryption and revelation: the production of some contents as secrets and their subsequent exposure to the public operate prior to democratic deliberation. The people can't deliberate if they don't know; as is often stated, the public has a *right to know*. My argument is that in contemporary technoculture, a dynamic of publicity and secrecy hurts rather than helps democracy. It produces communicative capitalism as the lure of secrets, and the promise of revelation circulates throughout cyberia's networks.

An Apple a Day . . .

These days, other than a few conspiracy theorists and those trapped in the camera-ed enclosures of reality television, not so many people worry about Big Brother. Instead, anxieties around technology, information, surveillance, and secrecy are linked to Little Brothers. Software designed to monitor workers' use of the Net goes under the label Little Brother.[6] The *New York Times* summons the specter of dangerous, secret-telling Little Brothers in a hand-wringing editorial on the websites, individuals, and corporations dealing information on the Internet.[7] Simson Garfinkel, in his account of the death of privacy in the twenty-first century, relies on the same image: "The future we're rushing towards isn't one where our every move is watched and recorded by some all-knowing 'Big Brother.' It is instead a future of a hundred kid brothers who constantly watch and interrupt our daily lives."[8]

Garfinkel's point is a good one, more accurately capturing the appeal of the poorly named television voyeuristic game show *Big Brother*. There isn't one controller behind the scenes; there aren't even that many watchers. The cameras are decentered—spread out and materialized as the possibility of multiple, discontinuous, differentiated watchers whose thoughts, desires, and opinions are no longer certain. As the "houseguests" on the American version of the show make clear, they have no idea how they are being seen, or how they appear in front of the cameras. They aren't performing for Big Brother at all (which may explain why the show is so boring).

Slavoj Žižek's application of the term "Little Brother" to Bill Gates clicks on accessibility as key to this new assemblage of power and information. For Žižek, Gates is "the average ugly guy" whose ordinariness combines with the monstrous uncanniness of an Evil Genius out for total world domination. Gates is nothing special, nothing particularly strong or impressive; he doesn't radiate authority. Nevertheless he has a capacity to control, a know-how that enables an incredible amassing of wealth and a capacity for structuring the conditions of communication. Žižek writes,

> Gates is not only no longer the patriarchal Father-Master, he is also no longer the corporate Big Brother running a rigid bureaucratic empire, dwelling on the inaccessible top floor, guarded by a host of secretaries and deputies. He is, rather, a kind of *little brother*: his very ordinariness functions as the indication of its opposite, of some monstrous dimension so uncanny that it can no longer be rendered public in the guise of some symbolic title.[9]

As a Little Brother, Gates is accessible. His power rests not on secrecy but on ubiquity—it can't be avoided; it's everywhere. It isn't symbolic. It's Real. Unlike the restrictive, totalitarian Big Brother, Little Brothers today don't need to set down the law. They can give us what we want, operating through dispersions and circulations, through the drive of the spectral Real of capitalism in the information age.[10]

And then there is the anti-Gates, Theodore Kaczynski, the technophobic Unabomber. He too is linked to a Little Brother, a sneaky Little Brother who can't keep a secret, who *tells*, who *makes public*, his suspicions about his big brother's activities. In 1995 David Kaczynski turned in his reclusive older brother, Ted Kaczynski, to the FBI. The preceding summer, he had read "Industrial Society and Its Future," the Unabomber manifesto, as it appeared in the *Washington Post* and the *New York Times*. Kaczynski saw in the text the critique of technology often voiced by his older brother and concluded that he must be responsible for the sixteen bombs that had killed three people and injured twenty-three others between 1978 and 1995. In frequent statements to the press, David depicted his big brother as a paranoid schizophrenic. By reconfiguring Ted's words and actions, David turned violent political protestation into politically irrelevant madness and irrationality.[11] The Unabomber's own Little Brother ended up using new technologies in precisely those ways the Unabomber most feared: David made Ted public and in so doing reduced him to the insignificance of the media event.

Until Big Brother was overthrown, there was no space for all these Little Brothers. So it's no coincidence that we find an ironic or critical distancing from Orwell's technocratic Big Brother present already in the early days of personal computing: "Little Brother" was batted around as a possible name for one of the first home computers.[12] We might even say that the link between individuals and computers so crucial to the era of the Little Brothers—the idea that the computer is a vital personal tool and consumer product—emerges through an engagement with, *even an attack on*, Big Brother.

Apple's famous commercial "1984" (created by Chiat-Day and directed by Ridley Scott) stages as well as wages this attack. Although the commercial officially aired only once, during the 1984 Super Bowl, its influence and renown are remarkable. The commercial's circulation as content in all sorts of televisual, print, and electronic media operates through precisely that dispersion of power and access that marks publicity in the age of the Little Brothers.[13]

As "1984" begins, bald, Heaven's Gate-ish drones shuffle through a gray corridor and into a well-guarded auditorium. From a large screen, Big Brother proclaims:

Each of you is a single cell in the great body of the State. And today, that great body has purged itself of parasites. We have triumphed over the unprincipled dissemination of facts. The thugs and wreckers have been cast out. *Let each and every cell rejoice!* For today we celebrate the first glorious anniversary of the *Information Purification Directive*.

We have created, for the first time in all history, *a garden of pure ideology*, from which each worker may bloom secure from the pests purveying contradictory and confusing truths. Our unification of thought is more powerful a weapon than any fleet or army on earth. *We are one people. With one will. One resolve. One cause.* Our enemies shall talk themselves to death, as we will bury them with their own confusion. We shall prevail![14]

At this point, a woman shatters the screen. An athlete in red shorts, she runs through the corridor, bursts into the auditorium, and hurls a sledgehammer, destroying Big Brother in an explosion that introduces the announcement for Apple's Macintosh computer.

Why does a woman enact the end of Big Brother? Perhaps because she represents the domestic female consumer or supportive secretary. Apple might have used a woman because the market it wanted to reach is typically thought of in feminine terms of home and personal life, on the one hand, and typist and data processor, on the other.[15] The woman could also be a postmodern Eve, an early adopter of the apple (a Macintosh) that will provide not knowledge or Truth, but know-how, access, and nifty graphics. Pomo Eve introduces the healthy, happy impurity of "contradicting and confusing truths" into the "garden of pure ideology." How like a woman. Maybe a woman destroys Big Brother because Apple, the world of computing that will transform 1984, and the new computer era itself all entail a collapse in the division between public and private that the figure of Big Brother secures. When computers are at home and at work, when they bring us together while we are apart and recombine our facts and fantasies, it is difficult to determine what sense a public/private division might make. Is it about space, action, access?[16] Maybe Pomo Eve is dressed as an athlete because, really, it's all just one big game.

Like the multiple possibilities figured by the woman runner, the difficulties in determining a plausible division between the public and private—the problem of, as Žižek suggests, "rendering public"—highlight the powerful ambiguity in Apple's evocation of Big Brother: he's more than IBM; he's the state. The attack on Big Brother is an attack on a particular mode of state power, one associated with the centralized, technologized, control of mainframes, with a capacity to dominate the production and dissemination of information, and with a monopoly on the secret and arcane knowledges associated with computers, codes, and cybernetics.[17] Big Brother controlled thought because he controlled computers; unity in thinking was a technological achievement. Consequently, confronting Big Brother entailed challenging his ability to unify thought, his monopoly on information and the tools that gathered, processed, and disseminated it. Whether IBM or the state, Big Brother's power relied on secrets: on secrets of technique, process, and arrangement; on secrets of programming that have more in common with Freemasonry's mythic knowledges of measurement, geometry, and building than with something that media people of a later generation would call "content." Thus the commercial holds out the promise of a power that stems from gaining access to secret knowledge: with Apple, we will be free, able to think our divergent and contradictory thoughts, because we will have the proper know-how. The dispersion of knowledge will liberate our (presupposed and repressed) multiplicity.

Employing a dynamic of secrecy and publicity, the "1984" commercial's attack on Big Brother suggests that the power to program need not remain the privileged secret of the few; the Macintosh makes it available to the many—and transforms the very meaning of computing power in the process. The commercial implies that the mysterious knowledge of computing can be seized from the sovereign and distributed throughout the population. Anyone can encrypt, reveal, or disseminate. Armed by Apple, the Little Brothers can appropriate the Master's tools: the techniques for arranging and accessing data; the capacity to uncover, produce, and disseminate information; the ability to program, organize, distribute, and connect what was previously the privileged domain of the state and its primary apparatuses.

The demise of the mainframe provides a technocultural variation on the old Freudian story of the death of the patriarchal Father.[18] Not only is the killing carried out by a woman (and not by a tribe of sons), but what was desire for the Mother now appears as desire for access to the Father's control over secrets. The Little Brothers want to know how it's done. They want a knowledge of techniques (as in the adage that discourages charitable giving: don't give a man a fish, teach him *how* to fish). Little Brothers recognize that power is like an assembly language—a way of organizing, like Weber's files, and naming, like Hobbes's sovereign. With their new techniques, the Little Brothers combat secret, centralizing, paternalistic authority, and in so doing they displace Big Brother. They destroy the Leader, the Master, the symbolic center of government (the state) and economy (IBM). In the resulting confusion, in cyberia's interconnected networks of communication, capital, media, and access, they wield the weapons of publicity, scrambling about the excesses of meaning and possibility that mark not simply the empty place of power but the very dissolution, the "de-placement," of a specific place for power to occupy.[19] Now that Little Brothers have acquired the assembly language for themselves, they can program, arrange, produce, circulate, and reveal whatever secrets they like.

You Say You Want a Revolution

The year before Big Brother was supposed to be watching everything, *Time* magazine swerved from its annual practice of naming a "man of the year" (a practice later renamed "person of the year") to declare the computer the "machine of the year" for 1982 (Margaret Thatcher was a runner-up). During 1982, *Time* had featured computers on its cover three times and had added a regular section on computers to the magazine. Significantly, the machine of the year was not just any computer; it was the personal computer. *Time* explains, "Computers were once regarded as distant, ominous abstractions like Big Brother. In 1982 they truly became personalized, brought down to scale, so that people could hold, prod and play with them."[20] One of the odd things about the *Time* feature was that the cover didn't show a real computer or even real people using a fake computer. No one holding, prodding, or playing with a computer appeared on the *Time* cover. Instead, there were two stark white George Segal sculptures of people sitting with models of computers by Richardson/Smith Design. The computer, the people, and the people's relation to the computer were imaginary. How could it be anything but? In 1983, few people had any idea what to do with a computer.

A fantastic sense of the personal computer also infuses Roger Rosenblatt's lead essay about the machine of the year. Written as the monologue for an unnamed, imaginary, masculine speaker, "A New World Dawns" links the computer to the American frontier tradition, a tradition romanticized as the love of open territory and the American capacity for invention. For Rosenblatt, computers reopen territory, providing new space by saving time. The space they open up, moreover, is "dreamspace." The nostalgic, frontier voice muses:

> This sweetheart here, this little baby, looks like any ordinary machine, isn't that so? . . . Think that's what the machine is made of, do you—the hardware and the software and the mouse? Not a chance. The computer is made of *you*, lady. It's got you all inside it. You wished it here. . . . You wished it here because the country was running low on dream time. Which provides *equal time*. I'm talking social equality. I'm talking freedom with a capital F, like when the railroad first rolled in 150 years ago, roaring and puffing over the countryside, scaring the chickens and the cows, but offering everyone a ride just the same, that's everyone, I say giving the Republic to the people. Just like the computer.[21]

Because Americans "were getting hungry to be ourselves again," the computer emerges to save the day, the dream, the fantasy of America.[22] In an inversion and incorporation of the maternal body—the "lady" is "all inside" the computer—the machine displaces the baby as the embodiment of hope for the future. The computer is infused with the American dream, with equality and freedom for everyone. Interestingly, however, Rosenblatt doesn't stop with these democratic hopes. Rather, he concludes his essay with reference to another American dream, revealing that the speaker behind the hokey frontier voice isn't just any American. The speaker is a salesman, a huckster, spinning a story with hype, hope, and an overwrought evocation of American history. The piece ends: "There's a New World coming again, looming on the desktop. Oh, say, can you see it? Major credit cards accepted."

By taking the American dream at its word, by bringing to the fore the element of the market always part of the American dream, Rosenblatt clicks on the fact that the personal computer is a commodity. It's part of a market. Like any domestic appliance, it has to be advertised and sold. Consumers have to want it.[23] Even in the early eighties, few American households had much use for computers. So they had to be taught; consumers had to be produced just as computers did. *Time*, using a rhetoric that by 1983 had come to dominate computer talk, refers to this change, to this production of computers and their consumers, as a revolution.

The idea of a computer "revolution" repeats the language of the Industrial Revolution—new mode of production, new economy, and so forth—but there is another sense of revolution that comes from the computer counterculture. Antiwar activists in the San Francisco Bay area wanted to use information technology for democratic politics. Attacking the centralization of information in the hands of corporate, government, media, and university authorities, they argued that participatory democracy depended on control over information flow. Computers provided this control. In the hands of the people, then, computers could be a liberating force. The activists emphasized that computers would enable people to bypass "electronic communications media, which broadcast centrally-determined messages to mass passive audiences" and communicate with each other quickly and directly.[24]

Computer liberation advocate Ted Nelson spoke frequently and passionately about universal access to computers, linking computers to personal freedom.[25] Stewart Brand, founder of the *Whole Earth Catalogue*, shared this enthusiasm, claiming that computers—the best news since psychedelics—"serving innumerable individual purposes can be healthful, can repair havoc, can feed life."[26] Access to computers, to the knowledges around programming and the capacities of networks, was the key to participatory democracy, to the empowerment of the oppressed and excluded. The newsletter for the People's Computer Company (which was not actually a company in the sense of making things or being incorporated—a nice foreshadowing of the changes to come in the information economy)—announced, "Computers are mostly used against people rather than for people, used to control people instead of to free them. . . . time to change all that."[27] In essence, as Theodore Roszak explains, the revolution in computers "would undergird a new Jeffersonian democracy based, not on the distribution of land, but upon equal access to information."[28] Computers were imagined as the bearers of, the vehicles for, democratic publicity. They would provide the information and communicative infrastructure that would enable America to realize its dream.

This emancipatory image of computer technology (minus the business component) fit well with a number of key countercultural themes. It continued Marshall McLuhan's utopian ideal of a global village (where everybody had to buy a television), of connections and relations extending beyond national and local boundaries to create a world community. With its promise of a world without paper, provision for alternate forms of affiliation, and potential for clean, environmentally sound industry, this technological image also reiterated ecological values. In the words of poet Richard Brautigan:

> I like to think (and
> the sooner the better!)
> of a cybernetic meadow
> where mammals and computers
> live together in mutually
> programming harmony
> like pure water
> touching sky[29]

The emancipatory fantasy of computer technology was also part of the technopopulism associated with Buckminster Fuller's geodesic domes. Once everyone had access to computers, they could find the information they needed to build simpler, better, lives for themselves. Communities of self-reliant individuals would spring up, healthy alternatives to the cold, impersonal, meaningless lives of complex, centralized societies. People would have the techniques to organize their intersubjective relations and arrange for their own work, consumption, distribution, and survival—sort of like cybernetic hunter-gatherers. Finally, the emancipatory image of computer technology reiterated countercultural technofetishism. It extended the experimentation in electronic music that had appeared in rock music with the synthesizer and the booming market in stereo equipment. And it suggested another version of "better living through chemistry"—the possibility for alternate experiences and states of consciousness associated with LSD.

These links between computers, emancipation, community participation, democratic communication, and individual creativity were not confined to the utopian imaginings of the counterculture. In the early seventies, academics, including computer scientists, were also thinking along these lines. At a conference held at the University of Pennsylvania in 1971, for example, a number of speakers emphasized the ways that the democratization of access to computers and computing knowledge would contribute to the dismantling of giant, centralized, bureaucracies and restore efficacy to individuals and small communities.[30] Admittedly, some in the audience were not impressed and criticized the speakers for not talking enough about meaning, cosmic values, humanism, and whether they were in favor of love. Nevertheless, speakers emphasized that changing the world depended on finding ways to communicate. Charles Dechert suggested that computers would personalize society, replacing hierarchical interactions with "dense webs of communication" and "increased facility for interpersonal contact."[31] And Victor Ferkiss argued, "Information technology could be devised which would make everyone a participant in social decision making even at the national or world level. People could participate in coordinated large scale communal activity without the feeling that they were mere cogs in a machine operated from outside."[32] Like countercultural computer activists, then, proponents of information technology like Dechert and Ferkiss envisioned the new technology in terms of idealized norms of publicity: communication, participation, and personalization.

Such emancipatory visions of the computer were raised as a direct assault on the programmed society associated with technocracy. Thus Ferkiss acknowledged the pervasive fear that technology would extend the reach of bureaucracy in people's lives. He asked, "But does the fact that in the past technology has been the source of hierarchical centralized bureaucratic political and economic systems mean that this must always be the case?"[33] Dechert similarly positioned his arguments against the depersonalized, bureaucratized society in which people feel overwhelmed by powerful, irresistible machines. Both challenged the notion that computers could serve only technocratic interests and, like the Bay area computer activists, reversed the terms of the discussion.

The overorganized, programmed society—one run by computers as in Jean-Luc Godard's film from the early sixties, *Alphaville*—was a particularly powerful conception up through the 1970s. "Many young people in the late 1960s," explains Steven Levy, "saw computers as something evil, part of a technological conspiracy where the rich and powerful used the computer's might *against* the poor and powerless."[34] Computers seemed to embody the very worst aspects of technocratic control.[35] In Ted Nelson's words:

> Public thinking about computers is heavily tinged by a pecu-
> liar logic which we may call the Myth of the Machine. It
> goes as follows: there is something called the Machine,
> which is Taking over the World. According to this point of
> view, the Machine is a relentless, peremptory, repetitive, in-
> variable, monotonous, inexorable, implacable, ruthless, in-
> human, dehumanizing, impersonal Juggernaut brainlessly
> carrying out repetitive (and often violent actions).[36]

This myth was embedded in a broader account of technocracy as the general systematization of social life in accordance with rationality, efficiency, and hierarchical organization.[37] By extending the quantitative standards of math and physics to society, the technocratic ideal held out the promise of a society free from conflict. There would no longer be strife between classes, the risk of political upheaval, or the graft and corruption associated with slimy party politics. Instead, science, the arbiter of reason, would render social and political issues more objective, ridding them of their inefficiency, arbitrariness, and irrationality. With proper research, surveys, and tabulations, experts would provide the guidance necessary for a rational society. Decisions would be centralized and made on the basis of efficiency, again, as defined by the experts.

The administration of President John F. Kennedy, for example, was seen by some as installing these methods in the U.S. government. One of the best and the brightest, Robert S. McNamara, was particularly fond of system approaches. As secretary of defense from 1960 to 1965, he set up a Program Planning Budget System that used cost-effectiveness to evaluate the social impact of governmental programs.[38] (And his subsequent tenure as head of the World Bank was characterized by disastrous, costly, megaprojects.)

Similarly, in the late 1960s there was considerable debate over the likely establishment of a national electronic data storehouse for all the information gathered by the federal government. Although the Social Science Research Council recommended in 1965 the establishment of such a center on grounds of increased efficiency, critics such as Vance Packard argued that it could easily threaten human values and encourage depersonalization.[39]

Critics of technocracy worried about the social costs of rule by experts. Not only did technocratic administration undermine democratic governance—for the opinions of the everyday citizen were nothing compared with the findings of trained experts—but it also led to mindless, robotic, coglike dependence. Because society was so complex, only experts could understand it; only they had the know-how to access, process, systematize, and analyze the relevant information. Everyday people, then, *had* to turn to them for guidance, defer to their expertise. This meant that individual hopes and dreams were unimportant, that individuality itself was a glitch, a nonquantifiable contingency that could only hurt efficient resolution of those technical matters that presented themselves as political problems. As Daniel Bell's discussion of technocracy admitted, "In its emphasis on the logical, practical, problem-solving, instrumental, orderly, and disciplined approach to objectives, in its reliance on a calculus, on precision and measurement and a concept of a system, it is a world-view quite opposed to the traditional and customary religious, esthetic, and intuitive modes."[40] Some basic modes of human experience, in other words, had to be sacrificed for the sake of the system. Depersonalization was the direct result of technocratic management.[41]

But why would people give up basic modes of human experience? What would make them buy in to a system that turned them into robots bereft of human attachment and imagination? Part of the answer involves computers. The authority of computers was so hard to resist, their capacity to accumulate and process information so vast, that it seemed nearly impossible for people to do anything but submit to the decisions uttered in their name—*the computer says* . . . As Arnold Toynbee explained in an address delivered in 1971:

Computers are now conquering the world by rapid strides because they provide an answer to the problem of how to deal with the quantities and magnitudes which are a feature of present day society. The computer can deal with vast quantities of information at lightening speed, and it can put this processed information at the disposal of administrators, managers, and governments. Computers can organize human relations on a colossal scale at the price of depersonalizing human beings. They deprive human beings of the possibility of controlling the demands on them by private agencies or public authorities.[42]

So part of the problem of computers and the organized society was this seeming inescapability. The complexity of contemporary life was pointing directly to the demise of democracy, community, and freedom, and apparently nothing could be done to stop it. The very imperatives of social control and organization, of economic efficiency and the administration of welfare, made the technological solution the rational solution. Paradoxically, people gave up basic modes of human experience because it was the rational thing to do.[43]

Not surprisingly, irrationality would provide the escape key, the point of entry into the technocratic Death Star. By the late 1970s, the rational image of the computer was deteriorating.[44] Not only had the computer, Hal, gone crazy in Stanley Kubrick's film version of Arthur C. Clarke's *2001: A Space Odyssey*, but the economic recession in the United States suggested that perhaps technology wasn't solving all our problems. On the contrary, it seemed to be creating a lot of new ones.[45] The nuclear standoff between the United States and the Soviet Union showed little sign of resolving itself. The environment was in a sorry state. Skylab was falling. In 1979, there was the near meltdown of the nuclear reactor at Three Mile Island. Developments of this kind complicated the idea of the programmed society. Computers and technocrats weren't controlling things. Society wasn't efficiently administered or organized at all. Instead, there was "runaway technology," a technology run amok, filled with inexplicable glitches, out of control.[46]

The "runaway technology" line differs significantly from the complaint of "total control." It breaks ranks with the critique of technocracy as it points toward the system's failures. The problem, in other words, no longer stemmed from the successful functioning of the system. It stemmed from its malfunctioning. And this emphasis on technology's failures pointed to an important gap in the system: the human element. As one magazine complained, "The computer is running into trouble—because of shortcomings in man, not the machine. In just two decades, the electronic marvels have grown so complex and intricate to operate that man is hard put to maintain the proper control."[47] Thus, the target of criticism shifted from technocracy to the technocrats, from the program to the programmers. Computers, it was argued, are simply tools. The question was how to use them, who controls them.

Once the target of technocratic criticism shifts from the system to the people, the solution to the problems posed by computers becomes clear: people have to take matters into their own hands. They have to do it themselves. As the title of a popular book announced, "small is beautiful." Computer advocates Nelson and Brand repeated the slogan "Garbage in/garbage out," installing the message that computers are only what people do with them, that there is no automatic link between technocratic authority and the ability to store and quickly retrieve vast amounts of information. The computer revolution, then, would take the master's tools and make them weapons in the hands of the people. Once people knew how computers worked, they could fix them themselves. They could also have the information, the files, that had empowered technocratic bureaucracies. No longer the victims of an impersonal system, the people would have reclaimed their voice, their agency, and their rights. The knowledge of how to acquire, arrange, and access information, the secret techniques of the technocratic system, would now be public.

But who controlled the technocratic system in the first place? On the face of it, the question is oddly stupid: systems run on their own; they are self-reproducing. Cybernetic systems in particular rely on feedback loops "through which the output of the system is linked to its input in such a way that variations in output from some pre-established or 'programmed' norm result in compensatory behavior that tends to restore the system output to the norm."[48] The system runs without a controller. Indeed, as the predominant critique of technocracy makes clear, at issue was a whole set of practices and ways of thinking, the techniques and norms that emphasized rationality, organization, predictability, and efficiency and that sought to contain individuality, spontaneity, creativity, and play. By shifting the focus to the experts and technocrats, the "runaway technology" thesis sidesteps these issues in favor of a more manageable, entertaining, and heroic account of revolutionary struggle. The problem of systems, of technological practices and presumptions, falls to the wayside as computers become more personal.

Priests and Play

The shift from systems to people was eased by the fact that the rise of the mainframe in the media imaginary had been accompanied by stories of a mysterious, elite, computer priesthood.[49] In a 1965 cover story on the "cybernated generation," for example, *Time* magazine describes the mainframe and its new computer elite as if they were the bearers of a new religion: "Arranged row upon row in air-conditioned rooms, waited upon by crisp, young, white-shirted men who move softly among them like priests serving in a shrine, the computers go about their work quietly and, for the most part, unseen by the public."[50] In case readers miss the point, the accompanying photographs feature the obligatory wall of computers and a group of bishops using punch cards to cast ballots at St. Peters (real priests!). The magazine depicts the new elite as young, smart, well-paid men, "a sort of solemn priesthood of the computer, purposefully separated from ordinary laymen."[51] Their differences stem from their specialized knowledge and problem-solving expertise, on the one hand, and the way they combine this expertise, this work, with an odd playfulness, on the other. The magazine explains: "Lovers of problem solving, they are apt to play chess at lunch or doodle in algebra over cocktails, speak an esoteric language that some suspect is just their way of mystifying outsiders. Deeply concerned about logic and sensitive to its breakdown in everyday life, they often annoy friends by asking them to rephrase their questions more logically."[52] Like priests, or, perhaps, those initiated into a secret society, the computer elite had a mysterious language that gave them access to powerful forces. And, at the same time, they participated in pleasures that the rest of us, somehow, were denied.

The computer elite was mysterious, alien: because mainframes were new, few people understood what they did.[53] During the 1950s and 1960s, for example, popular media blurred discussions between computers, robots, and artificial intelligence. Computers seemed animated, powerful beings that knew things, that had thoughts and memories. Those who worked with them seemed touched by, encompassed within, the aura of these exotic thinking machines. Indeed, like Catholic priests, members of the computer priesthood served as intermediaries: they were the medium through which those who wanted information had to pass in order to get it. They mediated the relations between executives, managers, technology, and data.

Significantly, like Catholic priests, the computer priesthood was predominantly male. The very idea of a select, esoteric group bound together by arcane knowledge helped format the clerical activities associated with female secretaries into the more exclusive, masculine domain of information technology. The link between computer workers and a priesthood, then, was gendered, and this gendering reconfigured the mundane, supportive tasks of office work into the mysteries and secrets of a highly trained cadre of professional men with their own particular quirks and talents.[54]

Like priests, the computer elite also relied on the power of words. As one popular writer observed, those who use the computer had to learn "secret and cumbersome languages with cabalistic names—'Fortran,' 'Algol,' 'IPL-V.' "[55] Moreover, in *The Network Revolution: Confessions of a Computer Scientist*, Jacques Vallee admits, "Computer engineers, with their initiation practices, their words of power, their rituals in specially designed rooms, their incomprehensible jargon, already form a cult."[56] Vallee's remarks point beyond the power of words to click on a deeper mystery of the computer elite. What made them a priesthood was the perception that their knowledge was secret. Computer people's allure was the allure of secrets, of access to information and capacities and languages and ways of thinking that no one else had. These weren't your ordinary experts with some particular knowledge of particular facts and formulae. No, the computer priesthood had a know-how that was a "meta-knowledge." Programming a mainframe required a kind of sorcery or alchemy that conjured the life force, that could see beyond the visible, that could change the world. Like Freemasons or Illuminati, these priests had knowledge that was esoteric, and it linked them into new affiliations of those who breathe, con-spire, together. One programmer remarked, "Some call it an art and some call it black magic."[57] Is it an accident that one of the most popular database programs is called Oracle?

Again, like the worries over organization, rationalization, centralization, and hierarchicalization, the worries over the computer priesthood's secrecy were embedded in a broader critique of technocracy. Jean Meynaud, for example, emphasized the incompatibility of democracy with technocracy because the technocrat likes "to act in secret, preferring confidential discussion to open debate."[58] Technocrats shroud even the smallest detail in secrecy, turning their activities into holy mysteries even as their secrecy casts doubts on the legitimacy of political decision-making more generally. Meynaud called into question just what the technocrats might be doing behind their closed doors:

> Today, the risk of a technocratic infiltration gathers strength
> from perfected techniques aimed at working on the minds
> and taming the wills of men without recourse to violence:
> because of the rate of progress in the field of psychological
> analysis, man runs the increasing risk of falling into the
> hands of the engineers of souls. We could add to this already
> ominous picture the prospects of automatic regulation
> opened up by cybernetics. Although it is not so sensational
> or terrifying in nature . . . this branch of knowledge seems
> capable of making a further contribution to the "condition-
> ing" of human beings.[59]

Who knew what the technocrats were doing with their powerful computers? No one—and that's part of the problem of the computer elite's esoterica, their odd manner of being, and their exclusivity. "We" don't know what they are up to. (More precisely, the fantasy of a "we" is held open through the suspicion that there are secrets.)

The idea of a powerful computer priesthood operating secretly at the heart of an ostensibly democratic state was not simply a manifestation of people's fear of the new or even of a fear of technology. From its earliest days, computing was linked to secrets, to surveillance and encryption.[60] Alan Turing, one of the first to conceptualize the computer, worked in British communications during World War II with the team trying to break the German codes. The German encryption device ENIGMA was based on an invention by a Dutch businessman, Hugo Koch, who was trying to protect business secrets.[61] Thus anxiety about the secret operations of those empowered by computers was not pointless: secret knowledge had won the war. What else could it do?

Computer advocates, presumably because they knew something about computers, were particularly critical of the privilege of secrecy that was attached to those employed as programmers and experts. IBM, with its white-shirted, tight-lipped, robotic army, came under special attack.[62] Ted Nelson referred to the company as Big Brother, the International Brotherhood of Magicians, and the Institute of Black Magic. Rejecting the "stranglehold on the operation of all large organizations" that companies like IBM held, Nelson worked to spread knowledge of computers, to educate people and demystify the machine. "Guardianship of the computer," he exhorted, "can no longer be left to a priesthood."[63] Consequently, Nelson emphasized the people-friendly dimensions of the computer: animation, learning, and, most importantly, fun. Computing wasn't a mysterious, arcane knowledge demanding years of devotion. It was so easy a kid could do it.

Of course, in the early seventies when Nelson was writing, disconnecting computers from their priesthood and linking them with child's play was no easy task. It took a while for this idea to catch on. Three things made it possible: games, hackers, and sex. Pleasures would help transform programming's esoterica into a know-how that was worth having, that was so worth having, in fact, that the ideal of its dissemination and circulation would reconfigure technocracy into technoculture.

The idea that one could play games on computers was already part of the general description of the computer priesthood. Recall, these guys were so strange, so different, so in tune with the computer that they could have fun with it. They could program it to play games, like an imaginary playmate in a box. Stewart Brand focused on this play as evidence that "computers are coming to the people." Remarking on the popularity of the game Spacewar in computer labs, Brand used the game to argue that computers need not automatically be associated with top-down organization. "Spacewar serves Earthpeace," Brand proclaimed; "so does any funky playing with computers, any computer-pursuit of your own particular goals, and especially any use of computers to offset other computers."[64] Popular media picked up on the safe, fun, idyllic version of computers as child's play. They frequently illustrated articles on computing with photographs of children at terminals and promoted the educational value of computer games. *Time* gushed: "Probably the most important effect of these games . . . is that they have brought a form of the computer into millions of homes and convinced millions of people that it is both pleasant and easy to operate, what computer buffs call 'user friendly.' "[65]

Kids weren't the only link between computers and games. Hackers also contributed to the reconfiguring of computers around fun and play. Rather like technological apostates, hackers represented a counter-element within the computer priesthood, an element that had the esoteric knowledge but wanted to use this knowledge to disrupt the system. Indeed, hackers provided a kind of perverse antithesis to the bureaucratized, robotic experts associated with IBM. Whereas the mainframe culture relied on hierarchy, centralization, formulae, and procedures, hackers emphasized anarchy, decentralization, creativity, and innovation. And whereas the computer priesthood relied on secrecy, hackers championed the slogan "Information wants to be free."[66] Hackers were the wild gamers pushing technology to its limits and making a mockery of the rule of experts.

Beating the system was the key. One of the most common stories in hacker lore tells how Apple founders Steve Jobs and Steve Wozniak spent their early years making blue boxes—devices that allowed users to make free long-distance telephone calls—and selling them on the Berkeley campus.[67] (Jobs even claimed to have used a blue box to get through to the Vatican: he said he was Henry Kissinger and, allegedly, almost spoke to Pope Paul VI.)[68] Of course, even with this "bring it to the people" ethos, hackers remained their own sort of elite, priding themselves on macho, and often childish, tricks and exploits. Like Han Solo and Luke Skywalker destroying the Empire to restore the Republic, the hackers were techno-revolutionaries working—or, better, *playing*—for the good of the people.

Finally, the link between computers and play was eased into place with sex. Many have commented on the role of sex in popularizing communication technologies; this is definitely true with respect to the initial popularization of computers. Sex contributed to disconnecting computers from the antihuman, deadening association with technocracy and reconnecting them with play, creativity, and spontaneous human affection. How? Computer dating. As early as 1965, *Time* was extolling the possibilities of a "punch-card cupid."[69] Such articles playfully eroticized the computer in terms of everyday hopes and dreams. Twenty-years later, the women's fashion magazine *Mademoiselle* published an article in which owning a computer was equated with dating a computer. The author takes the "personal" aspect of the personal computer seriously. Treating the computer like a nerdish engineer, she recounts their courtship and ongoing relationship.[70] *Time* made the sexual connection even more explicit by renaming CompuServe CompuSex and announcing that computer flirting was rapidly being replaced by "all sorts of obscene propositions right on-line."[71] The imaginary friend moves out of the box and into a body.

The shift from priesthood to play was a shift in the cultural configuration of computing, the imagination of the computer in terms of everyday knowledges and techniques for living. Anyone who knows how to play a game, beat the system, or get a date has the know-how that will enable successful interaction with a computer. The power of naming, assembling, accessing, and informing is within reach. Whereas the idea of a computer revolution suggests a kind of direct political engagement between technocracy and technoculture, the reconfiguration of the computer in terms of play points to a different sort of change, one at the level of ideas and representation.

Indeed, one might say that the computer revolution wasn't a revolution at all. It was a reconfiguring, a trumping, a displacement that reimagined technology in terms of hopes and dreams that could alleviate fears of technocracy. The language of revolution then looks a lot like a baby boomer's marketing ploy, like taking a Beatles' song and attaching it to sneakers. Countercultural ideals of publicity, of democratic participation, access, and communication, don't engage technocracy. They are instead aspects of a broader reversal of terms whereby computers turn work into play, isolation into sex, and systems into vehicles for individual creativity.

If we return to Apple, we find that its earliest publicity didn't focus on the corporation, something cold and impersonal. It focused on the hippy, hacker, garage-based founders, Jobs and Wozniak. As John Sculley, who headed Pepsi-Cola before he became president of Apple, describes *Time*'s 1982 cover story on Jobs: "It told an amazing tale of a passionate folk hero whose enduring dream was to allow individuals the power that only large corporations and institutions were able to wield."[72] Sculley emphasizes the Apple ethos: the company wanted to change the world. "Their abiding faith was in the power of tools made available to everybody," he says, "one person, one computer was the route by which they planned to change the world."[73] When Apple went public, one hundred of its employees became millionaires.

The company presented itself as leading a revolution. Apple was saving democracy by bringing technology to the people. It was enabling the fulfillment of the American dream of freedom, equality, and self-reliance. It was also restoring the dignity, creativity, and fun to work. The problem of a democratic revolution for and by millionaires wasn't even hidden. It was blatantly advertised. In 1984, Apple ran an ad for the Macintosh that placed an image of the computer next to one of Karl Marx. The slogan was "It was about time a capitalist started a revolution."[74]

That the so-called revolution reversed the terms of the critique of technocracy appears clearly in Sculley's chart setting out the "contrasting management paradigms" of "second-wave" (read technocratic) executive approaches and "third-wave" corporations:

Characteristic	Second Wave	Third Wave
Organization	Hierarchy	Network
Focus	Institution	Individual
Style	Structured	Flexible
Strength	Stability	Change
Mission	Goals/strategic plan	Identity/values
Expectations	Security	Personal growth
Status	Title and rank	Making a difference
Resource	Cash	Information[75]

The third-wave company captures the ideals of the counterculture. These ideals are more than guidelines for running a corporation. They are the techniques of a new way of life. The revolution goes "all the way down." Of course, third-wave values, as even Sculley admits, were never so simple as his chart implies. For one, an open management structure was already part of Fairchild electronics, the precursor to Intel before Silicon Valley was Silicon Valley. For another, the egalitarian atmosphere of Apple was supplemented by the cult of Steve, a culture of celebrity that emphasized Job's evangelical capacity to produce a "reality distortion field" and excused his abusive debasing of employees. Moreover, it is difficult to reconcile a company's claim of dedication to employees' personal growth when its employees have a work norm of ninety hours a week, unless one is making some kind of complicated and presumably ironic argument about the need to produce the new revolutionary subject of technoculture. Nonetheless, even with these contradictions, it's clear that what is at stake in technoculture is the morphing of the critique of technocracy into a set of values that markets, supports, and renders the information economy beyond criticism.

Who could oppose empowering the people? Who could oppose restoring democracy by giving people access to computers and information, by educating, teaching, and disseminating know-how throughout the population? No one (*teach a man to fish . . .*). In this format, technoculture seems rational, desirable, unavoidable. The public has a right to know (how).

Communication and the Informatization of Society

The technocratic nightmare of a secret technology of mainframes administered by an esoteric, hierarchical, unapproachable elite was countered by a vision of the personal computer as a tool of democratic publicity. Computing know-how need not be the privileged secret of the few; it could be a tool for the many, providing them with new possibilities for access, communication, creativity, and play. As I've shown, this reassuring dynamic of publicity against secret know-how formatted technoculture in response to the critique of technocracy. The ideals underlying the critique are reconfigured as the benefits, the products and achievements, of new technologies. If technocracy relies on centralized, expert knowledge for programming the system and producing a society of compliant, one-dimensional cogs, technoculture relies on the accessible know-how of amateurs who creatively reconstitute their identities and communities in an endless flow of morphing enjoyment. Put somewhat differently, the critique of technocracy is reconfigured through an ideal of publicity such that democratizing computer know-how solves the problem of "runaway technology," even as the computer's new image displaces technophobia.

Consequently, "new economy" corporations are disconnected from the state as symbols of Big Brother. In technoculture, computer companies are presented as vehicles for democracy, now formatted in terms of the access enabled by the Internet and consumer electronics such as the palm pilot, cell phone, and other portable, digital communication devices. Technoculture is an ideological formation that uses democracy, creativity, access, and interconnection to produce the subjectivities of communicative capitalism.

This is not say that technocracy wasn't itself ideological, although supporters and critics alike frequently presented it as the end of ideology. Proponents of technocracy emphasized that technocracy was a form of governing that moved beyond the ideological divide of the Cold War. As they saw it, both communists and capitalists relied on the centralized administration of persons and processes. Both systems required expertise, organization, and planning. Technocratic rule was simply the rational mode of governance for complex societies. Cybernetics emerged in the United States, beginning in 1942, over the course of meetings sponsored by the Josiah Macy Foundation, as the interdisciplinary study of steering systems, self-regulation, and animal–machine feedback loops; it was popular in the Soviet Union as the "general science of control over complex systems, information, and communication."[76] As a science, cybernetics held out the possibility of a rational society, one in which knowledge and productivity replaced conflict and crisis. For proponents of technocracy, then, the demands of the welfare state, military preparedness, economic efficiency, and the space race seemed incontrovertible demonstrations of the fact that efficient administration and the avoidance of conflict were the keys to global as well as national stability.

For critics of technocracy, however, this similarity with Soviet-style centralization and control indicated how far from freedom America had moved; bluntly put, cybernetics looked a lot like mind control. Compliance with the efficient plans of expert planners had little in common with the mythologies of frontier freedom and creative individuality that had long been part of America's self-understanding and were crucial to the image it used to differentiate itself from communism during the Cold War. If technocracy was post-ideological, this was part of the problem: it had purchased bland efficiency and security at the cost of the American adventure, of freedom and meaning. Critics of technocracy thus emphasized the interventions of welfare state capitalism, interventions into the economic and social fields not unlike those

undertaken in Soviet-style centralized economies. The big advertisers of Madison Avenue deployed arsenals of propaganda techniques that made those used by the Soviets look amateurish and
naive. Madison Avenue could produce desires, fears, and longings
as well as tastes and opinions. It could create consumers.

Taking the argument yet another step, Frank Webster and Kevin
Robins explain that from the standpoint of the scientific managers
of the technocratic order, consumption was too important to leave
to the irrational whims of the consumer.[77] It had to be rationalized
just as production had been. They write: "If one side of [modern
marketing] was an attempt to regulate distribution and to intensify
consumption, the other entailed making sure the consumer was
known about and open to persuasion. Information was to be
sought about income levels and spending patterns, and publicity
was to be disseminated to promote the appeal and desirability of
the product."[78] What consumers wanted, from their deepest desires and fantasies to their more transient preferences and fancies,
would be gathered, compiled, analyzed, and delivered.[79] Building a
better consumer, in other words, required an entire apparatus of inquiry, investigation, production, and dissemination.

Not everyone accepted the idea that technocracy was post-ideol-
ogy. Some of the strongest analyses of the ideological dimensions
of technocracy came from the critical theorists of the Frankfurt
school. They rightly emphasized that technocracy was an ideological formation differing significantly from industrial capitalism: in
technocracy, the process of production itself provides the justification, the logic, the matrix for understanding the social system.
Technology, moreover, appears as its fascinating, spectralized
fetish.[80] Technological achievements justify themselves; knowing
how things worked, the trick, the magic, the power behind the
scenes, is more important than whatever particular discovery or
event the technologies enable (the American space program provides a clear example).[81]

Herbert Marcuse's account of the one-dimensional society
works through the ideological functioning of technocracy. Unlike
those critics who stressed the hostile, inhuman aspects of technocratic rule, Marcuse recognizes that the problem with contemporary society is not alienation. On the contrary, people are overiden-
tified with the social order; they are too connected with, too
undifferentiated from society. They lack critical distance. Marcuse

observes that the postwar United States seemed to give people exactly what they wanted—better working conditions, more leisure time, prosperity. It did so by focusing on economic efficiency and individual satisfaction. Conversely, when assessed by these measures, the United States was generally successful, even rational. The problem is that although technocracy may be rational, it is also unfree. On the one hand, technology and new techniques of social organization actually provided new solutions to the demands of human needs. Technocratic decisions and policies improved efficiency and helped individuals prosper. On the other hand, this seemingly rational society was "irrational as a whole." Marcuse argues that rather than emancipated through efficiency, people were crushed, controlled, and regulated into docile, compliant, conformist one-dimensionality. They were disciplined into acquiescence so great that they were unable to contest the cold war politics that threatened global survival. Marcuse describes this technocratic society: "Its productivity is destructive of the free development of human needs and faculties, its peace maintained by the constant threat of war, its growth dependent on the repression of the real possibilities for pacifying the struggle for existence—individual, national, and international."[82] Marcuse thus finds U.S. economic efficiency, or instrumental rationality, to come at the cost of the freedom to criticize.

From this, Marcuse concludes that Marx was wrong. Capitalism doesn't create the conditions for its own destruction, overcoming, or sublation. Instead, capitalism's technological progress leads in the opposite direction, to a situation in which criticism is pointless because any problem it might reveal can only be solved by the very strengthening of the capitalist, technocratic system. For example, poverty could be addressed by providing the poor with the training and education that would enable them to prosper in the capitalist economy. Or poverty could be dealt with through better forms of welfare and administration. In either case, the solution furthers technocratic intervention and strengthens the system. At the same time, most any other solution (redistributing the nation's wealth, providing wages for unpaid labor, raising the wages for less desirable jobs) seems inefficient, and rejecting the system seems stupid, pointless, or hopelessly romantic.

Faced with capitalism's resilience, its ability to transform criticisms into strength, Marcuse revises Marx's theory of ideology. For

Marx, ideology mystifies the relations of production in ways that prevent people from recognizing their true interests. For Marcuse, people's individual pleasures and desires cause them to accept the relations of production (*I know that the system is exploitive; nevertheless, I accept it because it lets me buy what I want, gives me the opportunity to get ahead, and so forth.*). Technocracy is a system of "repressive satisfaction" in which people's very freedoms and pleasures prevent them from critically understanding and resisting how they are dominated. Marcuse explains:

> The technical achievement of advanced industrial society, and the effective manipulation of mental and material productivity have brought about a *shift in the locus of mystification*. If it is meaningful to say that the ideology comes to be embodied in the process of production itself, it may also be meaningful to suggest that, in this society, the rational rather than the irrational becomes the most effective vehicle of mystification.[83]

Technocratic rule is ideological not because it uses all sorts of irrational ideas to get people to buy into the system. It is ideological because it uses the system, the process of production itself, to secure compliance. Technological development, economic efficiency, and market success are represented as general interests. They establish the terms of freedom and the conditions for pleasure: favoring inefficiency or wanting markets to fail *is* irrational. Indeed, this apparent immunity from or boundary against critique indicates that we're working with ideology: "rationality" displaces attention from more fundamental underlying antagonisms. Marcuse gives the example of the specter of mutual annihilation presupposed to be the enforcer of the nuclear standoff between the United States and the Soviet Union. Rational accounts of fallout and kill ratios mask the underlying irrationality of killing everybody on the planet.

If we set aside the general theory of ideology on which Marcuse's argument rests, we can benefit from his insight that technology and the process of production no longer need to be masked. The transparency of the process itself has ideological effects: everyone can see that it is rational. As Habermas explains, the technocratic consciousness is not a "wish-fulfilling fantasy, not an 'illusion' in Freud's sense, in which a system of interaction is either represented or interpreted and grounded."[84] Instead, it is a way of thinking that represses ethics and depoliticizes the mass of people by anchoring the justification of forms of social organization in the requirements of the system. Again, according to technocratic governance, efficiency is value-neutral; the system is rational, based on knowledge and expertise beyond politics. Technocracy removes the social framework from reflection, substituting calculations of means and ends for other political and ethical criteria. System imperatives, what Habermas describes in terms of "purposive-rational action," legitimize the technocratic order, and this is what gives technocracy its overwhelming, seemingly unavoidable logical power.

Like Marcuse, Habermas rejects "this cybernetic dream of the instinct-like self-stabilization of societies."[85] But Habermas differs from Marcuse in the alternatives he provides: he rejects Marcuse's suggestion of a new attitude toward nature (a new-agey kind of position I don't address here) as well as Marcuse's tendency to restore the "political innocence of the forces of production."[86] Habermas is referring to Marcuse's occasional shifts from a systemic analysis of technocracy to what I referred to above as the "technology run amok" thesis. An example of this sort of shift appears when Marcuse writes: "the facts are all there which validate the critical theory of this society and of its fatal development: the increasing irrationality of the whole; waste and restriction of productivity; the need for aggressive expansion; the constant threat of war; intensified exploitation; dehumanization."[87]

Habermas's solution to the problem of technocracy is to complicate the idea of rationality. To escape from what he sees as Marcuse's totalizing approach to technocracy, Habermas argues that Marcuse is mistaken in assuming that purposive or instrumental rationality is the only kind of rationality. Marcuse ignores what Habermas calls "communicative rationality," a form of rationality as deeply rooted in fundamental human interests as purposive rationality. "This interest," Habermas explains, "extends to the maintenance of intersubjectivity of mutual understanding as well as to the creation of communication without domination."[88] So efficiency isn't the only measure of a rational society. Also important is unrestricted and uncoerced communication, the kind of communication necessary for organizing society in keeping with those consensual norms on which human individuation and sociality depend. Habermas writes: "Public, unrestricted discussion free from domination, of the suitability and desirability of action-orienting principles and norms in the light of the sociocultural repercussions of developing subsystems of purposive-rational action—such communication at all levels of political and repoliticized decision-making is the only medium in which anything like 'rationalization' is possible."[89] Habermas wants to solve the problem of technocracy's removal of the social framework from critical reflection by subjecting it to another form of rational assessment—the communicative rationality of public debate.

As I see it, Habermas responds to Marcuse not by providing a way beyond technocratic ideology but by setting out the ideology of technoculture. For him, publicity is the solution to the problem of instrumental reason: the system shouldn't run things, people should, and the way they should do this is by communicating and discussing in a free and open manner. People have to take things into their own hands, politicize the processes of decision-making, and stop allowing scientific and technocratic imperatives to organize all of social life. But whereas Habermas understands this extension of communication as a "process of generalized reflection" and a "rationalization of social norms," we might also analyze it in terms of the integration of media, a reflexivization of the social that contributes to the disintegration of trust, and the consolidation of the logic of the network society. In short, what looks to Habermas like communicative rationality is better theorized in terms of technocultural ideology.

"Communication free from domination," the "free flow of information"—these are the very terms that support communicative capitalism. From the idea that information wants to be free to the idea that the access facilitated by global telecommunication is the kind of access necessary for democratic politics, one finds an ideal of ever-proliferating discussion, of interaction and intersubjective connection, driving the production of the information society. Universities, local governments, NGOs, and activists as well as entrepreneurs, venture capitalists, software companies, long-distance telephone companies, Internet service providers, and media corporations urge open discussion and community building. They all agree that communication is rational, that it's the key. But to what?

One of the odd things about the feeding frenzy of the nineties network mentality was the way that no one knew what the Internet was for. What do we do with it? It's as though the early days of the Internet repeated the uncertainties that appeared in Segal's sculptures and Rosenblatt's imaginings of the personal computer. The Internet would do something—it would express a kind of and hope—but how it would do this wasn't clear at all. Buzzwords appeared every few months with the next new thing—multiuser dungeons and role-playing, chat rooms, push technology, shopping (books, pets, groceries), portal sites, content and destination sites, virtual communities, webcams, business-to-business. Often it seemed that all new media ever did (and do) was market themselves in an elaborate, self-reflexive web. And this is precisely the point: the information economy has shifted to where the question is no longer what computer networks are supposed to do. In fact, the information economy was never about one thing. It's about know-how, process, and procedures. The communicative infrastructure of the Internet provides the interconnectivity, the network, for the global economy. Like a hegemonic signifier that uses the chain to signify itself, the Net is the language, the media, the currency, the system of systems—rules, representations, ideas, expectations—not exactly on which communicative capitalism rests but through which it realizes itself as itself. Communicative rationality and instrumental rationality converge: communication is the means for achieving communication as the end. Talk has replaced sex in a new version of Marcuse's repressive desublimation—new media rely on the ways that talk and sex are really just the same thing.

In technoculture, communication is the fetish that fascinates, that transfixes us as the ultimate, total, answer. On the one hand, the fetishization of communication appears as a radicalization of the notion of technology as ideology. Communication technologies are the paradigmatic form of the technological changes marketed as the digital, information, networked revolution. These particular technologies—from the Internet, to satellite and cellular communication, to nano-and biotechnologies that themselves revise notions of the communicable—are fetishized as weapons that destroyed Big Brother and brought power, the power of publicity, to the people, or at least to the Little Brothers in the name of the people. For example, the Internet has been celebrated as a decentralized communications network that ingeniously protects people from domination. This isn't wrong—but it assumes that power today still emanates from the state and still operates through control over information. And insofar as proprietary know-how becomes the measure of freedom, technocultural ideology obscures the ways that Net freedom is the freedom of the market, the freedom of corporations to extend market forces throughout the domain of the social. Erasing distinctions between form, function, and content, new media rewrite the social in terms of demands for and expectations of access, communicability, and publicity.

On the other hand, the fetishization of communication appears as the manifestation of Habermas's rationalization of communication. Given the inscription of new technologies within the ideology of publicity and given their subsequent capacity to "remove restrictions on communication" at the institutional level, computer-mediated interaction furthers the reflexivation of postmodern life.[90] The past twenty years have witnessed all sorts of debates over practical matters—over reproductive and cloning and global warming ethics and what to do about the Internet and the impact of globalization—but these debates should not be understood in terms of an increase in rationality. On the contrary, they are often vehicles for selling and promoting precisely what they aim to criticize. Easy examples include the prurient appeal of antiporn tracts, list serve discussions devoted to the critique of the Internet, and cable news talking heads criticizing other television talking heads. Criticism abounds—and it reinforces the system in a twisted variation on Marcuse's account of instrumental reason in the one-dimensional society of technocratic capitalism.

Not only does the extension of communicative reflection, the exposure of ever more aspects of life to media(ted) surveillance and inquiry, reinforce the primary dynamics of communicative capitalism, but it also contributes to the materialization of suspicion and the belief that the secrets are there to be discovered. As with Habermas's communicative ideal, networked media bring anything and everything into the discussion. There are always multiple, competing opinions. A plethora of clashing experts are available for consultation on most any conceivable question. There are always other options, links, and sites. Something else is always already out there and available to us.[91] But rather than making people more informed and discussions more rational, the proliferation of competing expert opinions puts us in the horrible position of having to choose even when we lack the criteria for choice. How do we know which expert to believe? In many aspects of contemporary life, the wrong choice is potentially disastrous: from individual medical decisions to judgments about product safety to experiments in particle physics, the wrong choice could be deadly. The high stakes often push against making a decision, reinforcing the imperatives of publicity as they command a search for more information. At the same time, they necessitate that no decision will ever be fully informed because new information could emerge exactly after a fateful decision is made—"if only we had known."

Given the reflexivization of everyday life, increases in communicative rationality suggest not the maintenance of the lifeworld but its radical reconfiguration. As Žižek writes, "what is increasingly undermined is precisely the symbolic *trust* which persists against all skeptical data."[92] He gives the example of the emergence of "ethical committees" in the context of risk society theory. Like ideal speech situations or mini-versions of Habermasian practical discourses, these committees are supposed to help find ways of making ethical decisions about complex issues such as global warming, nuclear energy, cloning, genetic engineering, and similar low-probability/high-consequence issues. Viewed from a Habermasian perspective, these committees appear as vehicles for the restoration of a disrupted consensus regarding matters of common concern. What Žižek makes clear, however, is that such ethical committees are better understood as symptomatic expressions of the fact of pervasive disagreement, of the fact that there is disagreement even about the ways that disagreements are to be understood, regulated, evaluated, and assessed. In such a setting, new procedures and rules and guidebooks and regulations don't reassure. Rather, they express the ways that crucial issues remain undecidable. Why would anyone accept a decision simply because it was the result of deliberations from an ethical committee?

Like ethical committees, the generalization of reflection Habermas understands in terms of the extension of public discussion is neither a solution to the problem of loss of trust and legitimacy nor an alternative to technocracy. Instead, it extends the suspicions characteristic of publicity as a system of distrust and subjects ever more aspects of everyday life to the unrelenting brutalities of the networked economy's global market. To cite just one example, in a speech at the Global Internet Summit held in Barcelona in May 2000, a member of the European commission responsible for Enterprise and the Information Society presented his "e-Europe action plan" as necessitated by the economic imperative and social objective "to open up the 'last mile' to competition." The proposed policies include digital literacy, changing legal frameworks to ensure business confidence, and "protecting the interests of all market actors." Yes, this plan aims to provide cheaper, better, faster access to the Internet. Yes, it wants a more robust economy and cohesive society. These goals are part of the project of restructuring and extending law and communication in order to succeed in the information age. More communication is necessary for capitalist market expansion.

In his response to Marcuse, Habermas doesn't deny that instrumental reason is rational. His argument is rather that efficiency, instrumentality, is not the only form of rationality, and that the ideal of public deliberation provides another standard for assessing societal rationality. The consolidation of communicative and instrumental rationalities in the networked economy suggests otherwise. Today, communication is that which cannot be challenged, that which is presupposed as the measure, the end, the goal to be reached, the value to be maximized. To criticize communication seems a performative contradiction, a kind of irrationality, a lapse into precommunicative or noncognitive nonsense. Why shouldn't everyone be wired, turned on, tuned in? Why shouldn't we all have access, equal opportunity to get our views heard and hear the views of others?

The paradoxical horror of this position comes when we realize that it's ultimately as depoliticizing and totalizing as technocracy. The critical thrust of publicity has been reappropriated as the slogan of the information age. Corporations and activists can all support expanding discussion and increasing access. Activists want exposure, corporations want mindshare, and we all want to know.

Technoculture is not a nightmarish technocracy ruled by an autocratic Big Brother. Instead, it is a new power formation in which the ideals of publicity, of equal access, free information, and nonstop, multichanneled communication support the digital networks of communicative capitalism. In this context, publicity serves the information age. If technocracy aimed to eliminate politics in the name of efficient administration, technoculture forecloses politics in the name of communication. We're all connected, all linked together with cell phones, satellites, and the World Wide Web. Communication, the network of the networked economy, brings us together.

CHAPTER FOUR

Celebrity's Drive

What does the emergence of Little Brothers as a variation on the old story of the death of the father mean for technoculture's mode of subjectivization? This is the question I explore in chapter 4. My central claim is that publicity establishes the ideological matrix within which individuals in mediated, capitalist technocultures subjectivize their condition. People's experience of themselves as subjects is configured in terms of accessibility, visibility, *being known*. Without publicity, the subject of technoculture doesn't know if it exists at all. It has no way of establishing that it has a place within the general sociosymbolic order of things, that it is recognized. (The dot-com version of this notion might be something like "without a website, you're not even there.") The technocultural mode of subjectivization, in other words, is celebrity. Celebrity is the form of subjectivity that posits—that presupposes and reproduces—the ideology of publicity. Publicity in technoculture functions through the interpellation of a subject that makes itself into an object of public knowledge.

I raise this question of technocultural subjectivity as a counter to the more prominent emphasis on identity in cybercultural studies. In the early moments of the Internet, the pre-Web days of MUDs and MOOs, theorists emphasized sexual experimentation, role-playing, gender-bending, and multiplicity.[1] Networked communications, it seemed, were the ideal laboratory for postmodern theories of fluid or fragmented selves. Regardless of whether a theorist celebrated cyberian identity play, condemned it, or even worried about the reinscription of old, unappealing identities, that cyberia should be theorized in terms of its impact on identity was generally taken for granted.

With the emergence of the World Wide Web, however, this emphasis on identity seems quaint, a nostalgic evocation of a pre-political time of freedom and possibility that was never there.[2] The fluid identities celebrated by early theorists now look more like consumers (being) driven to find the next new thing, to produce and reproduce themselves via images, technologies, entertainment, and commodities. Anonymous cybersex brings less a flourishing of desiring selves than does the ready availability of immediate satisfaction close off desire in a new circuit of entertainment and stimulation. Indeed, as the prevalence of conspiracy theory suggests, in technoculture the desire to know characteristic of the public-supposed-to-know is configured through and as a never-ending process of searching, linking, and (re)producing information. Cyberian subjects are enjoined to know, to keep up to date, whether they want to or not. With permanent, easily accessible information, there is no excuse for not being up on the issues. (This injunction to know is of course accompanied by its obverse, the dismissive ridicule of news junkies and Net cruisers as couch potatoes who spend all their time consuming media and ignoring "real life.")

To return to the terms I introduced in chapter 1, the question becomes: What kinds of subjects are interpellated when everyone is supposed to know and the technologies believe for us? In chapter 2, I emphasized the interpellation of the conspiring subject. Technologies that encourage us to search and link, databases of information from which something always seems to be missing, and democracy as a system of distrust call subjects into being as conspiracy theorists. Here, I consider another mode of subjectivization, celebrity. The same technologies that call on us to link also call on us as known, as sources of content that are of interest to cameras, websites, and credit-card companies. The knowing subject, in other words, is first interpellated as a known subject. Introducing the celebrity mode of subjectivization thus enables me to complicate the account of secrecy and publicity I've presented thus far: whereas the conspiring subject emerges as a subject of desire, the celebrity emerges as a subject of drive.

I take this language of desire and drive from Slavoj Žižek. In some readings of psychoanalytic theory, drive is synonymous with instincts. The drives are prior to language, a kind of basis for the desire that emerges later, as the child comes into language. In Lacanian theory, however, drive is something different. As Žižek explains, drive for Lacan is "a montage of elements which emerges as a kind of 'necessary by-product' of the instinctual body getting caught in the web of the symbolic order."[3] For example, what this means with respect to an infant is that an instinctual need starts to take on a specific meaning even as it continues to be a need. The object that satisfies this need thereby becomes more than a simple satisfaction; it becomes an element in a signifying economy that has to do with giving and receiving love. In this economy, the need for the object is experienced as a kind of enslavement to the Mother (or Other) who can fulfill the need. The intervention of the symbolic Law, then, does two things at the same time. By prohibiting satisfaction, it provides a way out of the deadlock of enslavement: because the object is off limits, the subject can never have it, so it isn't enslaved to the Other. Of course, this means that the subject's desire is never satisfied. So breaking out of enslavement to the Other comes at the cost of the full satisfaction of desire. This is why, says Žižek, desire, at its most elementary level, takes the form of nonsatisfaction; to remain as desire, it can only be a desire for desire.[4]

So where does drive come in? "Drive," Žižek writes,

stands for the paradoxical possibility that the subject, forever prevented from achieving his Goal (and thus fully satisfying his desire), can nevertheless find satisfaction in the very circular movement of repeatedly missing its object, of circulating around it: the gap constitutive of desire is thus closed; the self-enclosed loop of a circular repetitive movement replaces infinite striving.[5]

Drive is a loop, a cycle in which the subject is caught. The subject is caught in that its ever-repeated efforts to fulfill its desire become a source of satisfaction. Repeatedly trying, doing the same thing over and over and over again, even when, *especially when*, the actions are doomed to fail, is a pleasure in itself. Even as the efforts represent a failure to fulfill desire as constituted within the Symbolic, they become "stained" by an extra or surplus enjoyment. One might consider the efforts of religious ascetics to become pure or worthy. Their activities of penance and renunciation, of denial, humiliation, and pain, create their own pleasures. Nietzsche, in his vivid and entertaining account in *The Genealogy of Morals*, describes these ascetic practices as inducing an "orgy of pleasure." So no matter what one does in the economy of drive, *jouissance* sticks to it. Just as the subject of desire is grounded in lack, so is the subject of drive grounded in surplus: it gets its pleasure without even wanting it; indeed, it can't escape it.

Žižek emphasizes how desire and drive presuppose one another. Yes, they involve two notions of subjectivity, two economies of *jouissance*, and two modes of reflexivity. But they are interconnected insofar as each reacts to the other. Žižek clarifies this point by way of a parallel with hysteria and perversion: desire is hysterical, and drive is perverse. The hysterical subject of desire perpetually postpones fulfillment, reflexively turning the impossibility of satisfying desire into a desire for unsatisfaction. Accompanying this desire for unsatisfaction, moreover, is a fundamental uncertainty. The hysterical subject incessantly questions her position, asking "What am I for the Other?" The perverse subject of drive knows what he is for the Other. He is certain. And rather than never attaining satisfaction, this subject always gets it; in fact, he gets it through the very movement of trying to repress it. Put somewhat differently, the reflexivity of drive relies on a failure to achieve satisfaction that then becomes itself as source of satisfaction insofar as the gestures taken toward the goal become themselves the goal.[6]

What does this have to do with secrecy? My argument is that desire and drive explain two economies of secrecy in technoculture. These two economies reproduce the ideology of publicity insofar as they are the circuits within which technocultural subjects come into being. Thinking about technocultural subjectivity in terms of these economies, I suggest, helps us understand how the contemporary subject of democracy is at the same time the consuming subject of communicative capitalism. I'll explain this with a brief recounting of my argument thus far.

In chapter 1, I introduce Bentham's account of publicity as a system of distrust. I show how within this system the public is structured as a disavowal held in place by the secret. The secret sustains the fantasy that a democratic "all" is possible, that the public is limited only by that which is hidden (and will eventually be revealed). In this system, the secret is an empty form that marks the limit of the public as it relies on but disavows the split between the public-supposed-to-know and the public-supposed-to-believe.

In technoculture, the secret functions differently. With the extension of the idea that everyone has the right to know and the materialization of this idea in the ideals and infrastructure of communicative capitalism, the gap between the public-supposed-to-believe and the public-supposed-to-know is closed off. Now everyone knows, and the technologies believe for us: we don't have to believe each other; we can search and link and find the truth that is out there. The technologies, then, materialize the ideal of the public posited in publicity as a system of distrust, and in so doing, they interpellate their users as conspiracy theorists enjoined to discover for themselves, to make links and find evidence. Accordingly, as I conclude in chapter 3, the same technologies that are lauded as realizing democracy undermine it, rendering it an impossibility insofar as they, paradoxically, eliminate the very interconnections of trust necessary for democratic institutions.

The conspiring subject, then, is like the hysterical subject, always seeking, always uncertain, never satisfied. *If the truth is out there, then the truth about me may be out there. Who knows about me? What do they know?* In this chapter, I explore an answer to these hysterical questions as it appears in the perverse economy of drive: everyone knows about me. I'm a star, a celebrity. In this mode of subjectivization, the secret functions differently. Instead of searching for the secret, one posits oneself as the secret, as that which is known.

The shift from looking for oneself to understanding oneself as looked at, even as it suggests a way out of the hysterical uncertainty of the conspiring subject, comes at a cost, namely, that the secret in this economy is less something precious than it is a simultaneously repellent and attractive nugget of content circulating through the networks of global capitalist entertainment culture.[7] I think of this shift as one from the secret to the "scoop." "Scoop" connotes the intriguing bit of news that is immediately out of date (but is nevertheless presumed to be something that everyone wants to know), a serving of sweet and sticky ice cream, and a tool for handling, ladling out, something that is mucky, unstable, or not already easily divisible. "Scoop" also resonates with tabloid elements of scandalous, obscene content that have always supported the materialization of ideals of publicity in popular media. It thus encapsulates the way publicity in technoculture smears everything with a kind of crassness or inauthenticity, the way it produces cynicism, as my discussion of secrets on the Net in the following section demonstrates.

Finally, understanding publicity as configured through the economies of desire and drive helps explain why communicative reflection provides not a mode of democratic freedom but a more insidious basis for global capitalism. In technoculture, more specifically, in a technocultural context characterized by the decline of symbolic efficiency, communicative reflection reproduces the silent, repetitive cycle of drive. Communicative capitalism, we might say, relies on publicity without publics.

Priceless

People today tend to worry about their secrets spilling out and circulating all over the Net. This strikes me as odd. Admittedly, the Internet poses major problems with respect to the accumulation, aggregation, and dissemination of personal data—indeed, this is key to the power of Little Brothers, as I point out in the previous chapter. But the issue of secrecy is usually presented as a kind of "outing," as a way that one's personal life becomes a matter of mass, public interest. This is strange. Who really cares? As every promoter, advertiser, and public relations agent knows, it's not as though mass audiences of people are out there, waiting and ready for our revelations, completely interested in the mundane details of our individual lives—or even in our most personal fantasies. But this is precisely the anxiety that accompanies communicative capitalism. A recent survey of more than two thousand American households—some with Internet users and some without—showed extreme concern about personal privacy online.[8]

Satirical appropriations of Mastercard's recent ad campaign click on this anxiety about our personal secrets oozing out all over the Net. The pseudo-ads circulated through e-mail. They all have the same format: a sexually explicit photograph and a text that itemizes the costs that went into producing the depicted—and disseminated—moment. The text accompanying the image "Limbo" reads:

Dinner & dance at the "BIG" Company Xmas party $ n/c
Bottle of Wine before the function to "Loosen up
   a little" $17.00

| Disposable Camera, "Just in Case anything happens" | $6.00 |
| Prize for being the "Limbo Queen" | $50.00 |

Underneath the text is what appears to be an authentic, candid photograph (caught by the disposable camera) of the Limbo Queen (loosened up from the wine) at the party. Predictably, the woman in the picture isn't wearing underwear. Thus, the punch line beneath the image: "Picture of you displaying your 'Special Talent' all over the free world . . . PRICELESS!!" (I should add that the images in the various spoofs are not only of women. There are also "candid" photographs of men who have urinated on themselves, just finished masturbating, or unwittingly displayed their genitals.)

To understand the parody, it's helpful to recall the official Mastercard campaign. Again, various items and activities are listed as objects of consumption. Again, the culmination of the list is a "priceless" experience. Of course Mastercard implies that this is an experience that "money can't buy." It's a precious moment, beyond valuation. Nevertheless, in the commercial itself the precious moment is stained by the obscene costs that went into getting it—the priceless experience still required a credit card. The precious moment, in other words, isn't priceless. It isn't outside the network of capital at all. It's stained by its very circulation within this economy.

The parody both inverts the opposition between precious and obscene in the official campaign and highlights the excess that circulates in a network. Put somewhat differently, in the parody, obscenity is doubled. Now the moment that money can't buy is clearly not a precious moment; instead, it is openly, admittedly, explicitly obscene. It is a moment marked by drunkenness, genitals, and excreta. But the image, although obscene when considered as an inversion of the official priceless series, is not where the real obscenity highlighted by the parody rests. It is not where we find the underlying supplement or excess analogous to money's stain of the precious moment. In the pseudo-ad, this obscene supplement comes from information, from the humiliation that arises from becoming content that circulates on the Net. So, again, there is an excess that circulates in a network, but this time in the network of information. What stains our evening's adventures is not the moment in the picture but the circulation of the moment as a picture on the Internet (just like in the official ad—what stains the moment is its place in commercial exchange).

One should thus resist the urge to read the pseudo-ads in terms of reputation, as simply cautionary tales against excessive use of alcohol and in favor of underwear. None of the pseudo-ads gives names, addresses, or dates. None identifies anyone. No identifiable person is really humiliated. In fact, the other people in the photographs are generally paying no attention whatsoever to the exposed person. The people closest to the victim, in other words, aren't scandalized in the least. Despite the clear presence to those in the picture of some "obscene content"—the visible genitals or sex act—nothing seems to have been revealed. There is a scoop but no secret. And what makes the scoop obscene, of course, is not its content but its circulation. What might have once been precious is now just another vulgar element amid all the other flotsam and jetsam of the Internet.

See and Be Seen

I am reading these "priceless" ads in terms of their inversion of the precious into dreck and their circulation in networks in order to highlight "scopic drive" as the larger circuit of the drive to make oneself seen that is crucial to publicity in technoculture.[9] Scopic drive is characterized by a kind of reflexivization or key reversal. As Žižek explains, "insofar as I cannot see the point in the other from which I'm gazed at, the only thing that remains for me to do is to make myself visible to that point."[10] So, to break this down, desire would entail a subject looking for something, trying to find it, trying to discern where and what it is. One thing that can never be found, though, one point that can never come within the desiring subject's field of vision, is the point from which that thing the subject is looking for looks back at it. In drive, the subject makes itself visible to that point. I'm no longer simply fascinated by some hidden thing, say; rather, I make myself open, accessible, available, visible to that mysterious, unknown, secret thing, to the place from which I am gazed back at. In my very looking, I make myself visible to this object, the gaze.[11] Drive, then, connects the way I make myself seen when I look to my act of looking. It designates the kind of transmutation into a new network that occurs when one's act of looking is what is looked at by that hidden, secret thing one is looking for (but hasn't found).

The "priceless" series of pseudo-ads presents the gaze as an object of drive in a double sense. First, the limbo queen is caught by her own camera. The photo is produced by the gaze as it is turned back on her. Second, the circulation of the pseudo-ad series via e-mail suggests that recipients can be caught in the very medium they are using. Recipients may very well, unbeknown to themselves, end up displayed on the screens they are viewing.

I'm particularly interested in this second sense of drive. Insofar as the pseudo-ads invoke the likelihood of an image *of us* circulating in front of the "free world," they suggest a celebrity subjectivity: only some sort of celebrity would presume her own "known-ness." In whatever it is that she is known for, the celebrity makes herself seen, accessible, available to others. She is a "public" person.[12] As Daniel J. Boorstin writes, *The celebrity is a person known for his well-knownness.*"[13] The "being known-ness" part of celebrity, in other words, involves a certain reflexivity. The celebrity is not just known; he is known for being known. In celebrity, publicity is reflexivized, turned back in on itself such that not only is something seen, but it *makes itself* seen—accessible to, information for—others.

But who, exactly, are these others? Technoculture posits them as everyone, as the all-inclusive public of all of us, all of us who are universally included in the domain of rights, all of us who have *a right to know. Everyone* knows a celebrity.

On the face of it, this makes no sense at all. No one and nothing is known to everyone—indeed, the impossibility of the public is a key contention of this book. But celebrity is a form of subjectivization that actually produces our sense that there is a public. That we understand ourselves as known is what makes us think that there is a public that knows us. As Žižek explains, "when the subject recognizes himself in an ideological call, he automatically overlooks the fact that this very formal act of recognition creates the content one recognizes oneself in."[14] The ideology of publicity thus works via a particular sort of subjectivization, one that hails subjects into being as celebrities known to everyone. The public (what one takes as the public) emerges through this process of interpellation.

The premise of being known needs to be linked to the fundamental diversity and opacity of cyberspace: we are known, but the terms of this being known are never transparent to us.[15] Celebrity as a subjectivity founded in drive stems from this excess.[16] I'll take up these points in turn.

Žižek writes that "in the case of the gaze, the point to which the subject makes himself seen retains its traumatic heterogeneity and nontransparency, it remains an object in the strict Lacanian sense."[17] With respect to cyberspace, this means that we are never quite sure to what we have made ourselves visible; we don't know who is looking at us or how they are looking. We can't even be certain whether there is a single perspective or multiple perspectives. What databases are we in? Who has looked us up and why? We might think here of the unsettling feeling of being "looked up" by people from our past. Who has not gotten the surprise e-mail or phone call from someone who just happened to *search* for them on the Internet? The cameras, the searchers, the information gatherers are anywhere and everywhere. Insofar as it materializes "knowing," then, technoculture produces subjects who are well aware of the fact that they are known and that they have no control over—or even full comprehension of—the ways they are known.[18] One of the ways that subjects are called into being in technoculture, then, is as known, as contents of knowledge. In their answering of the interpellative call, moreover, subjects posit a public—indeed, the public-supposed-to-know, a public that technoculture promises as a public of *everyone*.[19]

But what about excess? The diversity and opacity of cyberspace install a profound insecurity in the subject. Because one is never sure how one is being known, one is never certain of one's place in the symbolic order. How, exactly, are we being looked at? One never really knows who one is—despite all the cameras, files, media, and databases. An academic big shot, for example, is just another schmoe among organic farmers. A top reggae star may have zero recognition among physicists or oil company executives. Again, who one is in the sociosymbolic order is uncertain—and ever changing. The order is never fixed; it is in constant flux. In response, then, the subject is driven to make itself visible over and over again. It has to understand itself as a celebrity, precisely because the excesses of cyberia make it uncertain as to its place in the symbolic order.

Celebrity should therefore not be understood as a form of symbolic identification. One is not looking at oneself from the perspective of an ego ideal, judging and evaluating oneself from the perspective of an Other with whom one's acts register.[20] Rather, the gaze to which one makes oneself visible is a point hidden in an opaque and heterogeneous network. One is compelled to make oneself visible precisely because of the uncertainty as to whether one registers at all.

Celebrity as a mode of technocultural subjectivization is also not a kind of idealization or an instance of imaginary identification. One is not simply imagining oneself as a movie star or going through life as if on a stage. Instead, one is driven by the sense that one is known combined with the unbearable excess of ways in which one might be known repeatedly to make oneself visible, accessible. This inescapable dimension of celebrity appears even more strongly when we think of the terms that designate those who to some extent have failed (to register in the symbolic domain): they are unknown, nobodies, "you don't know who they are."

Put somewhat differently, the sense of being known should not be reduced to some kind of naive fantasy whereby one imagines oneself as a celebrity. Rather, most people in technoculture know full well that they aren't *really* celebrities. In fact, this anxiety about not being known, this tension between the conviction that one is known and not known, is a key component of the celebrity mode of subjectivization.[21] And it is materialized in new communication technologies, in the screens and sites of networked technoculture. So even if one knows that she isn't a celebrity, she acts as if she believes she were. The technologies believe for her.

I disagree, then, with the current preoccupation with wounded, victimized, or infantile citizens. These vulnerable, dependent subjects have been presented as key figures in contemporary ideological formations. Lauren Berlant, for example, draws out the infantile citizen in whose name regulatory interventions into the social are mobilized.[22] Wendy Brown theorizes the inordinate emphasis placed on injury in identity politics.[23] And Žižek argues that the Real of Capital exerts its rule through the ideology of victimization.[24] These accounts miss the way the subject of technoculture is the extreme realization of an ideal of publicity, a literalization of the notion of the actor in the public sphere. In technoculture's flows of capital and entertainment, celebrities seem to be the only actors, the only persons who can act. (That celebrities generally follow scripts, that their "acting" isn't action, doesn't merely illustrate the appeal of "outtakes" and "behind the scenes" footage; rather, it points to the ideological inversion at work in celebrity as a mode of subjectivization—it is easier to imagine oneself acting out a script than it is actually to act, to break free of the script. This may explain as well the initial media response to the U.S. presidential election of 2000: the media were more upset about deviations from the script of elections—the *New York Times* called for a quick decision—than they were about ballot irregularities, problematic machines, and racist election procedures.) For the victim to matter politically, it has to become public, to be made visible, accessible. It has to be known. Those who aren't known are not victims. They simply are not—they don't "exist" at all. Instead, they are the remainders of an unrelenting system that has reduced real suffering to the challenge of acquiring and retaining mindshare in a media that moves from victim to victim in an endless search for the new and the shocking.[25]

To register as a subject in technoculture, one has to present oneself as an object for everyone else. The phenomenon of the celebrity criminal effectively illustrates this point.[26] Here, the dynamic of celebrity culture reconfigures the terms through which criminality is understood. Arthur Bremer, who, after failing to assassinate Richard Nixon decided to shoot George Wallace, both scripted his activities and understood his crime as a way to end his anonymity. (In fact, his failure to kill Nixon was the result of a fashion faux pas: Bremer wasn't wearing the right suit and went home to change, thereby missing his opportunity.) Similarly, the primary goal behind the Unabomber's bombings was getting publicity for his antitechnology manifesto: "In order to get our message before the public with some chance of making a lasting impression, we've had to kill people." With an eye to his celebrity status, John Lennon's assassin, Mark David Chapman, lost fifty pounds before his *People* magazine interview. Timothy McVeigh, executed for the Oklahoma City bombing, approached his case as a publicity campaign. He and his lawyers sought to grant an interview to a celebrity journalist like Barbara Walters or Diane Sawyer and then to have the interview air during fall sweeps.

Interestingly, Lacan's original research involved a detailed study of a celebrity criminal, "Aimee." In a case widely reported at the time, Aimee had attacked a famous actress because she believed the actress was spreading slanderous rumors about her. An unsuccessful author, Aimee was also convinced that she was being plagiarized by well-known writers. In short, she thought of herself as known. Lacan concluded that Aimee suffered from "self-punishment paranoia" and that in attacking the actress she was attacking her ideal version of herself.[27] Criminality, we might say, is not the paradigmatic form of subjectivity in contemporary surveillance society. Celebrity is. Before the cameras, even criminals are celebrities.

Contingency, Celebrity, Obscenity

The celebrity subject of technoculture does not desire fame, that is to say, the desire for fame doesn't define or constitute this subject (it is not a hysterical subject of desire but rather a perverse subject of drive). Instead of desiring fame, the celebrity subject finds herself in a game of chance where the odds are that she will be known, and known in ways she neither wants nor controls. Thus, the excesses of technoculture stain celebrity with contingency, on the one hand, and a kind of obscene, pathetic, concreteness, on the other.[28] The chance involved with celebrity was already apparent in the early years of American mass entertainment culture when celebrity had an "everyman" sort of quality.[29] It was detached from specific excellences and talents and available to anyone who happened to be in the right place at the right time.[30] Indeed, this was key to the Hollywood myth of being discovered. Talent and hard work didn't create stars. Discovery did—and discovery depended on being in the right place at the right time and on the chance of being seen.

In the contemporary era of permanent news media, the World Wide Web, and reality television, this contingency is concretized and managed. Two websites in particular capture this point well. The Hollywood Stock Exchange serves as a market in celebrity. Those movie and television stars who are the most popular, who have the most social capital, are traded at higher valuations than are those whose popularity is waning. R U HOT OR NOT has a somewhat different assessment scheme, one that evaluates "everyday" people, treating and hence recognizing them in terms of celebrity. People can send in their photographs and then be judged on a "hot scale" of 1 to 10. In fact, the actual caption for the photographs is "judge me." (When I first visited this site, I was entangled in feeling sorry for the overreachers who really are not very hot and gleeful at the way I could put them in their place by giving them a low score.) Ratings systems, hits, mindshare, awards shows—all assert the chance involved in celebrity even as they attempt to measure or capture it. Given this contingency, those who seek celebrity seem all the more pathetic.

Because celebrity is something that happens—something that the "public" does, that is an attribute of publicity—grasping for it is repellant. This may explain the failure of the American version of the game show *Big Brother:* surrounded by cameras, the "house-guests" could be nothing but disgusting; they were openly struggling for celebrity, trying to be known. Their very participation in the show exemplified their drive to make themselves seen. In contrast, the American version of *Survivor* was much more successful—the cameras were outside the field of vision. But again, once the contestants were off the island, once the sociosymbolic frame of the game dissolved, they too seemed pathetic, deprived of the aura that the televisual illusion created. They were "just people," in all their specificity, not really "survivors" caught up in a set of games and strategic machinations. At the same time, they remained celebrities—of interest, known, even if this being known brought with it no connotations of respect or regard.

The "priceless" series brings home the obscene, pathetic, concrete stain of contemporary celebrity with a vengeance: one is known to all the "free world"—for one's genitals, drunkenness, or sexuality. "Being known" stains an evening, activity, or set of events that should be chalked up to personal fun or, at worst, to momentary indiscretion. This stain is part of subjectivity in technoculture: we depend on, require, "being known" in order to exist at all, but this very "being known" tarnishes, makes disgusting, whatever it touches. One might think here of the stereotypical celebrity photo in the tabloids—sunglasses, hat, arm outstretched to block the camera, to hide. We now read it simultaneously as a cynical gesture—Didn't they really seek the cameras, after all? Isn't their attempt to hide really an enacting of their own sense of being known?—and a legitimate endeavor to secure a space beyond the unrelenting gaze of the public. Here the death of Princess Diana comes to mind.

If new media technologies materialize publicity in practices of concealment and revelation, of posting and linking, and if in so doing they establish the conditions for contemporary experiences of subjectivity, celebrity is that mode of subjectivization in which individuals present themselves as content. Faced with cameras, microphones, and screens that question and search, that want to know, contemporary individuals are compelled to make themselves available as answers. Why? Because they are aware that they are already known, that they are already informationalized, and because the excesses and uncertainties of the terms in which they are known drive them repeatedly to seek to stabilize these terms. At the same time, they know that they aren't *really* known, that being in a database or having a website or getting their name in the paper doesn't *really* make them a celebrity. Yet they act as if they didn't know this. They let the technologies believe for them, and by doing so they "conspire in their own subjection."[31]

That individuals would consider themselves content for ever-present screens should hardly be surprising. The most obvious reason is the historical link between mass democracies and entertainment industries.[32] As P. David Marshall writes, "celebrities articulate agency and activity in democratic culture"; they are public representations of individuality.[33] Similarly, popular biology—from the Human Genome Project to cloning to evolutionary biology—presents people in terms of their information pattern, their code. The culture of confession in its religious, therapeutic, and media forms also presents disclosure as a method for getting at who people "really are." Finally, identity politics has taken who people are to be the primary matter of democratic politics, the key to locating patterns of oppression and exclusion. A key theme in queer activism, for example, has been that "invisibility is the great enemy."[34] Indeed, one might say that celebrity subjectivity presents an exaggerated version of the modern sense of life as something that is narrated, that it is a story we tell ourselves about ourselves. We are the content of our stories.

Technoculture's unendingly circulating information stream casts doubt on the value of this content. This is the creepy part of drive, of the reversal involved in making oneself seen: once we offer ourselves up, once we are displayed on the screens of technoculture, we are as trivial as everything else. To express this in banal terms, the celebrities of popular media are always viewed according to their entertainment value. Do they scandalize, seduce, or amuse us? The actual answer, though, is contingent. If escalating sexual display is the key, then someone may gain mindshare through further display *or* through covering up. If books on making millions are best-sellers, then someone will try to make a name by "returning to the simple things in life." Any particular (contingent) offering, then, is hardly a mysterious secret. Rather, it's only a scoop, a content that, although momentarily appealing, may and will easily turn to dreck.

The mode of subjectivization I've analyzed in terms of celebrity is thus rent by some unsettling contradictions. As celebrity, the subject emerges from an awareness that media contents are contingent, in flux, and trivial, yet the subject can't help but understand itself as something that warrants being known. It acts as if it's "being known-ness" is warranted, not contingent. In so doing, it posits a public-supposed-to-know as that which knows it, that which has hailed it as something worth being known. Likewise, this subjectivity is characterized by an awareness that "celebrity is everything," that everyone will be famous for fifteen minutes, that the Web and television are overflowing with celebrities. Nevertheless, it still understands itself as "more than" everyone else. Despite the resoundingly democratic ethos of entertainment culture—especially given its presumption that anyone can be discovered, that everyone is unique, that everyone counts, that everyone has a voice, that on the Web everyone has a home page, a place, an address—the celebrity subject believes that it is *not equal* to everyone else. It is better. And this sense of being more, better, a star, shifts immediately into a sense of utter banality. Precisely because one's "being known-ness" is content, one realizes that one may well be unique but trivial. As content, one doesn't have a secret that marks the mysterious kernel of one's being. One is instead stained by the scoop. The celebrity mode of subjectivization is thus weak and uncertain. It is characterized by the paradoxical awareness that even if everything is public, publicity is not all there is.

The Decline of Symbolic Efficiency

Publicity in technoculture can be understood as an ideological matrix. Two economies—desire and drive—configure this matrix. On the one hand, we can never have publicity. On the other, we can never escape it.

I've argued that the networked screens of contemporary technoculture interpellate subjects as conspiracy theorists and celebrities. As they respond to the interpellative call, subjects posit the public as everyone with a right to know. In the economy of desire, therefore, publicity means full revelation, the disclosure of the secret that can guarantee the public's claim to unified fullness. That everything will be (made) public is held out as the democratic ideal. With technologies that believe for them, conspiring subjects search and link, endeavoring to get the information that makes them good participatory democrats. But they never can. In the economy of drive, publicity designates the making of oneself visible to a heterogeneous gaze. The celebrity subject understands itself as known but doesn't know how or by whom or in terms of what.[35] One makes oneself visible to the screens of networked technoculture, becoming so much media content, another bit of Web drivel, nothing more than a scoop. Here, publicity is what we can't escape; it taints everything as it collapses democracy into the circulation of ideas, slogans, memes, and images.

Another way of designating the uncertainties of contemporary technoculture, the way that excess of information becomes lack of information, is in terms of what Žižek (borrowing a term from Claude Lévi-Strauss) theorizes as the decline of symbolic efficiency. This designation is useful in that it enables us to specify some of the problems pressuring technocultural subjects and thus better understand the effects of communicative capitalism on subjectivity. As I demonstrate through a discussion of Žižek's account of three fathers and through a reading of the film *Lola Rennt* (*Run, Lola, Run*), technocultural subjects are, first, plagued by uncertainties to which they often respond by creating little authorities, even as they reject their authority and play the odds. A matter of predicting and estimating the likelihood of adverse effects, life is a gamble. Second, technocultural subjects inhabit a political and cultural domain in which the smear of obscenity renders transgression no longer shocking and hence unable to provide a challenge to or escape from everyday experience. And, third, technocultural subjects encounter their own ideals, their own play, as demands to achieve, compete, and "be somebody." In a nutshell, the decline of symbolic efficiency helps explain why communicative reflection fails as an ideal of freedom. Increased and expanded communication fails to address technoculture's demands and uncertainties because it intensifies them.

Of course, before we can talk about the decline of symbolic efficiency, it makes sense to think about what symbolic efficiency involves. In the loosest, most general sense, symbolic efficiency refers to structures of trust and belief. A symbol is efficient when it can travel without being stopped and questioned. This in no way implies that people actually believe the symbol, that what the symbol says is true or right; rather, it simply means that people are willing to let it pass, to take it at face value because that's the way things are. Consequently, symbolic efficiency can coexist nicely with deception or distrust—as long as the general system remains intact. Bentham's system of distrust, for example, relies on symbolic efficiency not least of all because of the importance of the public-supposed-to-believe. Without their belief, distrust couldn't function as a system for the generation of a public. Žižek writes that symbolic efficiency "concerns the minimum of 'reification' on account of which it is not enough for us, all concerned individuals, to know some fact in order to be operative—'it', the symbolic institution, must also know/'register' this fact if the performative consequences of stating it are to ensue."[36] Keeping with the Bentham example, we can say that for a fact to be operative, it has to register with the public-supposed-to-believe. Or to return to the metaphor from chapter 3, we can say that Orwell's Big Brother was that symbolic institution that had to know a fact for it to be operative: until Big Brother knew, it didn't exist; and, conversely, if he stopped knowing or registering something, it no longer existed.

The decline of symbolic efficiency thus designates the breakdown of this generalized trust in the symbolic institution. I describe this breakdown in chapter 1 in terms of the generalization of suspicion, which occurs as publicity is materialized in technoculture. I describe it in chapter 3 with the move from Big Brother to Little Brothers. Indeed, we might say that the rhetorical shift in contemporary democratic theory from the language of "public" to the language of "publics" marks the decline of symbolic efficiency insofar as it acknowledges the inability to posit some kind of whole today. Taking this further, the currently popular move of adding an "s" to *everything*—globalizations, realities, sexualities—as if general terms such as globalization, reality, and sexuality were not themselves already abstract and contested terms, similarly suggests the roadblocks and detours hindering the movement of terms and symbols.

The decline of symbolic efficiency refers therefore to a fundamental uncertainty in our relation to our world. We aren't sure what will happen; we can only speak about probabilities, about how good or bad our chances are. Likewise, we aren't sure whom to rely on, who has the best data or the most impressive credentials. Arguments or authorities persuasive in one context can have no weight in another one—primarily because there are lots of different kinds of authorization. The identity we perform in one setting may have little to do with the one we perform in another. There isn't an automatic connection or coordination among contexts. Most people in wired cultures experience this uncanny excess and lack of meaning with ever-increasing frequency: we get conflicting information from nonstop multiple media; we more frequently come into contact with views and opinions different from our own; we don't know what to believe, whom to trust, or the criteria with which to decide questions of trust and belief. Strangeness, unassimilated weird things, is familiar; the everyday is uncanny.[37]

Žižek theorizes the decline in symbolic efficiency in terms of the collapse of the big Other. On the face of it, this is a little weird because Lacan emphasizes that the big Other never actually existed. So, what's going on?

The big Other is an intersubjective network of norms, expectations, and suppositions. As such, it isn't whole or "solid." There are always different interpretations, ideas, and assumptions at work in the symbolic order. We can also understand the big Other as an order of appearances, as that for whose sake we keep up the appearance that everything is fine, say, even if, deep down, we don't think it is. In this regard, Žižek sometimes describes the big Other in terms of a kind of "principle of charity" wherein people presume that they understand what another is saying.[38] This supposition of understanding is what makes the big Other an "order of double deception."[39] Not only is the big Other that for whose sake we might keep up appearances (lying that things are really fine), but because of the big Other we can also tell the truth and still be interpreted as if we were lying (as if we had said everything is fine when we actually said everything is miserable). The notion of the big Other, then, relies on the way we can pretend to deceive; we can say something that is factually true, intending that our hearer will assume we are lying. (I sometimes wonder if the Kantian injunction to tell the truth even when a murderer asks us where someone is may in fact rely on this dimension of the big Other. The murderer would assume that no one would really tell him where to find his potential victim, and thus the murderer would then go off in a different direction, leaving the Kantian happy both to have done his duty and not to have lead the murderer to the other.)[40]

The big Other has effects even though it doesn't really exist, even though it is just how things seem to be, how they appear (in the same way that magic can affect us even if it doesn't *really* work). This helps explain how the big Other functions with regard to ideological interpellation: "we effectively *become* something by pretending that we *already are* that."[41] When we act as if we are something, we adopt a particular position in the symbolic order. This place in the network of intersubjective relations determines who we are.[42]

We can now move to the other hand, namely, to the fact that the decline of symbolic efficiency refers to the demise of something that never existed in the first place. What this means is that the intersubjective network has broken down. There is no longer an underlying trust that persists even in the face of deception (such as the trust embodied in the public-supposed-to-believe, say). We're so attuned to deception, pretense, manipulation, and plausibility that we are reluctant to believe. Instead, we try to find out for ourselves, even as we suspect that we won't be able to hit on anything certain. In short, a repercussion of the decline of symbolic efficiency is a move into the repetitive cycle of drive.

Žižek locates the demise of symbolic efficiency in the changed functioning (the historicity) of the Oedipus complex. To this end, he revisits three Freudian accounts of symbolic authority as it is invested in the father: the standard Oedipal myth, the parricide in *Totem and Taboo*, and the willful, uncompromising God-the-father in *Moses and Monotheism*.[43] These three accounts provide three different combinations of the father function. First, the standard Oedipal myth unites the father as pacifying ego ideal (or point of ideal identification) with the father as ferocious superego or agent of prohibition. Here parricide is an unconscious dream; Oedipus is the only one who really kills his father. Second, in *Totem and Taboo*, all the sons kill the obscene father, the presymbolic, noncastrated father. But they don't end up sleeping with the mother because the dead father returns in the name of symbolic authority. Finally, in *Moses and Monotheism*, the father who is killed embraces the logos, the unified rational structure of the universe. What returns at the death of this rational father is God-the-father, the father of the uncompromising No!, the unforgiving father who prohibits everything.

The collapse of symbolic efficiency or the nonexistence of the big Other today can be thought of in terms of the absence of these three fathers. Beginning with God-the-father in *Moses and Monotheism*: because he provides a space of absolute willing, of pure decision, this God opens up the gap that establishes the domain of symbolic law as such. He represents the ultimate separation between the Symbolic and the Real because his word, his law, is grounded only in itself and accountable to nothing and no one. The repercussion of this is that with the demise of this father, there is no gap between the Symbolic and the Real. Žižek argues that the nonexistence of the big Other should be understood in terms of the demise of this father. The collapse of belief in a general structure of norms (a structure that never existed in the first place but nevertheless had actual effects) has led to all sorts of ethical committees, rule books, risk assessments and mini-authorities evaluating issues in the Real and using these evaluations to instruct behavior—even though everyone is already reflexively aware that these very assessments and evaluations may be faulty, tainted, or undermined by particular political or corporate interests.

This account of the decline of symbolic efficiency can be supplemented by attention to the repercussions of the collapse of patriarchal authority in the other two instances. With the demise of the dead father of *Totem and Taboo*, we have the return of the obscene father. On the one hand, this reappearance of the father of enjoyment smears symbolic authority with all sorts of obscene excesses. I think here of the kind of knowledge that U.S. senators and judges have when they investigate pornography. It's hard to take them seriously, to see them as authorities rather than as pathetic, dirty old men. They are simply despotic, authoritarian censors who want all the enjoyment for themselves. On the other hand, the return of the obscene father means that transgression is no longer possible. There is no symbolic order that demands complete sexual conformity. After all, the photos in the "priceless" series are nothing unexpected. Of course, there are mini-orders and rules still in play in particular instances. But transgression simply isn't shocking. Thomas Frank hammers home a similar point in his discussion of American market populism in the late 1990s. He describes the way transgression became a market angle, the way brands gained mindshare by presenting themselves as radical, "audacious." His examples include Benetton, Macintosh, Pepsi, Nike, and Duncan Yo-Yo. The slogan for the last is "Give us the finger; we'll give you the power."[44]

Finally, with the demise of the father as ego-ideal, the father emerges as the humiliated father, the rival. He no longer bars us from the objects of desire; they are no longer his alone; now we too have access to it, can achieve it or have it. It is within our reach. The prohibitive norms formerly provided by the father as ego-ideal are thus replaced by imaginary ideals of success, fitness, achievement. Released from the authority of the father, we can achieve perfection. Žižek describes this in terms of a kind of *direct 'super-egoization' of the imaginary Ideal*, caused by the lack of the proper symbolic Prohibition."[45] Here we can see especially clearly some of the compulsions of the celebrity mode of subjectivization as our imaginative ideals of ourselves come to bind us into global techno-culture. Dependent on recognition from elsewhere as they are "made visible," those very aspects of ourselves most connected with our own authenticity get caught up in the economy of drive. A good example can be found in the business of new technologies: the computer industry has been built on work's reconstruction as play (as I discuss in chapter 3). We might also think here of the way personal lives are rendered in terms of achievements and events that are staged, taped, catalogued, and evaluated. Describing a freakish extension of this rendering, Neal Gabler discusses the profession of "life coach" that appeared in the late 1990s. These coaches "advised clients on how to reorient their lives to reach what one coach called fulfillment but what someone else might have called a happy ending."[46]

Tom Tykwer's 1998 film *Lola Rennt* provides an account of the collapse of symbolic authority via the demise of the father in terms remarkably similar to Žižek's. Not only does the film aptly illustrate the collapse of symbolic efficiency but it highlights how this collapse reinforces the vigor of global capital.

The basic story of the film is that Lola has twenty minutes to save her boyfriend Manni from certain death. In so doing, Lola will prove that love can do anything. Manni has lost 100,000 DM and will be killed by a nasty gangster if this guy finds out. Manni both blames Lola for this loss—because she was late picking him up, he ended up taking the subway and losing the money there—and calls on her to save him. The rest of the movie consists of three alternate scenarios regarding what happens next. Now this overall structure itself suggests the collapse of symbolic authority. Why? Because no ending is complete. There is no real or authentic ending, just shifting parallel universes or alternate chains of causes and contingencies.[47] No one account of time wins out; there are always alternatives. As one of the film's epigraphs states: "After the game is before the game."

This general collapse of the big Other is reiterated in *Lola Rennt*'s three scenarios. In each, Lola runs for help to her father, an executive at Deutsche Transfer Bank. In none does he actually help her. When Lola arrives at the bank in the first scenario, the security guard refers to her as a little princess come to see Big Daddy. But as it turns out, he is not her Big Daddy. Entering the office, Lola interrupts a confrontation between her father and his mistress, who has just informed him that she is pregnant. To make matters worse, not only does her father refuse to give her any money but, as he throws her out of his office, he tells her that he isn't even her father, that her real father died before she was born. This scenario, then, suggests the return of the obscene father in the collapse of the big Other. With the father's authority smeared by obscenity to the point where he isn't a father at all, Lola is free to join Manni in robbing a store to get the money. And little, inept authorities try to reemerge: from the guard in the store who helplessly confronts the robbery to the inadequate little cop who accidentally shoots Lola. Her death is not even a tragedy: not only is it merely an accident, but given that there is another scenario, another universe or dimension, it is hard to get worked up about her death.

In the second scenario, Lola's father is the impotent obverse of the father as ego-ideal, the humiliated father who emerges when symbolic authority disintegrates. This time, the father's mistress is pregnant but by someone else. The father is now emasculated, not really a father, just an impotent guy whose mistress is sleeping around. The father's impotence frees up Lola to take control: when her father denies her the money, she takes him hostage. She's in control now, the perfect agent able to get things done and save Manni. But still she confronts the collapse of the big Other: no matter what she does, things don't work out, the world is ultimately senseless. For example, police surround the bank, but they are so inadequate that they let Lola go because they don't recognize her as the robber. And even though Lola gets the money, Manni is killed. Again death is an accident: Manni is hit by an ambulance.

Finally, in the third scenario, Lola's father is killed in a car wreck. Lola doesn't even get to ask him for the money because he isn't there; he's already gone when she arrives at the bank. Here the demise of the father is the demise of the commanding God of the uncompromising No! Accordingly, the mistress—the sign of the father's knowledge of *jouissance*—doesn't even appear. In this world, all of Lola's actions are gambles. She has to make choices, but under completely unclear and undecidable circumstances. Lola's situation illustrates Žižek's point that "far from being experienced as liberating, this compulsion to decide freely is experienced as an anxiety-provoking obscene gamble, a kind of ironic reversal of predestination: I am held accountable for decisions which I was forced to make without proper knowledge of the situation."[48] Lola's third world is ruled by chance: in fact, she gets the money for Manni by winning at roulette in a casino that she just happens upon. At the same time, a series of coincidences enables Manni to recover the money he originally lost. So they get the money, they even double it. But in this world of luck and chance, there is no meaning, no struggle, no tragedy. In this context, that the whole endeavor was supposed to prove the power of love makes no sense; love itself is lost.

Of course, the collapse of patriarchal authority in *Lola Rennt* is linked to the impact of another force, of another figure of the big Other—money. Everything is set in motion by the need to get money. The father's failure is his failure to provide money. Lola's success is measured by her capacity to get money. The very strength of her love for Manni depends on money. This too illustrates Žižek's point that "the spectral presence of Capital is the figure of the big Other which not only remains operative when all the traditional embodiments of the symbolic big Other disintegrate, but even directly causes this disintegration. . . . today's subject is perhaps more than ever caught in an inexorable compulsion that effectively runs his life."[49]

In sum, the collapse of the father function helps explain the contingencies, possibilities, and uncertainties that characterize the decline of symbolic efficiency and set the configurations of contemporary technoculture for the circulation of drive. Why can't Lola stop running? Because the loss of the "father almighty" installs drive as a loop of repetitively moving between alternatives. Communicative capitalism, of course, offers way too many analogies here. Some are serious: the movement of finance capital, the relocating of corporations, the migration of peoples.[50] Some are trivial: channel surfing, Web cruising, fashion finding. All click on the inexorable compulsions wrought by communicative capitalism.

Communicative Drive

Perhaps surprisingly, Habermas's description of "the fragile, dynamic, and fuzzy shape of a decentered, even fragmented public consciousness" resonates with the idea of the decline of symbolic efficiency.[51] Not only does Habermas acknowledge postmodernity's (which he describes in terms of "detraditionalization") effects on subjectivity, but he agrees that what is at work is a process of reflexivization. What is at issue, then, is how this reflexivization impacts democracy. Is it a form of rationalization that represents positive momentum for democratic freedom, as Habermas's response to Marcuse suggests? My answer is no. Habermas misconstrues the problem of subjectivity in technoculture as the solution. For him, the transformations in communication (transformations that he also presents in terms of an orientation to an audience) suggest increased freedom, a vehicle for emancipation from the constraints of instrumental reason. In contrast, I read the reflexivization of communication as entrapping the subject in a network of drive. And this entrapment, this problem of communication and the network today, is *the* crucial question facing democracy in technoculture.

Seyla Benhabib has demonstrated how the critical theory of the early Frankfurt school comes up against a fundamental aporia—the conditions of its own impossibility.[52] Horkheimer and Adorno accept this aporia and use it to theorize a negative dialectics. Habermas (as well as Benhabib and others) rejects this alternative.

They seek instead to provide a positive justification for the promises of enlightenment. As I explain in chapter 3, communicative rationality, understood as an interest in maintaining the intersubjectivity of mutual understanding as well as communicating without domination, is a central concept of this philosophical project. My argument is that communicative reason, especially as developed in discourse ethics, does not solve the problem of critical theory's fundamental antagonism or gap but repeats it, endlessly, as drive.

Renata Salecl's account of drive aptly describes the aporias of critical theory. She writes:

> The Lacanian term for this 'knowledge in the real' that resists symbolization is *drive*, the self-sufficient closed circuit of the deadly compulsion to repeat: the paradox is that which cannot ever be memorized, symbolized by way of its inclusion into the narrative frame, is not some fleeting moment of the past, forever lost, but the very insistence of drive as that which *cannot ever be forgotten* in the first place, since it repeats itself incessantly.[53]

The knowledge that critical theory needs, the foundation that can ground its critique, resists symbolization. This resistance compels a circuit of repetition, of never-ending repetitive efforts to symbolize, to include within the symbolic order. The fact that this symbolic inclusion is always "not yet" manifests itself in the justification program of discourse ethics: the outcome of any discourse on the validity of a norm is always deferred until the inclusion of everyone and every possibly relevant fact or consideration. In this respect, the typical criticism of Habermas misses the point. The problem with discourse ethics' universalization principle is not consensus. Rather, it is the endless discursive loop, the way that the procedure or discussion itself is the source of satisfaction instead of the norms it is supposed to justify.

Discussion, in theories of deliberative democracy such as those of Habermas as well as in the networks of the information age, involves an endless, circulating loop of reflexivity. Perhaps paradoxically, new communications media don't seem to increase the likelihood of a discursively generated agreement on normative validity claims at all. On the contrary, insofar as they promise to make available any information, at any time, they make all too clear how completely inadequate any solution, decision, or agreement will be. There are always alternatives, and the demand to consider them is absolute, never-ending, and ultimately unsatisfiable. (The proliferation of discourse types in Habermasian critical theory is an "intensive" version of this same problem. Here, instead of extending the justification procedure outward in time, a process of specifying different types of discourses and their rules comes into play. These discourses may be ethical, political, aesthetic, application, and so forth.)

Habermas's recent response to the endless, repetitive, cycle of discussion, to the inability of communication in and of itself to generate results, has been to turn to law.[54] Contemporary societies are fragmented, pluralistic, and complex. Neither custom nor consensus is capable of securing the basic conditions of social integration: traditional norms and values can no longer be relied on to determine action orientations, but we cannot use discussion to organize everything all the time. We have to rely on some patterns and procedures, on instruments, systems, and programs that relieve us from the burden of decision-making. Accordingly, complex societies rely on systems coded in terms of money and power. In this setting, Habermas argues, law helps secure the environment for the operation of these subsystems (for example, it establishes the terms and conditions of the market economy). But law does so not simply as a system or in accordance with some technocratic or cybernetic logic. Rather, law in constitutional democracies establishes the conditions through which the very "securing" of the environment can claim legitimacy. For Habermas, law is the vehicle for executing and enforcing expectations of behavior that carry with them the supposition of reasonableness, of collectively generated validity. It has, then, a dual character of justice (normativity and validity) and social facticity (efficiency and necessity).[55]

In the course of his turn to law, Habermas specifies and updates the concept of the public sphere that he introduces in *The Structural Transformation of the Public Sphere*. Two components of this updating stand out. Habermas expands the notion of the public to include any communicative act. Simultaneously, he contracts and redirects the political role of the public to the legal system.

Habermas's expansion of the notion of the public into a more general sense of communicative acts relies on the idea of net-works. He writes: "The public sphere can best be described as a network for communicating information and points of view."[56] In complex societies, this network is highly differentiated. It is bro-ken up according to function, topic, locale, complexity, temporal-ity. In the face of these breaks, what links these "partial publics" is their constitution in ordinary language. This renders them, in principle, porous to one another.[57] The idea, in a nutshell, is that the constitutive attribute of a public is its communicative struc-ture. Hence, any linguistically mediated interaction is (potentially) public. Anything that involves communication is public. Commu-nication and publicity are interchangeable.

In this version of publicity, "public" seems a matter of orienta-tion: it is not just about watching; it is about interacting, register-ing one's two cents, one's opinion. If something is interactive, it is public. All our little communicative exchanges, then, make up one great big public. How, exactly? By contracting into informational content. That is to say, Habermas suggests that the elision be-tween communication and publicity is possible because, in com-plex, highly mediated societies, communicative exchanges uncou-ple from their specific contexts, extend out into the virtual presence of those linked through media, and circulate as informa-tion.

Having expanded the notion of the bourgeois public sphere into an unbounded (because porous) universal public sphere, Habermas reduces the political role of the public. He explains: "The more the audience is widened through mass communications, the more in-clusive and the more abstract in form it becomes. Correspond-ingly, the *roles of actors* appearing in the arenas are, to an increas-ing degree, sharply separated from the roles of the spectators in the galleries."[58] The public denotes less a deliberative sphere, a set of discussions about norms and values, than an audience. Politics is what actors do; the public watches. Habermas's widening of the public thus seems to reconfigure its communicative structure: publicity now connotes an audience watching actors.

William Scheuerman has provided a powerful critique of Haber-mas's redirection of the political role of the public into the legal system. Focusing on Habermas's attempt to develop a two-track model of democracy, Scheuerman questions the "center-periph-ery" political spatiality Habermas takes over from the realist political theory of Bernard Peters.[59] In this political spatiality, the center denotes the legislation, adjudication, and administration of power by actors in the political arena. Out on the periphery of civil society is the audience. I agree with Scheuerman that Habermas's move leads him "to downplay worrisome trends in contemporary capitalist democracy."[60] And one of these trends, of course, is the increase in media, the increase in the means of communication, the proliferation of screens and cameras and sites and opportunities to express one's opinion and show one's face even as corporations tighten their global grip and democracy is reduced to a content. In this setting, clicking on an icon and expressing an opinion doesn't transform the audience into actors. (But it may very well interpellate them as celebrities.)

What is also striking is the weird way Habermas's contemporary reformulation of publicity echoes and endorses the account of technoculture I introduce in chapter 1. In Habermas's account, the system believes for us and everybody wants to know. Beginning from the position that no overarching norms can be relied on to hold people together today, Habermas reconfigures political will-formation as a property of law as a system, as a dimension of the institutions and decision-making structures of a constitutional state. The system, the processes and procedures, guarantee legitimacy; in effect, the system believes so that the audience is "unburdened" of the pressure of supposing its reasonableness (and the cynic, noting the extreme difficulty of supposing the current system to be reasonable, adds "good thing!"). But communicative power doesn't go away—people want to know. And the way communicative power is exercised in technoculture continuously reconfirms and reproduces this compulsion to know. Habermas describes the "exercise" of communicative power as "a siege."[61] This suggests to me the way media today swamp and overwhelm viewers and consumers and so transform them into audience. Corporations and advertisers depend on the porosity of communicative networks; they employ integrated campaigns that reproduce the message or image absolutely everywhere. They rely on publicity's reflexivization into celebrity such that persons, things, slogans, and events become well known for their well-knownness.

This siege-like dimension of communicative power is clearly not the same as an exchange of reasons and can in no way be detached from the material conditions of global capitalist technoculture out of which it arises. The problem, then, is how Habermas can defend the account of communicative power he describes, how he can suggest that communicative power is something that can "take responsibility," how he can assume that a kind of rationality inheres in the networks of technoculture, and how he can rely on a fundamentally normative sense of communicative action. To consider a more specific example, Habermas claims that public opinions lose credibility when they are discovered to be based on intrusions of power and money, when they are understood to be produced by particular groups or organizations.[62] This is clearly wrong. People today know full well that opinions are produced, and still they act as if they did not know this, as if they believed. Currently popular television series that go through the steps involved in creating teen bands are but one example. The shows depict the processes by which teens compete, are selected, and then trained and groomed to be in a band. There is no illusion of struggling artists in a garage or folks in it "for the sake of the music." In fact, the formula for making these bands is so successful that they all have produced chart-topping pop music hits.

People know that popularity is managed, part of a campaign or strategy. In the United States, everyone knows that winning an election is directly tied to how much money is spent. We know that corporations employ public relations managers and lobbyists (as in Nike's attempt to position itself as a leading opponent of sweatshop labor when it is in fact a leading employer of sweatshop labor), that corporations give to charities in order to appear to care about community interests (computer companies' donations of computers to schools are particularly interesting here insofar as they are clearly implicated in the production of new users, consumers, and markets). We know that "being convinced" is orchestrated, part of a carefully spun series of stories, leaks, and opinions. And still we are convinced.

Habermas links the "autonomy" of the public to whether its position on an issue comes out of "a process of becoming informed or in fact only a more or less concealed game of power."[63] But the opposition between revelation and concealment on which this formulation of the normative dimension of publicity relies is no longer persuasive. Habermas misses the way that in contemporary technoculture the very process of becoming informed, the very goal of knowing, reproduces capitalist domination. To know, one has to consume information and the media and technologies that provide it. One has to engage a program that runs surveillance, accumulation, aggregation, and dissemination. Put another way: the problem of technoculture is not simply that we are hailed as consumers all the time. Rather, the problem is that our very interpellation as citizens installs us in practices of consumption, conspiracy, and celebrity. Publicity as ideology does not simply emphasize information. It *openly* acknowledges information's imbrication in power. It's the way things are. No concealment is necessary.

In an analogous attempt to defend the continued normativity of an ideal of publicity that he has simultaneously expanded and depoliticized, Habermas tries to distinguish actors who "emerge from" the public from those who "appear before" it. Like his opposition between information and coercion, this one does not hold up. The ideal of "coming up out of" or "being extricated from" the mass of the people was always crucial to celebrity appeal. "Celebrities," P. David Marshall explains, "emerge from a legitimation process that is connected to the people."[64] To be sure, the key difference between "emerging from" and "appearing before" for Habermas seems to rest on a distinction between those who employ market studies, opinion surveys, and public relations campaigns and those who do not. But in an era of permanent media in which everyone has a camera and a website, this makes no sense. Not only does registering politically, does having a "public" presence, require some kind of expertise and awareness of public relations and the market, but the extension and reflexivization of communication brought about by networked computing and integrated media have made these tools readily available to more and more people. The independent media movement has shown, through demonstrations in Seattle, Sydney, Los Angeles, Prague, and Washington, D.C., the potentially radical uses of "appearing before"—or better, of what happens when the audience takes control of the cameras before which the actors want to appear. On the flipside, isn't a key tool of mainstream politics a story of emergence? Of how great figure X or significant policy Y became something out of nothing? In sum, the opposition between "emerging from" and "appearing before" adds nothing to Habermas's normative construal of the public as audience.

Problems also appear in Habermas's account of communicative power in terms of a complex network of porous, differentiated, and vaguely alternative publics. There's no fundamental conflict among them. There's no real struggle between them. Instead, there's an odd kind of parity or elision of potentially radically different kinds of groups, media, interests, and claims, as if they could just sit around a table and talk about their feelings. Nevertheless, the fundamental division within the social reappears in the gap between the actors and the audience. And what both conceals and sustains this division? Communicative power. (Bill Gates gives a cheer!)

Habermas's reflexive communicative power is a version of the drive for publicity. In the center–periphery model, the primary mechanism of political action is becoming public, gaining the attention of the audience.[65] One must make oneself visible. We might consider this visibility in terms of Habermas's continued commitment to universal publicity rights: if it is the case that everyone retains participatory and speech rights, then it makes perfect sense that everyone would think of themselves as actors or celebrities on a public stage. When communication makes everything potentially public, everyone is potentially a celebrity. At the same time, the networks of communication circulate endlessly, thereby avoiding the ultimate deadlock of the failure of normative justification. Reflexivity is not liberation—it is the circuit of drive.

An Audience but No Actors (or, "Leave Your Egos at the Door")

My treatment of communicative reflexivization in terms of celebrity may seem a distorted reading of Habermas. But how little it distorts is clear when one looks at Habermas's own account of subjectivity. In chapter 1, I discussed the orientation toward an audience that Habermas ascribes to the bourgeois subject in *Structural Transformation of the Public Sphere*. Emerging in the domestic sphere of the nuclear family, the subject is compelled to give an account of itself before an audience of others. In Freemasonry as well, subjects come into being in the context of filling out detailed questionnaires, of offering themselves to the opinion and judgment of lodge brethren. As Habermas makes clear, the public sphere emerges in private, and it emerges via a particular mode of subjectivization. Indeed, that there was a domain of privacy anchored the possibility of a public precisely insofar as it guaranteed this subjectivization.

In his later work, Habermas considers the pressures that postmodern societies place on "individualization" or the development of a "postconventional ego identity." Through a reconstruction of George Herbert Mead, he argues that this form of ego identity depends on the capacity to confront or view oneself from the perspective of "*all* others in every community."[66] One takes the position of those who look upon one, judging, and evaluating oneself from this perspective. For Habermas, this process is part of a rationalization of the lifeworld that cannot be reduced to the systems-theoretic accounts of risk society theorists. In fact, it points to the positive potential of a transformation in communication whereby postconventional individuals are more unique, more individuated, and more free than are those before. He writes:

> Not only as an *autonomous* being but also as an *individuated* being, the self of the practical relation-to-self cannot reassure itself about itself through direct reflection but only via the perspective of others. In this case I have to rely not on others' *agreement* with my judgments and actions but on their recognition of my claim to uniqueness and irreplaceability.[67]

Postconventional individuals, then, have to be reflexively reassured of their identities through their recognition by others. More precisely, they have to posit this acknowledgment of their own uniqueness on the part of all others.

Habermas presents this account of postconventional identity as an extension of the societal rationalization process into the communicative domain of the lifeworld. (Risk society theorists for the most part limit their account of rationalization to economic and administrative steering systems.) For Habermas, then, such an extension of communicative reason anticipates a better, more rational, and freer mode of social integration as well as individualization.

To me, however, the postconventional ego seems like a celebrity subject. The postconventional ego is insecure. It cannot rely on traditional or conventional norms and practices for security or even self-identity. To function in the reflexivized risk society that Habermas describes—one characterized by the decline of symbolic efficiency—this postconventional ego has to posit, continually, an audience of others before which it can justify and validate itself. This is the only way it can secure its own sense of itself, its own claim to uniqueness. Habermas suggests that relationships with concrete others cannot fulfill this imperative for two reasons: first, the brutalities of the economic and political system tend to disrupt or juridify these relationships; second, the destabilization of social roles is so complete that no concrete other can provide an assurance great enough to combat the more prevailing forces of normative and ethical uncertainty. In others words, my friends might be wrong about me. A subject adequate to the times, then, is one formed through positing itself before an audience of everyone.

Technoculture's computer-mediated interactions seem to have transformed structures of communication in precisely the way Habermas suggests is necessary for postconventional subjectivity. They provide the means whereby subjects can understand themselves as watched by, visible to, present before "*all* others in every community." Indeed, this mode of subjectivization seems to anchor a social formation rooted in publicity. These days, our very selves are already public. At the same time, however, the ever-presence of screens makes clear the fundamental anxiety permeating this form of subjectivity, an anxiety Habermas ignores: not only is it impossible to present oneself before all others in a community, but the demand to do so pushes the subject into spectacular modes of self-presentation in order to get attention. Additionally, the impossibility of watching all these performances, of actually being in the audience, marks the subject as guilty in advance.

Habermas's acknowledgment that the development of a postconventional ego identity is a "challenge" dramatically understates the impact of transformations in communication on subjectivity. The increased reflexivity he describes as a process of individualization also involves a direct externalization of the individual's feelings and experiences. How do I feel? Tons of self-help books and magazine quizzes flow through the data stream as if they were ways of figuring out an answer. What is my experience? In technoculture, the multiple levels of reflexivity and virtuality challenge any claim to authenticity. As Žižek explains, "in the thorough reflexivity of our lives, any direct appeal to our experience is invalidated—that is to say, I no longer trust my own direct experiences, but expect the Other to tell me how I really feel."[68] An account of the reflexivization of communication, then, needs to consider the new forms of domination that emerge, forms that, as I suggest above, might be linked to Little Brothers or demanding little authorities, or processes of super-egoization that attach us to communicative capitalism.

Similarly, it seems clear that the anxieties stimulated by technoculture's connections and virtualities have less to do with pornography and stalkers than they do with fears of what we don't know but should, fears rooted in the new technologies themselves. The speed of networked communications, for example, gives many of us the sense of being forever behind, of forever lacking what everyone else has. The promise of information gives us the sense of being always uninformed, unsure, never quite certain that what we think we know hasn't been proven otherwise and that were we diligent enough we would have discovered our error. Our fears, then, are linked to an overwhelming doubt that can never be resolved. And this brings with it the risk that our desires to know may become desires for relief, desires for some acquisition or authority that can release us from the overwhelming multiplicity of options, possibilities, facts, and fantasies confronting us daily.

Žižek links drive to a fundamental failure. He writes: "The most succinct definition of the reversal constitutive of drive is the moment when, in our engagement in a purposeful activity (activity directed towards some goal), the way towards this goal, the gestures we make to achieve it, start to function as a goal in itself, as its own aim, as a something that brings its own satisfaction."[69] This is a critical (psychoanalytic) version of the same mode of subjectivization that Habermas describes in terms of postconventional identity. The failure of the Habermasian subject to assure itself of its identity under the demanding conditions of a "detraditionalized" lifeworld is answered by a reflexivation of this goal—not the uniqueness of the subject but the *recognition* of the uniqueness of the subject by an *audience* of everyone.[70]

We might further describe the failure constitutive of drive in Habermasian terms of the disrupted consensus, the challenge raised to a particular norm, and the unending discussion this failure stimulates. Outside of the institutionalized will of law, Habermas cannot get from discussion to action. His postconventional subject, in other words, seems to want to present itself as an actor before an audience but not really to act; there is only the retroactive presentation and effort to win approval, justification, from an audience of everyone.

Nothing to Say

The horrible paradox of the endless circulation of discussion is that it results in a frightening silence, a kind of paralysis in which there are all sorts of plausible responses, all sorts of information available (out there, if we can find it)—but, ultimately, nothing we can say. Žižek describes drive in terms of a "sudden onset of silence."[71] He explains that this break into silence is a subjectivization; it marks the emergence of the subject of drive. This subject cannot talk. It is perverse, not really engaging subjectively at all.

Žižek presents the subject of drive as the subject of capital or late-capitalist market relations and the subject of desire as the democratic subject.[72] He argues that given the collapse of symbolic efficiency, the paradigmatic mode of subjectivity is a kind of polymorphous perversity. Correspondingly, political discourse has shifted from hysteria to perversion. For Žižek, this means that a pressing political problem is "how to hystericize the subject," how to break through drive and inculcate questioning and lack.

I think the problem here should be framed differently. The hysterical conspiring subject and the perverse celebrity subject are two aspects of the same subject, two modes of subjectivization that respond to the reflexivization of communication in the networked economy. Rather than needing to be hystericized, the subject of technoculture is already hysterical, perpetually unsure of who she is and what she wants, driven to all sorts of excesses in order to establish some kind of certainty about her identity. But this subject is perhaps not so much a desiring subject as she is a conspiring subject, a subject of conspiracy theory who keeps looking for answers, making links. She asks questions and tries to uncover the secret—not because she believes she will find an answer but because the technologies and practices believe for her. Her very questioning itself is reflexivized, offered up to the gaze. If drive's logic is *I don't want to do this, nevertheless, I'm doing this*, then the conspiring subject is the one who makes another link, gets a second or third opinion, reads something else, asks another question, even when she doesn't want to—in fact, especially when she doesn't want to but nevertheless is compelled to. To hystericize *this* subject, to inculcate lack, will do nothing but feed into the re-flexivity of communicative drive.

Perhaps another way to pose the question is to take the conspiring subject seriously and ask: Who's this for? Who is the other for whom all this is enacted? This question draws us toward the media apparatuses, the screens and cameras, the networked technologies who believe in our stead. These format publicity today via a celebrity subject who puts himself in the position of the secret and a communicative drive that results in silence. It is fashionable these days to express dismay over the excesses of surveillance in society; nevertheless, there are increasing quantities of various sorts of cameras (digital, video, Web, watch-based), increased inter-connectivity among databases, and increased integration of media more generally. We say that we worry about this proliferation, but still we proliferate. Why? In this chapter, I've suggested that it's because we enjoy being on camera, because we don't feel we exist as subjects unless we can think of ourselves as celebrities.

Reflexivized publicity secures the material conditions through which communicative capitalism reproduces itself today. Capitalism in its information mode functions as communication, as the circulation of messages and information. To fail to criticize this circulation, to fail to politicize communication as an ideal, results in the acceptance of global corporate power. Perhaps paradoxically, the very means of democratic publicity end up leading to its opposite: private control by the market.

Neo-Democracy

This book is a work of critical theory. In it, I use ideology critique to try to break the seemingly unquestionable connection between publicity and democracy that prevents contemporary theorists of democracy from challenging the basic premises of technoculture. The presumption that democracy relies on a public, I've argued, reinforces communicative capitalism. The ideal of the public materializes an economy of transnational telecommunications corporations, media conglomerates, computer hardware, software and infrastructure developers, and content (information and entertainment) providers. Democratic potentials are thereby collapsed into increases in access and information. Democratic governance becomes indistinguishable from intensifications and extensions in the circulation of information. Our deepest commitments—to inclusion, equality, and participation within a public—bind us into the practices whereby we submit to global capital.

That the ideal of a public has a continued hold should not be surprising. The fantasy of a unified public links together powerful utopian energies of inclusivity, equality, transparency, and rationality. It holds out the promise of democratic institutions in which free and equal citizens collectively deliberate over the principles that should govern their lives. It suggests the value of democratic spaces realized through shared practices of generosity and toleration. One might even say that the ideal of a public has taught us what to desire when it comes to democracy; it has provided the matrix through which we know what to claim, value, and defend.[1]

I have emphasized publicity's claim that everyone has a right to know. Publicity values suspicion, exposure, and information as components of the system that can secure this right. It defends practices, institutions, and technologies insofar as they materialize the system. Publicity's technocultural materialization as and through suspicions and screens, then, is not opposed to the aspirations that historically have been articulated together via the notion of the public. On the contrary, that the public has served as a vehicle for these aspirations is what gives the concept its ideological force. So my argument is that breaking out of today's technocultural matrix may well entail shooting ourselves in the foot, that is to say, it may require a willingness to challenge, perhaps to sacrifice, our deepest commitments.

To clarify this point, I turn again to Habermas in order to situate the aspirations of the public in the context of the nation-state and address how the networks of communicative capitalism change the conditions under which "the public" is invoked. I then return to my discussion of the ideology of technoculture to consider whether the material conditions that allow for the critique of the public suggest alternate configurations for democratic politics.

Public Aspirations

The aspirational quality of publicity features strongly in Habermas's work. But it is configured within a depoliticized—a legitimizing rather than an inciting—use of universality. From *The Structural Transformation of the Public Sphere* to *Between Facts and Norms*, Habermas has argued for the ultimately universal character of the public. As is well known, his early account of the public sphere's claim to universality extends from—and inverts— the legacy of critical theory. Theorists from Marx to Marcuse located the potential for universal political emancipation in the margins of society—in the revolutionary classes of the workers and then the students, racial minorities, and others excluded from the benefits of the capitalist state. In these and other accounts, the margin becomes the center. In contrast, Habermas's emphasis on the public sphere shifts critical theory's attention away from the agents to the sites of political change (or, more precisely, to the spaces that agents produce in the course of their communicative engagements). What the concept of the public sphere does is find *within* society and the state, *within* the norms of the bourgeoisie, the potential for, minimally, the democratic legitimation of the late-capitalist state and, maximally, the possibility of universal emancipation through the rule of law. By turning to this concept, then, Habermas replaces revolutionary energy with democratic procedure and political will with democratic will-formation. The "all" inciting the formation of the revolutionary class becomes the depoliticized "all" of deliberative democracy.

The universal claim for the public sphere appears in a somewhat different—although still depoliticized—version in Habermas's theory of communicative action: the presuppositions of ordinary language establish normativity as such.[2] Here, Habermas emphasizes the fundamental inclusivity of the public sphere, the primacy of reason (rational argumentation), and the ultimately legitimizing role the public plays. The public in this universal dimension is naturalized into the preconditions of language use and elevated into an intersubjective version of the categorical imperative.

As Habermas acknowledges, the aspirational and universalizing dimensions of the public that he systematically reconstructs have a historical context in the nation-state. That is to say, the public that has been invoked by theorists, critics, and constitutions has been a *national* public. Conspiracy theory, as I discuss in chapter 2, takes this absolutely seriously. In American history, invoking a conspiracy enabled not the extension of the universal claims of the British constitution but the establishment of a new national public. Likewise, in conspiracy theory the secrets that need to be exposed are those that challenge the sovereignty of a democratic nation or, more precisely, that reveal the obscene supplement of power already challenging it.

The nation-state is what gives unity to Habermas's public sphere. Habermas doesn't thematize the place of the public sphere in securing particular national identities; nevertheless, he appeals to these identities in *Structural Transformation* as he highlights the German *Tischgesellschaften*, the English coffeehouses, and the French salons. Moreover, he describes the political activity of the public sphere as targeting the state: discussions are to impact the actions of specific governments within specific nations. Habermas writes: "The public of 'human beings' engaged in rational-critical debate was constituted into one of 'citizens' wherever there was communication concerning the affairs of the 'commonwealth.' "[3] Although in his appeals to Kant, such citizenship is part of the cosmopolitan world of reason, with each account of the connection between discussion and law, discussion and the constitution, and discussion and fundamental rights, Habermas relies implicitly on the setting of the public sphere within the nation-state.

In *Between Facts and Norms*, Habermas continues to highlight the universality of democratic norms even as he acknowledges the historical link between popular sovereignty and "the nation." In fact, at the same time that he appeals to the possibility of a world public sphere produced through global telecommunications, he grants a certain priority to "the identity of the political community, which also must not be violated by immigration" and which "depends primarily on the legal principles anchored in the *political culture*."[4] Furthermore, he admits that "up to the present the political public sphere has been fragmented into national units."[5] So again, as in *Structural Transformation of the Public Sphere*, Habermas's appeal to a cosmopolitan public sphere remains bounded by the priority of the nation.

A typical response to this binding capacity of the nation is the critique of ethnocentrism. One treats as an exposure—a secret to be revealed—the particular ethnic, blood, racial, or linguistic suppositions of the nation as a constitutional state. The exposure of national particularity is supposed to subvert the claim to public universality. This is not my argument here. Rather, the point I want to make concerns the limits of the public sphere and how these limits establish the utopian dimension of publicity. I'm interested in boundedness per se. The matrix of democratic desire has been constituted through the nation—not through a global or universal ideal of a public. Bentham, for example, explicitly discusses an English public. The disavowed constitutive split that sustains his public is within the nation. Or, to use a different example, democratic desires for inclusion are for inclusion within the field determined by a constitutional nation-state. If we take this boundedness seriously, we see that Habermas mislocates the utopian core of publicity. Far from resting in abstract ideals of an open-ended public sphere, it depends on and is inextricable from the nation.[6]

Habermas's discussion is built around the thesis that "there is only a historically contingent and not a conceptual connection between republicanism and nationalism."[7] He takes the position that the practices of citizenship entailed in legal relations of recognition have a formal quality that can't be boiled down to the customs and culture of a particular community. Thus Habermas holds that it is possible and necessary to distinguish between the procedural components of democracy and the particular contours and history of a nation. So he renounces "an overly concrete reading of the principle of popular sovereignty" and interprets the sovereign will of a collectivity "as anchored in a procedure of opinion and will-formation."[8] Another way to say this is that Habermas emphasizes a reflexive account of sovereignty within the constitutional state.

Paul A. Passavant's work on the First Amendment to the U.S. Constitution clarifies the problems with this argument.[9] Far from "renouncing an overly concrete reading of the principle of popular sovereignty," Passavant demonstrates how procedures of opinion and will formation constitute embodied subjects within a particular community. To this end, he emphasizes the fact that the U.S. Constitution invests rights in (and through this investment produces) the American people. To claim a right is to claim membership in this community. One claims a right to free speech, say, as an American. Membership gives meaning to the claim for free speech. The claim is an address not to an amorphous, indeterminate, potentially global public but to a community willing to recognize and back up this claim. Passavant's examples include Martin Luther King Jr.'s mobilization of a *national* discourse of rights at the Montgomery bus boycott. Such examples enable him to establish the corresponding point as to how a rights claim incites a discussion about the identity of the community invoked to recognize it: who are "we," then, who recognize this claim? Are you who raise it *really* one of us? And what does it mean for us if you are? As Passavant writes: "To adjudicate a question of rights is, in some measure, to adjudicate the identity of the American people and the requirements that flow from this identity."[10] So, to return to Habermas: he is correct when he says that the connection between rights and nation is contingent insofar as it is implicated in national histories. But this connection is conceptual, nonetheless—rights and nation are linked together via the concept of the people in whom sovereignty is invested.

When one considers the process through which subjects capable of making rights claims are produced, or, to use a different language, when one takes up the question of the materialization of opinion and will formation in the bodies of citizens, the difficulties with Habermas's effort to extract procedures from national practices of subject formation are even more glaring. In Passavant's account, free speech is more than an enabling condition of rational democratic debate. His historical analysis documents the ways a normative account of discussion produces "civil" subjects through a variety of disciplinary regimes. Commenting on Walter Bagehot's concept of "government by discussion," Passavant explains: "The capacity for being a speaker and producing speech is created through a strict discipline of sexual desire, while discussion in turn regulates sexual desire, thus reproducing the conditions for free speech. In a broad sense, therefore, government by discussion describes a set of *economic* relations that reproduces a national people capable of exercising its rights of free speech."[11] What Habermas describes as procedures of opinion and will formation are more than just procedures. They presuppose and demand the production of subjects who can follow them, who can speak according to their rules, who can recognize themselves as part of the collectivity bound through the procedures themselves. Their activities have to be "decent," "civilized," in order to be recognizable in terms of national practices and customs. For the protections of free speech to apply, claimants have to conform to what is expected of one of the people. They have to be interpellated as members of a national public.

I've introduced this account of the deep connection between the procedures Habermas associates with the public and their embeddedness within the nation in order to draw attention to the external boundaries of the ideal of a public sphere. The public sphere has been configured in terms of a national public. Today, processes of globalization challenge this figuration. Worldwide communications networks (including the protocols establishing top-level Internet connectivity), transnational migrations and immigrations, and the force of global financial markets all disrupt the primacy of the nation.[12] The nation can no longer provide the fantasy of unity necessary for the ideal of a public.

Some think that contemporary technoculture realizes the promise of unlimited and uncoerced communication. Habermas finds that "the phenomenon of a world public sphere" is today "becoming political reality for the first time in a cosmopolitan matrix of communication."[13] To be sure, this world public sphere differs from the old bourgeois public sphere. In today's global media, Habermas acknowledges, "communication structures contract to information content and points of view that are uncoupled from the thick contexts of simple interactions."[14] Put somewhat differently, the digitalization of contemporary telecommunications doesn't simply enable the realization of the public sphere; digital communication *is* the public sphere. Habermas writes: "The public sphere can best be described as a network for communicating information and points of view (i.e., opinions expressing affirmative or negative attitudes)."[15] For Habermas, then, the circulation of content and points of view through communication networks *is* the democratic exchange of ideas.

What is astounding is that even as Habermas acknowledges—indeed, fully supports—the digitalization of communication or the reconfiguration of the public sphere in terms of information technologies, he says nothing about the ruthless economic preconditions of this digitalization. Dan Schiller, however, thoroughly documents the neoliberal market policies that drove the development of networked communications and the corresponding increase to corporate wealth and power.[16] Today, the circulation of information is also the paradigmatic form of capitalism.[17] Let's be clear: the growth of new media technologies both drives and has been driven by the global market. A democratic decision-making process did not produce the World Wide Web. There were no democratic debates in which people concluded, "Gee, what we really need is a global telecommunications infrastructure that will enable corporations to consolidate their power."

In his discussion of the oligopolistic practices of the contemporary computer and telecommunications industry, Robert McChesney makes clear what is at stake in the presumption of democracy that has formatted contemporary endorsement of new media technologies—an equation of democracy and markets. He writes:

> The anti-democratic nature of Web policy making is explained or defended on very simple grounds: the Web is to be and should be regulated by the free market. This is the most rational, fair, and democratic regulatory mechanism ever known to humanity, so by all rights it should be automatically applied to any and all areas of social life where profit can be found. . . . Indeed, by this logic, any public debate over Web policy can only be counterproductive, because it could only lead us away from a profit-driven system.[18]

As McChesney makes clear, the belief that the Web is already public, that it already best encodes ideals of freedom, exchange, reciprocity, and rationality, has driven the information economy, preventing its politicization by presenting it as democratic in advance.[19] Moreoever, this supposition of publicity depends on the idea that the public is realized through the market.

Debates around the creation of new global top-level domains (gTLDs—the dot-whatever suffixes that designate addresses on the Internet—.com, .gov, .org) further illustrate the equation of democratic communication with the securing of global markets. In testimony before the Telecommunications Subcommittee of the House Committee on Energy and Commerce, speakers from the Center for Democracy and Technology collapsed free communication into the protection of competition. This testimony is especially significant because the Center for Democracy and Technology presents itself as a progressive, not-for-profit organization working on behalf of the "public" interest. Not only did the center adopt the typical public sphere value of "transparency" as a goal for the process of creating domain names (as if the opacity of the procedures was as much a problem as the $50,000 fee for entering the domain name auction or, better, as if a gTLD auction could ever conceivably be a matter for a global public, something the center fudges by talking about proper "representation"), but it presumed no difference between market and democratic interests. It criticized ICANN (Internet Corporation for Assigned Names and Numbers—the organization that assigns domain names) for failing to live up to its mission of promoting "speech, commerce, and civic discourse."[20] Indeed, the biggest worry of the center seemed to be that ICANN will become some kind of Big Brother, deciding on domain names like .democrat instead of .gop—as if *this* were the problem of global technoculture.

Put somewhat differently, the Center for Democracy and Technology rendered as a problem of arbitrary authority what is better understood in terms of the increasingly relentless force of the market. In this vein, it sympathetically interjected that "Trademark holders have . . . raised concerns about their ability to police their marks in a multitude of new spaces." (This sets up a nice Žižekian point about the center's awareness of the decline of symbolic efficiency in cyberia; the center worried about the proliferation of names that are neither authorized nor policed. In this regard, its remark that "it is increasingly difficult to find descriptive and meaningful new names" can be read psychoanalytically in terms of psychosis: psychotics are unable to create new metaphors. Language in cyberspace—as in psychosis—operates through the absence or failure of a central organizing metaphor, through the foreclosure of the paternal function.[21] As the name-granting authority, ICANN is supposed to provide a remedy to this psychosis because it registers addresses and structures the terms and conditions of naming in cyberia.)

Global telecommunications depend on massive transnational corporations. When communication understood in terms of the ideals of publicity is collapsed into technoculture's information networks, this economic dimension disappears. Put more strongly, the telecommunications network can appear as a democratic public sphere only if its role as and in the market is disavowed.

Such a disavowal appears in Habermas's emphasis on a "self-limiting radicalism" in his discussion of the communicative rationalization of the lifeworld. In his view, the complexity of contemporary society requires that steering systems like the market not be politicized but be allowed to follow their own logics. In technoculture, though, "following their own logics" has meant not simply capital's annexation of ever more social practices but a digitalization and informatization such that communicative networks and practices are no different from the circulation of capital.[22] The division of the world Habermas presupposes certainly doesn't work now—if it ever did. Again, my point is that the historical conditions under which the public might be invoked as the democratic ideal do not hold in communicative capitalism.

The Matrix

The nation-state has functioned as a boundary for the public sphere. This external boundary has accompanied secrecy as the internal limiting condition of the public, a point I've emphasized throughout this book. The nation was never unified, whole, or coherent. The national public, as Bentham makes clear, was split. Indeed, publicity as a system of distrust mobilizes to overcome and produce this split. The failures, conflicts, and weaknesses of the public that appear as merely empirical barriers to its realization stimulate efforts on behalf of its realization, suspicious efforts to expose and disseminate, to make sure that everyone knows. Not only does this circulation of suspicion undermine that trust of a public-supposed-to-believe necessary to sustain the fantasy of the public, but it also becomes materialized in media and communication technologies. When everyone has the right to know, the technologies believe for us. We don't have to believe in the public anymore; we just act "as if" we believe, clicking for secrets and watching the screens. This acting "as if" materializes the "public" as if it were really there.

Publicity appears today as the matrix that regulates the relationship between the visible and the not-visible, the imaginable and the not-imaginable.[23] On the one hand, that which is public is presented as a secret. The best examples here are the tabloids screaming about secret romances, secret book deals, or secret diets, all of which they illustrate with completely public information. Promotional campaigns for film and television do the same thing: part of the success of *The Sixth Sense* stemmed from repetitions of the injunction not to tell the secret of the ending—as if something shown on thousands of screens to millions of people could be a secret. (Why were these audiences not a public?) Recently I saw a remarkably extreme example in an article on net porn: "Have you ever had a secret that you were slightly ashamed of? Have you had an embarrassing secret that you would prefer that nobody knew? The Internet industry has a secret like that. The secret is pornography, or rather the fact that it has consistently been one of the Internet's biggest revenue earners."[24] Here again, what is completely obvious, well known, and highly publicized is presented as if it were a scandalous revelation, as if it were a disclosure capable, somehow, of calling a public into being. Indeed, the "obviousness" that pornography is plentiful on the Net reinforces the sense of a public in the inverse direction as well: insofar as our response to this claim is that "everybody knows" the Net oozes with porn, our presumption of a knowing public is confirmed.

On the other hand, we find people reacting to matters that are fully public as if the matters were secrets they didn't know. That is, some completely obvious things illustrate the phenomenon of the public not supposed to know that I discuss in the chapter 1. Consider the U.S. presidential election of 2000. George W. Bush was not elected president. Al Gore received a majority of the popular vote; a partisan Supreme Court ushered Bush into office. Bush's assumption of the presidency was in large part a product of him acting as if he were president.[25] In fact, the more reports appeared with voting analyses and investigations into over-votes and various kinds of chads, the less effect they seemed to have. They never really registered symbolically at all (they had little symbolic efficiency). Similar examples can be found in reports of poverty, extreme concentrations of wealth, and the combination of increased stock valuations with corporate layoffs and downsizing. People know these situations are real and ongoing—but they act as if the circumstances were some kind of secret, as if they didn't know this at all.

Finally, we have global telecommunications as the networked economy. This is absolutely obvious and openly acknowledged; it is the very ether we breathe. At the same time, that the intensification of communications networks is not an extension of global democracy is like a secret kept from the public (one we keep from ourselves). Importantly, although corporate control of entertainment networks, radio, and print media is part of this secret, it isn't all: even the proliferation of noncorporate media enriches telecommunications, hardware, and software providers. It too stimulates processes of branding, public relations, advertising, and image consulting. The proliferation of screens and voices and links and contents intensifies an ever-circulating cycle of drive.

This same matrix can be seen in technoculture's extreme materializations of the ideology of publicity in conspiracy and celebrity. Both conspiracy and celebrity "positivize" (serve as inscriptions of) the impossibility of the public.[26] The prevalence of conspiracy theory today marks the decline of symbolic efficiency, the sweeping, disarticulating power of publicity to reflexivize everything and destroy any reference point. All sorts of different—wild—views and explanations circulate, and all we have to do is point, click, and link. But the mindshare occupied by conspiracy may also be understood as an inversion: that is to say, politics today may be too consultative; there may be too many opinions, too many consultants, too many options, too much inclusion such that one would like some kind of conspiracy to be at work behind the scenes just to stop the endless process of discussion. Conspiracy in this version satisfies a longing for the big Other. A particularly popular version of this longing—which has the added benefit of being true according to criteria accepted by those outside conspiracy circles—appears in accounts of ECHELON, a network of global electronic surveillance that links the security systems of the United States, Britain, Canada, Australia, and New Zealand.[27] ECHELON apparently integrates all electromagnetically circulating information in the world. Not only does it enable governments to eavesdrop, but, according to Christopher Hitchens's account, it informationalizes (digitalizes into one big soup) transmissions over baby monitors, the words of a "housewife," U.S. senators' illicit cell phone conversations, and negotiations for multibillion dollar defense contracts. Although Hitchens says he is not implying that big Brother is watching ("I'm not a conspiracy theorist, but . . ."), that is exactly what he is doing when he writes, "we do well to remember how much of the power of the state is invisible." Such suspicions and invocations reassure us in the face of technoculture's myriad, indeterminate screens—at least something, someone, is certain.

The celebrity mode of subjectivization employs this same matrix. New media, the demand to fill 24/7 content in an 800-channel universe, not to mention the ubiquity of databases, enable everyone to be famous for at least fifteen minutes. But then again celebrity is the predominant experience of subjectivity today precisely because no one can really be known; no one has the kind of star power to establish himself or herself as a point of reference. As with conspiracy, so with celebrity, we see accompanying the endorsement of an absence of authority a longing for authority.

In democratic theory, the public has been offered as a procedural substitute for this authority. Whether as an empty place or a communicative space, it has suggested a fantasy of authorization without the coercive inevitability of a king, dictator, or ruling party. The public serves as a reflexivization of authority, one in which consideration of the bases of authority comes itself to function as authority's basis. On this account, the strength of the ideal of the public stems from its openness: not only does the concept not designate in some sort of descriptivist way but its emancipatory promise stems from its very contestability. The efficacy of the public, some might say, arises from its openness and availability to contestation. I agree that "public" is open. I agree that this "openness" is critical to its political efficacy. But the crucial matter is efficacy *with respect to what?* My answer is that the contestability of the public is efficacious with respect to a particular formation of power. The openness of the category of the public is precisely what makes it functional as technocultural ideology. It has political effects that cannot be addressed through an appeal to openness—precisely because this openness—transparency, inclusivity, accessibility, rationality—is what functionalizes it for technoculture.

Contemporary critical theory, particularly in its Habermasian variants, locates possibilities for freedom and legitimacy in the reflexivization of authority. I argue that this mislocates the problem of democracy in technoculture and in so doing works ideologically in support of communicative capitalism. Technoculture's materialization of the public-supposed-to-know such that now everybody has a right to know is profoundly depoliticizing. Not only is trust displaced from persons to technologies (or, the public-supposed-to-believe becomes the technologies that believe in our stead), but the pressure to know, to find out for oneself, to be informed, sucks the life out of political action. Action is postponed until a thorough study is undertaken, until all the facts are known.

This postponement is a permanent deferral. All the facts can never be known; the very process of searching for them generates new ones. And even if the facts could be known, their very operation detracts from the likelihood of action: the facts become the explanation that one must understand, the apology or excuse designed to eliminate rage. The public relations industry has mastered the art of eliminating opportunities for action. It dumps tons of complicated information onto investigators, critics, and consumers.[28] It arranges for apologies and explanations of problems. Why organize against corporations when they are working to serve us better? How resist in the face of admissions of guilt and injunctions to move on and put it all behind us? In short, excesses of information and communication work in the ideological mode of truth that functions as a lie.

Even if the facts could be known and somehow a space for action could be opened up, one can never know whether the action is the right action or not. There are no criteria that can ground a particular action, because grounding in a technocultural network characterized by the decline of symbolic efficiency is impossible. Reflexivization has, paradoxically, yielded a situation not of transparency but of radically unbearable opacity: there is information without clarity because there are no terms through which clarity might be stabilized. We may be free to decide, but we have no criteria upon which to decide. As Žižek writes, "There is no guarantee that the democratic politicization of crucial decisions, the ac-

tive involvement of thousands of concerned individuals, will nec-
essarily improve the quality and accuracy of decisions, and thus
effectively lessen the risks."[29] The basic experience of reflexivization, in other words, is that decisions are experienced as anxiety-
provoking obscene gambles.

In technoculture we have ideology without hegemony (or, more
precisely, within the hegemony of contingency, flow, multiplicity,
mutability, and indeterminacy). Publicity establishes the contemporary democratic matrix as a kind of reflexivization program that
forecloses in advance possibilities for galvanizing resistance and
opposition. Paradoxically, publicity's very power to defamiliarize,
disarticulate, and skeptically challenge functionalizes it for communicative capitalism.

What Next?

One of the best things about the movie *The Matrix* is that the option chosen by the hero, Neo (Keanu Reeves), isn't clearly the best
choice. Suspecting that what he sees around him isn't all there is,
Neo comes into contact with Morpheus (Laurence Fishburne), a
terrorist-type figure wanted by the authorities. Morpheus presents
Neo with a choice: if Neo takes the red pill, he will know the truth
of the matrix; if he chooses the blue pill, he will forget everything.
Once Neo chooses, however, there is no going back. So, first, Neo's
very choice of the red pill is under impossible conditions: not only
does he have no way of evaluating potential outcomes in advance,
but he will not be able retroactively to undo his decision. Second,
once he chooses the red pill of knowledge and discovers that he
and the rest of the human race are batteries serving the energy
needs of intelligent machines in a post-apocalyptic hell, he has to
live a horrible life eating disgusting food, fighting the hideous machines, and trying to destroy people's illusions, even though their
only alternative is living underground on a destroyed planet. That
is the reward, the payoff, the benefit. In effect, he chooses the
worst.

Neo chooses the worst, but the choice isn't completely outrageous. There are already hints along the way that, at least in retro-
spect, can be understood as pushing him toward the red pill. One,
Neo has major doubts about the world, about what he sees around
him and is supposed to accept as true and real. Two, even though
he doesn't know Morpheus, Neo takes a gamble and trusts instruc-

tions he receives on a cell phone that arrives in an envelope he assumes (rightly) is from this Morpheus. Three, Neo's existing situation is bad: he's been threatened, interrogated, beaten, and implanted with a horrible bug-machine-Thing by the authorities. So, yes, Neo gambles. He doesn't have full information; he can't predict or evaluate the potential results of his choice. Nevertheless, given what he knows and what he suspects, his act makes sense in the concrete context of his situation.

Our actions today make the public real to us. They continuously materialize publicity as the only way to understand democracy. At the same time, the concrete realization of publicity in the screens and networks of technoculture hails us not just as members of a public-supposed-to-know but as celebrities whose lives are the content of this very knowledge. This matrix of knowing and being known collapses into the "scoop," the obscene object of publicity's drive. How can we break out of this?

The option I advocate is to choose the worst: to acknowledge that the public is an ideal whose materialization undermines its very aspirations. There are, of course, already strong theoretical pushes in this direction. William Connolly's argument for a multidimensional pluralism rooted in a generosity toward different modes of becoming is one such push.[30] Although I am not convinced that the plurality Connolly supports is as contingent as he suggests (because of its imbrications in communicative capitalism), I admire his emphasis on the diversity of political styles and modes of engagement. Rather than appealing to a "public," Connolly finds possibilities for enhancing democracy by multiplying "lines of connection through which governing assemblages can be constructed from a variety of intersecting constituencies."[31] Not only does Connolly accept the painful challenge of constructing and reconstructing governing assemblages today, a necessity in a global network within which states are only one set of often not particularly powerful actors, but also he recognizes the specificities around which constituencies are likely to intersect. Put somewhat differently, he posits links rather than social wholes. Another push to take the red pill comes from Michael Hardt and Antonio Negri's emphasis on the "multitude."[32] They theorize the multitude in terms of production, desire, and singularity, effectively distancing themselves from public sphere emphases on normativity, reason, and equality. At the same time, they associate the political activity of the multitude with specific actions arising in specific locales but attacking nonetheless key aspects of the current power formation, "Empire." To be sure, their ontological account of the multitude flounders in its attempt to avoid the terrain of representation, as if the multitude were always already political, as if politics didn't require division, taking a stand, indeed, the representation of particular harms as extending beyond themselves.[33] Nevertheless, like Connolly, they too find democratic potential in collective assemblages that are more complex than the old notion of the public and thus far more appropriate to political theory in global technoculture.

Despite the critique of technoculture I've raised throughout this book, I find the Web a source of democratic potential. That is to say, there we might find some of the material conditions that suggest alternate configurations of democratic politics. After all, it's highly unlikely that the world will become less technological, less mediated. Nevertheless, these alternatives should not be linked to some mistaken notion that the Web is a public sphere.

So, what, then, is the Web? What ways of conceiving the Web enable new ways of thinking about democracy in technoculture? Should the Web be considered a tool or medium of communication? No, not if by that one means to employ a model of technology that is not always already a materialization of particular ideologies, beliefs, aspirations. Perhaps the Web is better understood in terms of virtual reality. Absolutely not: not only is it real in the sense that real people use it, remaining within their bodies and retaining their physical capacities, but it is a very real component of the economic formation that now impacts the entire planet. To emphasize its virtuality displaces attention from its economic role. Perhaps the Web is best understood as a site at which multiple realities converge. Again, absolutely not. The idea of multiple realities is one of the most pernicious today. There is one reality. It is a site of conflict. It is multiple to the extent that there are multiple approaches to it, but each of these approaches has political effects, effects that reach far beyond those who allegedly accept a particular reality.

Admittedly, I often find myself holding the view that the Web is nothing at all—that all of contemporary society should be understood as cyberia, as awash in a sea of flows and links and networks such that to isolate one communicative infrastructure on the basis of technology alone makes no sense. Nevertheless, the Web plays a key role in configuring the contemporary communicative capitalist imaginary. It is a site of conflict over the meaning, practice, and shape of the global. To that extent, how and what it represents are inseparable from what it does. The Web is the architecture for communicative capitalism, both as an order establishing itself and as an order being resisted.

Consequently, I suggest that the Web be theorized as a "zero institution." This term comes from Lévi-Strauss as explained by Slavoj Žižek.[34] A zero institution is an empty signifier that itself has no determinate meaning but that signifies the presence of meaning. It is an institution with no positive function—all it does is signal the actuality of social institutions as opposed to preinstitutional chaos. Such zero institutions appear in political theory in Machiavelli's Prince and Rousseau's Legislator. As institutions they signify the beginning or founding of something, marking that instance of transformation from the chaotic period prior to the founding. Lévi-Strauss uses the idea of the zero institution to explain how members of a tribe are able to think for themselves as members of the same tribe, even when they are radically split, even when their very representations of what the tribe is are radically antagonistic to one another. Similarly, Žižek views the nation as a kind of zero institution, and he adds that sexual difference should also be understood as a zero institution. Whereas the nation is the zero institution of society's unity, sexual difference is the zero institution of society's split or fundamental antagonism.

The Web is also a zero institution: it enables myriad conflicting constituencies to understand themselves as part of the same global structure, even as they disagree over what the architecture of this structure should entail. Indeed, the Web is a particularly powerful form of zero institution insofar as its basic elements seem a paradoxical combination of singularity and collectivity, collision and convergence. It brings together both the unity and split, both the hope and the antagonism, the imaginary and the Real in one site. The fundamental constitutive antagonisms of communicative capitalism are alive and present, coursing through and structuring the Web in diverse, protean, and evolving networks. As the nation has collapsed as a zero institution capable of standing in symbolically for the possibility of social institutions (and we see this collapse all over the place, from the crisis of sovereignty engendered by the

World Trade Organization, to the crises in the Balkans, to the conflicts over migration and immigration, to the dismantling of the welfare state) and as global economic structures have made their presence felt all the more strongly, the Web has emerged as that zero institution signifying institutionality as such. Likewise, as sexual difference has been complicated by myriad other differences (sexuality, race, ethnicity, and so forth) and as experimentation and blurring and proliferation of sexual difference have thrown into disarray the very possibility of the term, the Web—precisely as a site at which all these differences emerge, mutate, and link up into and through networks—seems to take on this aspect of the zero institution as well. Hence, conflict over configuring the Web is at the same time a conflict over the configuration of the world of unity and difference.

So, representationally, the Web is a zero institution. It provides an all-encompassing space in which social antagonism is simultaneously expressed and obliterated. It is a global space in which many can recognize themselves as connected to others, as linked to things that matter. At the same time, it is a space of conflicting networks and networks of conflict so deep and fundamental that even to speak of consensus, convergence, equality, or inclusion seems an act of violence. So the Web is communicative capitalism's imaginary of uncontested yet competitive global flow. And it is the Real of communicative capitalism, configuring the networks and flows and markets and gambles of the global market. All of this is naturalized on, rendered as the nature of, the Web.

It might be objected that my argument to this point emphasizes communicative capitalism to the neglect of noncommercial forms of networked interaction. After all, not just corporations are on the Web. Activists too make important use of networked communications, as organizers of World Trade Organization protests and the emerging peace movement have made perfectly clear. And the dot-com meltdown proves that commercial applications of the Web are economically as well as ideationally bankrupt.

But the dot-com meltdown should in no way be read in terms of the demise of communicative capitalism. The introduction of commercially viable new technologies is always accompanied by phases of proliferation and meltdown as the new technology establishes itself. At points in the early to mid-1980s, as Commodore, Atari, and other PC companies collapsed, many thought that the personal computer was going the way of the eight-track tape player. Instead, it was a period of consolidation that relied on the efforts of precisely those companies that had died in the struggle, that had fought the good fight. In a more cynical vein, one might speculate that the consumer-oriented period of the late 1990s was really part of a strategy to naturalize the Web, to make it a part of everyday life, like banking, even as the real beneficiary was global capital.

The presence of activists is an argument in my favor: the Web is a site of conflict. And this conflictual, contested dimension of the Web needs to be emphasized. Recent work by Richard Rogers and Noortje Marres does just this, suggesting how one might think about democratic politics post-public.[35] Rogers and Marres have developed a set of software tools in conjunction with a research project on issue-fication on the Web.[36] In effect, these tools provide new imaginings of democracy. The tools themselves involve material practices of navigating differently through cyberia, practices that do not follow, reproduce, or presuppose the binary of publicity and secrecy. By following the movement of issues on the Web, Rogers and Marres have been able to identify "issue networks" that are neither publics nor actors. Networks are the flows of communication and contestation that turn matters into issues. For example, using their "netlocator" software to check the Web for information about television's spectacular presentation of French farmers marching in the streets of Paris, they discover a radically different political configuration: the farmers are absent. What the Web tells them, Rogers and Marres write, is that "the farmers are not farmers, but an organizational figuration that moves from the national to the global and from the political-ideological to the issue-activist. It is quite an organized picture, whereby neither farmers, nor 'phony farmers,' nor 'a bunch of disorganized anarchists' make up the protests, but a professional national–international network."[37]

As they follow issues on the Web rather than in more massified media, Rogers and Marres avoid some of the major problems of publicity in technoculture. They are not sideswiped by spectacle, suspicion, or celebrity. They do not presume a public or an audience in advance. They are not in the business of trying to decide which actors are worthy, which actors count as actors. They do not decide which knowledge has authority—they let the Web decide.[38] Contestation, argument over issues, is at the center of their analysis—not some fantasy of unity or dream of consensus. Furthermore, although Rogers and Marres treat the Web as a communications medium, they don't romanticize the connections it enables; instead they politicize them, investigating and challenging the practices of linking that are employed in issue networks. In fact, their research on the influence of dot-coms and dot-govs in "issue-fication" clarifies the ways in which all links are not equal. The configurations of networks change as various players enter or leave the network, as they strategically link to specific sites within the network, and as certain sites lose or gain in prominence. Additionally, Rogers and Marres demonstrate the difference in attention cycles between issues on the Web and news in the media. This is a powerful challenge to an idea of "real time" that has become limited to the time it takes to type a sentence, refresh a screen, or write and send e-mail before AOL cuts off the connection. Ultimately, then, this empirical research suggests possibilities of seeing through and manipulating the code that structures the ideological matrix of publicity in communicative capitalism. (I'm thinking here of the dissolution of the matrix into shimmering lines of code once Neo "did the impossible" and came back to life.)

What sort of democracy is without publics? If we take Rogers and Marres's advice and "follow the issues," we get not exactly a set of democratic norms and procedures, not a democratic public sphere, but more or less democratic configurations that we might think of as "neo-democracies."[39] Neo-democracies are configured through contestation and conflict. They reject the fantasy of unity and instead work from the antagonisms that animate political life. For heuristic purposes, to incite further thinking about the ways neo-democracies might do the impossible and bring politics back to life in a networked age, I supply the following table:

Attribute	Public Sphere	Neo-Democracies
Site	Nation	Web as zero institution
Goal	Consensus (legitimation)	Contestation
Means	Procedures (legal, rational)	Networked conflict
Values	Inclusivity	Duration
	Equality	Hegemony
	Transparency	Decisiveness
	Rationality	Credibility
Vehicle	Actors	Issues

I've argued throughout this conclusion that the public sphere has been bounded by the nation. Given the challenges to national sovereignty under globally communicative capitalism, this spatiality limits our political imagination, again, keeping it within the matrix of publicity and secrecy rather than enabling us to fight within it or, better, see our way out of it. As a beginning point, then, neo-democracies should be understood in terms of a different zero institution, the Web. Just like the nation, the Web is a zero institution that posits the possibility of institutionality over chaos. Unlike the nation and like sexual difference, the Web uses the very presence of conflict and antagonism to signify institutionality. Paradoxically perhaps, contestation itself signifies collectivity.

Thus, neo-democratic politics draw from the material conditions enabled by the Web to work through networks rather than nations (in "lines of connection," to use Connolly's term). Just like the nation, however, these networks are not spatially static. Rather they shift and move, enabling different sorts of affiliations, intersections, and invocations.[40] Neo-democratic networks provide a technocultural rendition of those to whom claims are made and who are willing to back up these claims (analogous to the America produced through practices of rights-claiming in Passavant's account).

As theorized by Habermas, the public sphere has been the site of political legitimation, that locus of discussion and debate that impacts collective will and opinion formation as well as the more "central" institutions of politics and law. I've argued, however, that this focus on legitimation is ultimately depoliticizing. As it posits in advance a unified community, it withdraws the revolutionary energy long associated with claims to universality. In contrast, neo-democratic networks are contestatory networks, networks of engagement around issues of vital concern to their constituents. These networks accept that democracy is animated by a split: they thrive on it rather than suppress it as a secret. By focusing on contestation instead of legitimation, then, neo-democracy acknowledges the unavoidable antagonisms of political life. This is especially important today as Third Way advocates seek to obscure the reality of the fundamental cleavages wrought by the new economy.[41]

I fully acknowledge, moreover, that some may find this emphasis on conflict obscene when millions around the world are victims of various forms of military, state, economic, and domestic violence. But precisely this perception of "distant violence" has to be rejected: power is always accompanied by an obscene, excessive supplement. Disavowing the ways that privilege enables some of us to inhabit zones of protection while violence remains "elsewhere," then, distorts and limits democratic politics even as it contributes to the production of spectacles for communicative capitalism's media machine. As Aida Hozic argues,

> Perhaps the most important aspect of the construction of war zones by and through the media is their de-contextualization from other, global, political and economic trends. There are no economic crises in war zones, only humanitarian. There is no politics in war zones, only the perennial struggle of good and evil. War zones are *zones* precisely because they are cut-off from the rest of the world, internally homogenized and externally policed. Violence is thus fetishized, turned into an object separate from "body politic" and, as such, voyeuristically adored.[42]

Clearly then, neo-democratic politics will not be a politics rooted in figuring out the best sorts of procedures and decision rules for political deliberation. Instead, it acknowledges in advance the endless morphing variety of political tools and tactics. What is crucial to these tactics, however, is whether they open up opportunities for contestation. Not all tactics are equal; those that are part of a neo-democratic arsenal are those that challenge rather than reinforce the powerful illusions of the matrix.

The values articulated together by the notion of the public are important to utopian imaginings of democracy. Unfortunately, they have been co-opted by a communicative capitalism that has turned them into their opposite. For this reason, it may well be necessary to abandon them—if only to realize them. Hence, instead of prioritizing inclusivity, equality, transparency, and rationality, neo-democratic politics emphasizes duration, hegemony, decisiveness, and credibility.

Any transformative politics today will have to grapple with the speed of global telecommunications and the concomitant problems of data glut and information dumping. Instead of giving into the drive for spectacle and immediacy that plagues an audience-oriented news cycle, the issue networks of neo-democracy work to maintain links among those specifically engaged with a matter of concern. Although the outcomes of these practices may be deeply embedded within already existing power relations, linking does not presuppose the technocratic rule of the experts. Rather, it builds from the extensions of access, information, and know-how enabled by networked communications and uses them to value various strengths, perspectives, and knowledges developed by people of varying degrees of interest and expertise. Put somewhat differently, the valuation of duration as opposed to inclusion prioritizes the interest and engagement brought to bear on an issue rather than inclusion for its own sake. Not everyone knows. Not every opinion matters. What does matter is commitment and engagement by people and organizations networked around contested issues.

If contestation and antagonism are at the core of democratic politics, then not every view or way of living is equal. What I mean is that the very notion of a fundamental antagonism involves a political claim on behalf of some modes of living and against others. These other views, then, are in no way equal: calling them that makes no sense; it basically misses the point of contestation, namely, winning. Usually, in a contested matter, one doesn't want the other view to coexist happily somewhere; one wants to defeat it. (Examples from U.S. politics might be guns or prayer in public schools. Each side wants to prevent the other side from practicing what it believes or values.) Accordingly, neo-democratic politics are struggles for hegemony. They are partisan, fought for the sake of people's most fundamental beliefs, identities, and practices. Admittedly, at one level, my emphasis on hegemony seems simply a description of politics in technoculture—yes, that's what's going on, a struggle for hegemony. I highlight it, though, out of a conviction that the democratic left has so emphasized plurality, inclusivity, and equality that it has lost the partisan will to name and fight against an enemy. (Indeed, it is precisely this will to name and fight against an enemy that makes Hardt and Negri's account of Empire so powerful.)

The replacing of transparency by decisiveness follows from the critique of publicity as ideology. The politics of the public sphere has been based on the idea that power is always hidden and secret. But clearly this is not the case today. We know full well that corporations are destroying the environment, employing slaves, holding populations hostage to their threats to move their operations to locales with cheaper labor. All sorts of horrible political processes are perfectly transparent today. The problem is that people don't seem to mind, that they are so enthralled by transparency that they have lost the will to fight (*Look! The chemical corporation really is trying. . . . Look! The government explained where the money went . . .*). With this in mind, neo-democracy emphasizes the importance of affecting outcomes. Fully aware that there is always more information available and that this availability is ultimately depoliticizing, neo-democratic politics prioritizes decisiveness. Of course, the outcomes of decisions cannot be predicted in advance. Of course, they can be rearticulated in all sorts of perverse and unexpected ways. But the only way out of communicative capitalism's endless reflexive circuits of discussion is through decisive action. For many, the ever-increasing protests against the World Bank and the G8 have been remarkable precisely because these are instances of decisive action that momentarily disrupt the flow of things and hint at the possibility of alternatives to communicative capitalism.

Similarly, the neo-democratic politics mapped by issue networks highlights the contemporary priority of credibility over rationality. The ideal of rationality linked to the public sphere highlighted a single set of competences, raising them to the category of the universal. That native knowledges, feminine strengths, and folk remedies, say, were occluded from this rationality has been well documented in recent decades. What we see on the Web, moreover, is the clash of these different levels and styles of knowledge production. What the issue networks show us is how credibility is managed, who is credible to whom, in what articulations, and under what circumstances.

Finally, the key to this imagining of neo-democracy is focusing on issues, not actors. Given the wide acceptance of the critique of the subject, the proliferation of cites to Nietzsche's dictum "there is no doer behind the deed," the ongoing experiments with identity and subjectivity throughout technoculture, and the recognition that decisions and actors are always already embedded in networks and systems, it makes sense for critical democratic theory to "follow the issues." Although this may not seem like such a radical move—after all, "concerned citizens" interviewed on television during presidential elections always complain that the candidates don't talk enough about the issues—given the emphasis on identity that has been so prominent in work inspired by the new social movements, it is not an insignificant one. Indeed, it seems to me that a democratic theory built around the notion of issue networks could avoid the fantasy of unity that has rendered publicity in technoculture so profoundly depoliticizing. It recognizes that fissures, antagonism, are what give democracy its political strength (something Machiavelli recognized long ago). Democracy, then, may well be a secondary quality that emerges as an effect or a result of other practices but that can never be achieved when aimed at directly.

Reimagining democracy under conditions of global technoculture is a project that is just beginning. The repercussions of the challenge that global financial markets pose to state sovereignty as well as the broader crisis of representation occasioned by the proliferation and expansion of global networks are only now starting to be addressed. One vision, that of communicative capitalism, should not be allowed to provide the matrix through which this reimagining occurs. For the sake of democracy, it is time to abandon the public.

Notes

Introduction

1. See my critique of this reading of cybersociety in Jodi Dean, "Cyber-salons and Civil Society: Rethinking the Public Sphere in Transnational Technoculture," *Public Culture* 13, 2 (spring 2001): 243–66.
2. Hubertus Buchstein, "Bytes That Bite: The Internet and Deliberative Democracy," *Constellations* 4, 2 (October 1997): 251.
3. For an account of the emergence of notions of the public and public opinion in early modern Europe, see Jürgen Habermas, *The Structural Transformation of the Public Sphere*, trans. Thomas Burger (Cambridge, Mass.: MIT Press, 1989).
4. I get the term "communicative capitalism" from Paul A. Passavant. Personal communication.
5. As Susan Buck-Morss writes, "The machinery of modern power was not so much hidden behind the ideology of mass utopia as it was produced by it"; *Dreamworld and Catastrophe* (Cambridge, Mass.: MIT Press, 2000), 220.
6. Saskia Sassen, *Globalization and Its Discontents* (New York: New Press, 1998).
7. For an analysis of the structural exclusion of people and territories, see Manuel Castells's discussion of the "black holes of informational capitalism." Castells emphasizes that the "territorial confinement of systemically worthless populations, disconnected from networks of valuable functions and people, is indeed a major characteristic of the spatial logic of the network society"; Castells, *End of Millennium* (Oxford: Blackwell Publishers, 1998), 164.
8. This is my argument in Jodi Dean, *Aliens in America: Conspiracy Cultures from Outerspace to Cyberspace* (Ithaca, N.Y.: Cornell University Press, 1998).
9. See Slavoj Žižek, *The Sublime Object of Ideology* (London: Verso, 1989), chap. 1; and idem, "The Spectre of Ideology," in *Mapping Ideology*, ed. Slavoj Žižek (London: Verso, 1994), 1–33. My discussion of Žižek's theory of ideology synthesizes the arguments in these two texts.
10. Michael Wolff, *Burn Rate* (New York: Simon and Schuster, 1998), 54.

11. Žižek, *Sublime Object*, 34.

12. Slavoj Žižek, *For They Know Not What They Do* (London: Verso, 1991), 245.

13. This emphasis on an underlying fantasy indicates the difference between Žižek's account of ideology and that of Ernesto Laclau and Chantal Mouffe, *Hegemony and Socialist Strategy* (London: Verso, 1985). They demonstrate how a given field of disparate elements is sutured together through the totalizing intervention of a hegemonic nodal point. Žižek argues that this needs to be supplemented by an analysis of enjoyment, by an investigation of the way "an ideology implies, manipulates, produces a preideological enjoyment structured in fantasy" (*Sublime Object*, 125). Also, Žižek does not see ideology as a problem of knowledge but views it in terms of the fantasies materialized through practices. Thus, he does not position the critic as outside of ideology but as fully within it.

14. Of course, this fantasy in no way must be positive. In *Totem and Taboo*, Freud gives an account of the fantasy constitutive of the primary unity of democracy as a fantasy of patricidal violence, the killing of the primal father by the horde. Describing the totem meal, Freud writes, "Each man is conscious that he is performing an act forbidden to the individual and justifiable only through the participation of the whole clan; nor may anyone absent himself from the killing and the meal"; Freud, *Totem and Taboo*, excerpted in *The Freud Reader*, ed. Peter Gay (New York: W. W. Norton, 1989), 499. Publicity is what gives legitimacy to the act; any secret remainder or exclusion would undermine its rightness.

15. Sisela Bok, *Secrets* (New York: Pantheon Books, 1982), 6.

16. As Georg Simmel writes, "Even as late as in the seventeenth and eighteenth centuries, governments kept anxiously silent about the amounts of state debts, the tax situation, and the size of the army." See Simmel, "The Secret and the Secret Society," in *The Sociology of Georg Simmel*, trans. Kurt H. Wolff (New York: Free Press, 1964), 336.

17. Ibid., 330.

18. See the discussion of the secretization of sexuality in Michel Foucault, *The History of Sexuality*, vol. 1, trans. Robert Hurley (New York: Vintage, 1980). For Foucault, the secret is "a way of giving shape to the requirement to speak about the matter, a fable that is indispensable to the endlessly proliferating economy of the discourse on sex" (35). It functions as a limit or internalized boundary to speaking that stimulates the urge to talk and channels this urge in particular directions. Describing the machinery operating in the industrial age to produce the truth of sex, Foucault writes that "sex gradually became an object of great suspicion; the general and disquieting meaning that pervades our conduct and our existence, in spite of ourselves; the point of weakness where evil portents reach through to us; the fragment of darkness that we each carry within

us: a general signification, a universal secret, an omnipresent cause, a fear that never ends" (69).

19. Slavoj Žižek, *Looking Awry* (Cambridge, Mass.: MIT Press, 1991), 168.

20. My ideas here were stimulated by a talk given by Judith Butler, "What Is Critique?" at the Society for the Humanities, Cornell University, July 14, 2000.

1. Publicity's Secret

1. Slavoj Žižek makes clear that the "ruling ideas are *never* directly the ideas of the ruling class." Instead, they incorporate the "motifs and aspirations of the oppressed . . . rearticulating them in such a way that they [become] compatible with the existing relations of domination"; Žižek, *The Ticklish Subject* (London: Verso, 1999), 186. So, of course, there are good, democratic things about publicity.

2. Georg Simmel writes, "The secret gives one a position of exception; it operates as a purely socially determined attraction. It is basically independent of the content it guards but, of course, is increasingly effective in the measure in which the exclusive possession is vast and significant"; Simmel, "The Secret and the Secret Society," in *The Sociology of Georg Simmel*, trans. Kurt H. Wolff (New York: Free Press, 1964), 332–33.

3. Slavoj Žižek, "The Spectre of Ideology," in *Mapping Ideology*, ed. Slavoj Žižek (London: Verso, 1994), 1. This essay analyzes Marxist debates over the concept of ideology. For an overview of these discussions that includes the Foucauldian critique, see the excellent study by Michèle Barrett, *The Politics of Truth* (Stanford, Calif.: Stanford University Press, 1991).

4. For historical accounts of the conflicting notions of the public, see Keith Michael Baker, *Inventing the French Revolution* (Cambridge: Cambridge University Press, 1990), esp. chap. 8; and Roger Chartier, *The Cultural Origins of the French Revolution*, trans. Lydia G. Cochrane (Durham, N.C.: Duke University Press, 1991), esp. chap. 2. Despite the usefulness of their accounts, both historians, in demonstrating the rise of a notion of the rational, universal public, underestimate the continued influence of the earlier notion of the inconstant and uncertain public. This notion is never simply trumped. Rather it continues to haunt and disrupt unitary accounts of the public.

5. Jeremy Bentham, "Essay on Political Tactics," chap. 2 in "Of Publicity" (1821), in *The Works of Jeremy Bentham*, ed. John Bowring (New York: Russell and Russell, 1962), 2:310.

6. I'm drawing here from the discussion of the *subject supposed to know*, by Slavoj Žižek, *The Plague of Fantasies* (London: Verso, 1997). Žižek explains that "when Lacan speaks of the subject supposed to know, one usually fails to notice how this notion is not the norm but the exception, which gains its value in contrast to the sub-

ject supposed to believe as the standard feature of the symbolic order" (106).

7. Bentham, "Essay on Political Tactics," 313.

8. One might compare Bentham with Rousseau here. For Rousseau, the unerring general will might be thought of as the public-supposed-to-know. The public-supposed-to-believe is captured in his notion of public opinion or the opinions of the people, opinions that can change, improve, be guided, become corrupt. Rather than linking the public-supposed-to-know with the public-supposed-to-believe in any direct sense, however, Rousseau emphasizes their distance and differences. The general will must remain separate from communication and the exchange of opinion. Likewise, whereas the object of the general will concerns general laws, the object of public opinion involves more particular judgments of honor, pleasure, and beauty. Interestingly, the one link Rousseau does establish between the general will and opinion of the people operates in secret: the legislator who provides the constitution. Rousseau writes, "I am speaking of moral habits, customs, and, above all, of opinion, a part of the law unknown to our political theorists, but upon which, nonetheless, the success of all the other laws depends, the part with which the great lawgiver concerns himself in secret, while he appears to limit himself to particular regulations that are only the sides of the arch, of which moral habits, slower to rise, form at length the unshakeable keystone"; Rousseau, "On the Social Contract," in *Rousseau's Political Writings*, ed. Alan Ritter and Julia Conaway Bondanella, trans. Julia Conaway Bondanella (New York: W. W. Norton, 1988), 118.

9. See Žižek, *Plague of Fantasies*, 110.

10. Bentham, "Essay on Political Tactics," 312 (italics in original).

11. Ibid., 311.

12. Ibid., 310.

13. See also Slavoj Žižek's account of the agency of the big Other as both reassuring and terrifying. Žižek notes that these contradictory aspects appear as well in Lacan's account of the analyst as the "subject supposed to know." Crucially, these two aspects are linked together rather than simply opposed. The subject that secures meaning also menaces enjoyment. Žižek, *Enjoy Your Symptom!* (New York: Routledge, 1992), 39–40.

14. Bentham, "Essay on Political Tactics," 314 (italics in original).

15. Francois Furet analyses the French Revolution in similar terms: "Once it had become power, opinion had to be at one with the people; language must no longer serve to hide intrigues but reflect values as in a mirror. In the frenzied collective preoccupation with power than henceforth shaped the political battles of the Revolution, representation was ruled out or perpetually put under surveillance"; Furet, *Interpeting the French Revolution*, trans. Elborg Forster (Cambridge: Cambridge University Press, 1981), 48.

16. Jürgen Habermas, *The Structural Transformation of the Public*

Sphere, trans. Thomas Burger (Cambridge, Mass.: MIT Press, 1989), 28.

17. Reinhart Koselleck, *Critique and Crisis* (first published in German, 1959; Cambridge, Mass.: MIT Press, 1988), 166. For a critical comparison of Habermas and Koselleck, see Jean Cohen and Andrew Arato, *Civil Society and Political Theory* (Cambridge, Mass.: MIT Press, 1992), chap. 5.

18. Koselleck, *Critique and Crisis*, 33.

19. Ibid., 55.

20. Koselleck links the philosophical exposition of moral interiority with important socioeconomic changes. Tensions created by the exclusion of a rising strata of socially and economically powerful groups from the institutions of the absolutist state exacerbated the split between morality and politics. With political decision-making foreclosed to them, these men and women from various classes created new social institutions. Koselleck sees the new society as a coalescing of anti-Absolutist nobility, a financially powerful bourgeoisie (increasingly insecure about the arbitrariness of state fiscal decision-making), the more than 80,000 émigrés forced to leave France in 1685, and a free-floating layer of writers and enlighteners or philosophers (ibid., 62–65).

21. Ibid., 74.

22. Ibid., 77.

23. Ibid., 79.

24. Ibid., 82.

25. Ibid., 83.

26. Ibid.

27. Ibid., 115.

28. Habermas, *Structural Transformation*, 53.

29. Ibid., 35.

30. Margaret C. Jacobs develops this point in *Living the Enlightenment: Freemasonry and Politics in Eighteenth-Century Europe* (New York: Oxford University Press, 1991).

31. This is probably a good place to note the shifting articulations of publicity and secrecy in the Enlightenment. Frances A. Yates, *The Rosicrucian Enlightenment* (New York: Routledge, 1972), traces the history of commentary on manifestos allegedly linked to the secret society of the Rosicrucians in the sixteenth and seventeenth centuries. This commentary characterizes Rosicrucianism in terms of (1) an interest in science and (2) an adaptation to the styles of the countries the Rosicrucians inhabited. The commentary then treats these attributes as diabolical secrets and seductions designed to attract the curious. Yates argues that the resulting articulation of Rosicrucianism with witchcraft contributed to the ability of Cartesianism to triumph over Renaissance animism. During this period, avoiding Rosicrucian secrecy was important for the new sciences to separate themselves from conjuring, magic, alchemy, and religion. For ex-

ample, having traveled in Germany in 1619 on a search for Rosicrucians, Descartes returned to Paris in 1623 only to be accused of being one. Yates quotes the 1691 biography of Descartes by Adrien Baillet:

But he confounded those who wished to make use of this conjunction of events to establish their calumny. He made himself visible to all the world, and particularly to his friends who needed no other argument to convince him that he was not one of the Brotherhood of Rosicrucians or Invisibles: and he used the same argument of their invisibility to explain to the curious why he had not been able to find any of them in Germany. (116)

Especially compelling is Yates's discussion of the fiction of Rosicrucianism: she never found any evidence of an actual secret brotherhood of the Rosy Cross. She suggests, however, that the idea of secret societies of enlightenment furthered by the Rosicrucian manifestos contributed to the popularity of Freemasonry. Yates writes:

the theme of secrecy is of importance, for it connects the Renaissance with the early scientific revolution. The great mathematical and scientific thinkers of the seventeenth century have at the back of their minds Renaissance traditions of esoteric thinking, of mystical continuity from Hebraic or "Egyptian" wisdom, of that conflation of Moses with "Hermes Trismegistus" which fascinated the Renaissance. These traditions survived across the period in secret societies, particularly in Freemasonry. (219)

The secret society that isn't there, we might say, serves as a placeholder to be occupied later. It establishes the empty place that will enable later thinking about secrecy and publicity.

32. Habermas, *Structural Transformation*, 46.
33. Ibid., 51.
34. For a more thorough and nuanced account of the Kantian will, see William Connolly, *Why I'm Not a Secularist* (Minneapolis: University of Minnesota Press, 1999).
35. Quoted in Koselleck, *Critique and Crisis*, 121.
36. For a discussion of the public's right to know in connection with freedom of the press, see Bok, *Secrets*, 254–64. She argues (in agreement with Ronald Dworkin) that the First Amendment to the U.S. Constitution should not be understood as entailing or justifying the public's right to information.
37. Joseph S. Nye, Jr., and William A. Owen, "America's Information Edge," *Foreign Affairs* (March/April 1996): 20. See also Aida Hozic's analysis of the "digital coalition" constituted through the convergence of technological, entertainment, and military-political sectors, "Uncle Sam Goes to Siliwood: Of Landscapes, Spielberg, and Hegemony," *Review of International Political Economy* 6, 3 (autumn 1999): 289–312. Hozic explains that in the networked global economy,

technology is both the means and the ends to U.S. economic power and global hegemony: information technology is inextricably linked with U.S. military dominance, with the development and daily functioning of the global financial system, and an absolutely necessary ingredient in the coordination of geographically dispersed activities in global commodity chains. But information technology is also a product itself, and the sectors which most directly engulf its development—telecommunications, computer industry, entertainment—are among the fastest growing in the United States. (298)

38. Nancy Fraser, *Justice Interruptus* (New York: Routledge, 1997) 70. Fraser is one of many scholars who find the concept of the public sphere invaluable to democratic theory. In his introduction to *The Phantom Public Sphere* (Minneapolis: University of Minnesota Press, 1993), for example, Bruce Robbins notes that the contributors to the collection share that "qualified but steadfast commitment to the concept of the public that any supporter of democracy *must* share" (xxii). Similarly, Craig Calhoun, in his introduction to *Habermas and the Public Sphere*, ed. Craig Calhoun (Cambridge, Mass.: MIT Press, 1997), notes that the continued resonance of *Structural Transformation of the Public Sphere* thirty years after its initial publication "suggests that the recovery and extension of a strong normative idea of publicness is very much on the current agenda" (42).

39. Jürgen Habermas, *Between Facts and Norms*, trans. William Rehg (Cambridge, Mass.: MIT Press, 1996).

40. For a discussion of Habermas's use of Fraser, see William E. Scheuerman, "Between Radicalism and Resignation: Democratic Theory in Habermas's *Between Facts and Norms*," in *Habermas: A Critical Reader*, ed. Peter Dews (London: Blackwell Press, 1999). Scheuerman provides a persuasive account of the tensions that accompany Habermas's attempt to combine Fraser's radical democratic socialism with the "realist" model of Berhard Peters.

41. Habermas, *Structural Transformation*, 232. Habermas has since reevaluated his pessimistic assessment of consumer-oriented publicity, finding the continued democratic potential of the public sphere more promising than he had first thought. See Habermas, "Further Reflections on the Public Sphere," trans. Thomas Berger, in Calhoun, *Habermas and the Public Sphere*, 421–61.

42. Habermas, *Structural Transformation*, 195.

43. Ibid., 201.

44. Ibid., 209.

45. Žižek, *Plague of Fantasies*, 21.

46. Douglass Rushkoff, *Coercion* (New York: Riverhead Books, 1999), 209.

47. Lauren Berlant accounts for this positive possibility in her useful and nuanced discussion of "Diva Citizenship," in *The Queen of*

America Goes to Washington City (Durham, N.C.: Duke University Press, 1997), 221–46. Berlant writes, "The centrality of publicity to Diva Citizenship cannot be underestimated, for it tends to emerge in moments of such extraordinary political paralysis that acts of language can feel like explosives that shake the ground of collective existence. Yet in remaking the scene of public life into a spectacle of subjectivity, it can lead to a confusion of willful and memorable rhetorical performance with sustained social change itself" (223).

48. Žižek notes that "such an oscillation is an unmistakable sign that we are dealing with *jouissance*" (*Plague of Fantasies*, 54).

49. Žižek, *Enjoy Your Symptom!* 39.

50. Ibid., 40.

51. Ibid., 39–41.

52. Žižek, *Plague of Fantasies*, 76.

53. I make a similar argument in Jodi Dean, *Aliens in America* (Ithaca, N.Y.: Cornell University Press, 1998).

54. For example, in her defense of the Habermasian discursive public sphere against Hannah Arendt's agnostic public sphere and Bruce Ackerman's legal-liberal public sphere, Seyla Benhabib considers the American debate over pornography, *Situating the Self* (New York: Routledge, 1992). We "simply cannot know" whether pornography should be thought of as a private issue, a question of aesthetic sensibility, or a reasonable limitation on the First Amendment right of free speech, Benhabib maintains, "before the process of unconstrained public dialogue has run its course." But in the very next sentence, Behabib implies that she in fact does know: "I no more want to live in a society which cannot distinguish between *Hustler* magazine and Salinger's *Catcher in the Rye* than Ackerman does, or in a society that would place Henry Miller and D. H. Lawrence in the company of *Deep Throat*" (99). The answer to pornography is there, prior to the debate. In a further illustration of the way in which consensus precedes discussion, Benhabib worries about the "less than noble majorities" who could rush in to "challenge the principles of neutrality and the lines between the right and the good" should "the flood gates open for the whim of majoritarian decisions" (102). Given the "radical proceduralism" of the discursive model of the public sphere, we might say that democratic debate refers to the process through which those affected by general social norms come to understand and accept the norms already established in discourse ethics. Benhabib, following Ken Baynes, refers to this process as one of "recursive validation" (79), "Toward a Deliberative Model of Democratic Legitimacy," in *Democracy and Difference*, ed. Seyla Benhabib (Princeton, N.J.: Princeton University Press, 1996), 67–94.

55. Lisa Disch, "Civic Virtue and the Uncertain Promise of Electoral Fusion," delivered at the Annual Meeting of the Western Political Science Association, Seattle, March 25–27, 1999, 14.

2. Conspiracy's Desire

1. Kathleen Stewart, "Conspiracy Theory's Worlds," in *Paranoia within Reason*, ed. George Marcus (Chicago: University of Chicago Press, 1999), 13.
2. S. Paige Baty emphasizes plot; see Baty, *American Monroe: The Making of a Body Politic* (Berkeley: University of California Press, 1995). Richard Hofstadter emphasizes style; see Hofstadter, *The Paranoid Style in American Politics and Other Essays* (Cambridge: Harvard University Press, 1996). Daniel Pipes emphasizes pathology; see Pipes, *Conspiracy: How the Paranoid Style Flourishes and Where It Comes From* (New York: Free Press, 1997).
3. Slavoj Žižek, *The Plague of Fantasies* (London: Verso, 1997), 53–54.
4. Hofstadter, *Paranoid Style in American Politics*, 5, 39.
5. Robert S. Robins and Jerrold M. Post, *Political Paranoia: The Psychopolitics of Hatred* (New Haven: Yale University Press, 1997), 18–19.
6. Such an account appears in Jim Keith, *Mass Control: Engineering Human Consciousness* (Lilburn, Ga.: IllumiNet Press, 1999), 125.
7. Slavoj Žižek, "Holding the Place," in *Contingency, Hegemony, Universality*, Judith Butler, Ernesto Laclau, and Slavoj Žižek (London: Verso, 1997), 313.
8. Žižek, *Plague of Fantasies*, 54–60.
9. Jonathan Vankin and John Whalen, *The 60 Greatest Conspiracies of All Time* (Secaucus, N.J.: Citadel Press, 1997), 288–94.
10. Robins and Post do a particularly intricate version of this dance in *Political Paranoia*.
11. Eve Kosofsky Sedgwick, "Paranoid Reading and Reparative Reading; or, You're So Paranoid, You Probably Think This Introduction Is about You," in *Novel Gazing: Queer Readings in Fiction*, ed. Eve Kosofsky Sedgwick (Durham, N.C.: Duke University Press, 1997), 6.
12. Ibid., 19.
13. Pauline Maier, *American Scripture: Making the Declaration of Independence* (New York: Alfred A. Knopf, 1997), 123.
14. Ibid., 105.
15. Ibid., 106.
16. Ibid., 115.
17. Ibid., 156.
18. Bernard Bailyn, *The Ideological Origins of the American Revolution* (Cambridge: Harvard University Press, 1972), 95.
19. Gordon S. Wood, *The Creation of the American Republic, 1776–1787* (New York: W. W. Norton, 1972), 32.
20. Ibid., 39.
21. Bailyn, *Ideological Origins of the American Revolution*, 144.
22. Wood, *Creation of the American Republic*, 40.
23. Ibid., 40–41.
24. Ibid., 3.
25. Bailyn, *Ideological Origins of the American Revolution*, 138.

26. Françoise Fouret, *Interpreting the French Revolution* (Cambridge: Cambridge University Press, 1981), 53.

27. Ibid.

28. See Michael Rogin's analysis of the realist and symbolic approaches to political demonology prominent in American political science during the 1950s; Rogin, *Ronald Reagan, The Movie and Other Episodes in Political Demonology* (Berkeley: University of California Press, 1987), 272–300.

29. William E. Connolly, *The Ethos of Pluralization* (Minneapolis: University of Minnesota Press, 1995), xiii–xvi.

30. Seymour Martin Lipset and Earl Raab, *The Politics of Unreason: Right-Wing Extremism in America, 1790–1970* (New York: Harper and Row, 1970), 6.

31. Pipes, *Conspiracy*, 38.

32. Rogin, *Reagan, The Movie*, 278.

33. This is not a new criticism. Theories of pluralism have coexisted with their critiques. For example, in a critical analysis rooted in political realism, E. E. Schattschneider writes, "The flaw in the pluralist heaven is that the heavenly chorus sings with a strong upperclass accent. Probably about 90 per cent of the people cannot get into the pressure system"; Schattschneider, *The Semi-Sovereign People: A Realist's View of Democracy in America* (Hinsdale, Ill.: Dryden Press, 1960), 35.

34. Lipset and Raab, *Politics of Unreason*, 6.

35. Robins and Post, *Political Paranoia*, 8. See also Pipes, *Conspiracy*, 44.

36. Robins and Post, *Political Paranoia*, 42.

37. Ibid., 9.

38. Robins and Post employ the virus metaphor (ibid., 61); Pipes, *Conspiracy*, 2.

39. Hofstadter, *Paranoid Style in American Politics*, 39.

40. Indeed, Robins and Post go so far as to take Patricia Turner to task for failing to condemn paranoia in her excellent study of rumor in some African American communities (*Political Paranoia*, 64). See Patricia A. Turner, *I Heard It through the Grapevine: Rumor in African-American Culture* (Berkeley: University of California Press, 1994).

41. Pipes, *Conspiracy*, 183.

42. Ibid., 163.

43. Ibid., 33.

44. For an example, see ibid., chap. 8.

45. Robins and Post, *Political Paranoia*, 95.

46. See my work, Jodi Dean, *Alien in America: Conspiracy Culture from Outerspace to Cyberspace* (Ithaca, N.Y.: Cornell University Press, 1998). See also Diana Tumminia, "How Prophecy Never Fails: Interpretive Reason in a Flying Saucer Group," *Sociology of Religion* 59, 2 (1998): 157–70. Tumminia argues that working through failure, skepticism, and disbelief enabled the Unarius Academy of Science to strengthen the bonds among group members. They pursued a pro-

cess of "collaborative reinvention" in the face of the failure of the Space Brothers to return as expected.

47. For an alternate account of the relationship between conspiracy, skepticism, and paranoia, see Lee Quinby, *Millennial Seduction: A Skeptic Confronts Apocalyptic Culture* (Ithaca, N.Y.: Cornell University Press, 1999).

48. Hofstadter, *Paranoid Style in American Politics*, 31.

49. Quote available at http://home.att.net/~joserojas/conspiracy.html.

50. Philip Weiss, "The Clinton Haters," *New York Times Magazine*, February 23, 1997.

51. Found at http://www.geocities.com/Pentagon/2783/lewinsky.html.

52. William F. Buckley, "Are You a Right-Wing Conspirator," *National Review* 50, 3 (February 23, 1998): 62–63. I am indebted to Dawn Rooth for bringing this article to my attention.

53. Howard Krutz, "Clintons Long under Siege by Conservative Detractors," *Washington Post*, January 28, 1998, A1, 20. I am indebted to Meredith Maslich for bringing this article to my attention.

54. Robins and Post use the virus-spread infection as a metaphor for conspiracy, *Political Paranoia*, 23, 47.

55. Pipes, *Conspiracy*, 49.

56. Slavoj Žižek, *Tarrying with the Negative* (Durham, N.C.: Duke University Press, 1993), 200.

57. See William Wresch, *Disconnected: Have and Have-nots in the Information Age* (New Brunswick, N.J.: Rutgers University Press, 1996).

58. See Laura J. Gurak, *Persuasion and Privacy in Cyberspace: The Online Protests over Lotus Marketplace and the Clipper Chip* (New Haven: Yale University Press, 1997).

59. Wendy M. Grossman writes, "Many Net surfers don't realize it, but the average Web site can tell what browser you're using, what domain you're coming from, and what type of computer and operating system you're using as well as what pages you've looked at and for how long. A lot of Web sites put this information into a small bit of text called a 'cookie' and store it on your hard drive, to streamline your next visit to their site, which some people feel is an invasion of privacy"; Grossman, *net.wars* (New York: New York University Press, 1997), 188.

60. Esther Dyson, "The End of the Official Story," *Brill's Content*, July/August 1998, 50–51.

61. Howard Fineman, "Who Needs Washington?" *Newsweek*, January 27, 1997, 52. Fineman is quoting Doug Bailey, whom he identifies as "the pioneering founder of the Political Hotline."

62. I disagree with Stephen Johnson's claim that "on the World Wide Web, where this imaginative crisis is most sorely felt, it is the link that finally supplies that sense of coherence [supplied by narrative links in the novels of Charles Dickens]"; Johnson, *Interface Culture: How New Technology Transforms the Way We Create and Commu-*

nicate (New York: Harper Collins, 1997), 116. Not only is coherence not a goal—What would it even mean in this context? Why would one need a coherent vision of millions of networked computers?—but there is no such thing as "the" link. There are always more links opening up and extending our interaction on specific sites into interactions on other ones. Indeed, there are different practices of linking as well as different kinds of links.

63. Although I do not agree with Baty's rendering of conspiracy in terms of coherent, narrative plots, her account of the link between conspiracy thinking and mass media technologies of reproduction is insightful. Baty writes: "The meshed networks of dissimulation 'revealed' by conspiracies and conspiracy theories in the cartographic mode of remembering also correspond to mass-mediated forms of circulation, for the conspiratorial net is itself woven through plots and channels of information" (*American Monroe*, 116).

64. Amy Harmon, "NASA Flew to Mars for Rocks? Sure," *New York Times*, July 20, 1997, 4E.

65. For example, see Grossman, *net.wars*; David Shenk, *Data Smog* (New York: Harper Collins, 1997); and Chris Toulouse and Timothy W. Luke, eds., *The Politics of Cyberspace* (New York: Routledge, 1998).

3. Little Brothers

I'm indebted to Andrew Heitman for the long, creative, and voluntary hours of research that went into this chapter.

1. See Michael Hardt and Antonio Negri, *Empire* (Cambridge: Harvard University Press, 2000), 294.

2. Manuel Castells, in his discussion of decentralization and diffusion in new technologies, surveillance, and information distribution, uses the term "little sisters." He writes: "*Rather than an oppressive 'Big Brother,' it is a myriad of well-wishing 'little sisters,' relating to each one of us on a personal basis because they know who we are, who have invaded all realms of life*"; Castells, *The Power of Identity* (Oxford: Blackwell Publishers 1997), 301 (italics in original). Instead of going with Castells's term, I've adopted "Little Brothers" as a break against interpretations of the present as a feminine age or as a time of full female equality. There is also something a tad condescending in Castells's evocation of these well-wishing, invasive "little sisters" that I want to avoid. Finally, I find it useful that the term "Little Brothers" has already appeared in the computer industry.

3. Hardt and Negri, *Empire*, 300.

4. See an account of financial markets and corporations as contemporary loci of "economic citizenship," in Saskia Sassen, *Losing Control: Sovereignty in an Age of Globalization* (New York: Columbia University Press, 1996). See also a discussion of the freedom of commercial speech as an extension of the idea of the free flow of information, in Armand Mattelart, *Networking the World, 1794–2000*,

trans. Liz Carey-Libbrecht and James A. Cohen (Minneapolis: University of Minnesota Press, 2000).

5. See Hardt and Negri's discussion of the assault on the disciplinary regime (*Empire*, 272–76). For an account of the fugitivity of truth, see Jodi Dean, *Aliens in America: Conspiracy Cultures from Outerspace to Cyberspace* (Ithaca, N.Y.: Cornell University Press, 1998), chap. 1.

6. In an essay on electronic surveillance, Matt Richtel writes: "Computer users these days may have a right to feel paranoid. A new generation of software is making it easier than ever for employers and parents to keep an eye on everything that workers or family members do on their computers"; Richtel, "Software to Watch over You," *New York Times Magazine*, July 4, 1999, 12–13.

7. Thomas L. Friedman writes: "Rule No. 1 of the Internet is this: We are all connected, but nobody's in charge. That is, the Internet is Orwellian in its reach, but there's no Big Brother. Instead of Big Brother, there are a lot of Little Brothers. They are going to be a problem. The Internet super-empowers individuals, Web sites, corporations, and even hotels—the Little Brothers—so they can amass huge amounts of information outside of any government supervision"; Friedman, "Little Brother," *New York Times*, September 26, 1999, sec. 4, 17.

8. Simson Garfinkle, *Database Nation* (Sebastopol, Calif.: O'Reilly, 2000), 3.

9. Slavoj Žižek, *The Ticklish Subject* (London: Verso, 1999), 347.

10. For a discussion of capital as Real, see Slavoj Žižek, *The Fragile Absolute* (London: Verso, 2000).

11. See Michael Mello, *The United States of America versus Theodore John Kaczynski: Ethics, Power and the Invention of the Unabomber* (New York: Context Books, 1999).

12. In the midseventies, Ed Roberts, owner of the electronics company MITS (Model Instrumentation Telemetry Systems), which produced the first home computer available for hobbyists, considered calling his minicomputer Little Brother as a swipe at computing's Big Boy, IBM. As it turned out, however, Lauren Solomon, the twelve-year-old daughter of *Popular Electronics* technical editor Les Solomon, named the computer. *Popular Electronics* had agreed to feature the MITS computer on its January 1975 cover before the machine was even built. Roberts hadn't decided what to call it when Solomon asked her daughter the name of the computer on *Star Trek*. Because it was called, simply, "computer," Lauren suggested "Altair," the Enterprise's destination on that week's episode. See Steven Levy, *Hackers* (New York: Dell Publishing, 1994), 187–89; Paul Freiberger and Michael Swaine, *Fire in the Valley: The Making of the Personal Computer* (Berkeley: Osborne/McGraw Hill, 1984), 34; and, H. Edward Roberts and William Yates, "Altair 8800 Minicomputer, Part I," *Popular Electronics* 7, 1 (January 1975): cover, 33–38.

13. I'm indebted to Tom Dumm for this point.

14. Quoted in Steven Levy, *Insanely Great* (New York: Penguin Books,

1994), 169–70. The commercial is available at http://www.
chiatday.com/product/historicalwork/tv/1984/1984.html.

15. With regard to the association between women and computers in the
    workplace, Paul E. Ceruzzi notes that up until the 1940s, the term
    "computer" meant person and was applied, typically, to women. He
    writes: "The tradition of women as computers has been traced back
    as far as Babbage's time, where women assisted male astronomers in
    their calculations. By the 1890s it was common for university obser-
    vatories to employ women computers to classify stellar spectra. . . .
    In the modern office environment, women are the principal users of
    computer keyboards and terminals"; Ceruzzi, "When Computers
    Were Human," *Annals of the History of Computing* 13, 3 (1991):
    240.

16. N. Katherine Hayles makes a similar point: "When the emphasis
    falls on access rather than ownership, the private/public distinction
    that was so important in the formation of the novel is radically re-
    configured. Whereas possession implies the existence of private life
    based on physical exclusion or inclusion, access implies the exis-
    tence of credentialing practices that use patterns rather than pres-
    ences to distinguish between those who do and those who do not
    have the right to enter. Moreover, entering is itself constituted as
    access to data rather than as change in physical location"; Hayles,
    *How We Became Posthuman: Virtual Bodies in Cybernetics, Liter-
    ature, and Informatics* (Chicago: University of Chicago Press,
    1999), 40.

17. See Theodore Roszak, *From Satori to Silicon Valley* (San Francisco:
    Don't Call It Frisco Press, 1986).

18. For a different reading of Little Brothers and the decline of patriar-
    chal authority, see Juliet Flowers MacCannell, *The Regime of the
    Brother* (New York: Routledge, 1991).

19. The most interesting theorist of "the empty place" of democracy re-
    mains, of course, Claude Lefort. See Lefort, *Democracy and Political
    Theory*, trans. David Macey (Minneapolis: University of Minnesota
    Press, 1988), esp. 17–20.

20. See "A Letter from the Publisher," *Time*, January 3, 1983.

21. Roger Rosenblatt, "A New World Dawns," *Time*, January 3, 1983,
    13.

22. This link between computers and the restoration of the American
    dream had already been made in *Time* the previous year in a cover
    story on Apple founder Steve Jobs (February 15, 1982).

23. Jerry L. Salvaggio provides a compelling account of the advertising
    efforts undertaken by telecommunications and information indus-
    tries in the United States during the 1970s and early 1980s. He
    points out the ways that advertisements tried to change the image of
    the information society by portraying it in warm, humanistic terms,
    by emphasizing the idea of networks, and by announcing that the in-
    formation age had already arrived and people had to learn how to

succeed in it. See Salvaggio, "Projecting a Positive Image of the Information Society," in *The Ideology of the Information Age*, ed. Jennifer Daryl Slack and Fred Fejes (Norwood, N.J.: Ablex Publishing Corporation, 1987), 146–57.

24. From a remark by Michael Rossman, one of the theoreticians of the Community Memory Project in Berkeley in the early seventies. Quoted in Theodore Roszak, *The Cult of Information* (New York: Pantheon, 1986), 140.

25. Theodor H. Nelson, *Computer Lib* (South Bend, Ind.: University of Notre Dame Press, 1974).

26. Stewart Brand, *Cybernetic Frontiers* (New York: Random House, 1974), 39. The pieces in this book appeared originally in *Rolling Stone* (December 1972) and *Harper's* (November 1973).

27. Quoted in Bryan Pfaffenberger, "The Social Meaning of the Personal Computer: Or, Why the Computer Revolution Was No Revolution," *Anthropological Quarterly* 61 (January 1988): 1, 40.

28. Roszak, *Cult of Information*, 147.

29. Roszak, *From Satori to Silicon Valley*, 37.

30. The proceedings of this meeting were published as Charles A. Thrall and Jerold M. Starr, eds., *Technology, Power, and Social Change* (Lexington, Mass.: D. C. Heath, 1971).

31. Ibid., 126.

32. Ibid., 32.

33. Ibid., 30.

34. Levy, *Hackers*, 130.

35. The critique of technocracy is only loosely related to the technocracy movement that gained in popularity in the early years of the Depression. This movement extended out of a loose circle of Greenwich Village intellectuals who began meeting in 1919. Thorstein Veblen's *The Engineers and the Price System* was a key text for this group, and Veblen himself was an active participant. The term "technocracy" was coined by William H. Smyth in several articles published in *Industrial Management* in 1919. In 1932, in part because of increasing publicity given to Howard Smith's message that capitalism was in crisis, technocracy received media attention as a possible solution to the United States's economic problems insofar as it claimed that the problems were technical, not political. The way out was the vaguely conceived "energy state." Howard Smith, however, was a scammer, "a gorgeous, entertaining myth, traveling down the age as a man of infinite abilities and gargantuan feats, the type of character Paul Bunyan is in the lore of the logging camps"; Allen Raymond, *What Is Technocracy* (New York: McGraw-Hill, 1933), 105.

   For a thorough history of technocracy and technocratic reason (one that includes an analysis of Veblen and the Progressive movement as well as a detailed history of instrumental reason in the Enlightenment), see Frank Fischer, *Technocracy and the Politics of Ex-*

pertise (Newbury Park, Calif.: Sage Publications, 1990). Fischer emphasizes the crucial connection between technocracy and the abolition of politics, the very collapse of a space for the political in the technocratic vision of the organized, programmed society. Central to the Progressive idea of scientific management, for example, was the elimination of class conflict (82).

36. Nelson, *Computer Lib*, 2.
37. Particularly strong and influential versions of this critique came from Jacques Ellul, *The Technological Society*, trans. John Wilkinson (New York: Vintage Books, 1964); Erich Fromm, *The Revolution of Hope: Toward a Humanized Technology* (New York: Harper and Row, 1968); and Lewis Mumford, *The Myth of the Machine* (New York: Harcourt, Brace, Jovanovich, 1967). As I discuss below, the critique of instrumental reason associated with the Frankfurt school also figured significantly in the antitechnology discourse.
38. Daniel Bell, *The Coming of the Post-Industrial Society* (New York: Basic Books, 1973), 357–58.
39. Vance Packard, "Don't Tell It to the Computer," *New York Times Magazine*, January 8, 1976, 44ff.
40. Bell, *Coming of the Post-Industrial Society*, 349.
41. Nolan E. Shepard provides the following summary of the worries of the antitechnologists: "(1) Contemporary technological trends dehumanize people; they are made to be anonymous and lose significance and individuality. (2) Work loses dignity, creativity, and meaning. (3) Cybernation encourages nonreflective conformity. (4) Materialism and technolatry replace traditional religious values. (5) Technique becomes autonomous and human beings its slaves"; Shepard, "Technology: Messiah or Monster?" in *Monster or Messiah? The Computer's Impact on Society*, ed. Walter M. Mathews (Jackson, Miss.: University Press of Mississippi, 1980), 149.
42. Arnold Toynbee, *Surviving the Future* (New York: Oxford University Press, 1971), 117.
43. Theodore Roszak explains, "Within such a society, the citizen, confronted by bewildering bigness and complexity, finds it necessary to defer on all matters to those who know better. Indeed, it would be a violation of reason to do otherwise, since it is universally agreed that the prime goal of the society is to keep the productive apparatus turning over efficiently"; Roszak, *The Making of a Counter-Culture: Reflections on the Technocratic Society and Its Youthful Opposition* (New York: Doubleday, 1969), 7.
44. Johnny E. Tolliver writes, "The fear that society will become a technocracy pervades American society"; Tolliver, "The Computer and the Protestant Ethic: A Conflict," in Mathews, *Monster or Messiah?* 157. For a description of antitechnology sentiment in the United States in the late seventies, see Samuel C. Florman, *Blaming Technology: The Irrational Search for Scapegoats* (New York: St. Martin's Press, 1981).

45. See also Anthony Lewis's editorial, "Time to Remember," *New York Times*, May 26, 1980, for further discussion of "growing public hostility to technology." Lewis quotes former MIT president and science advisor to the Kennedy administration Jerome B. Wiesner: "We have outrun the processes by which we make our decisions and manage our society."

46. For a detailed account of the idea of runaway technology, see Langdon Winner, *Autonomous Technology* (Cambridge, Mass.: MIT Press, 1977).

47. "Computers: The 'Software' Snarl," *Time*, August 18, 1967, 75.

48. Charles R. Dechert, "The Development of Cybernetics," in *The Social Impact of Cybernetics* (South Bend, Ind.: University of Notre Dame Press, 1966), 12.

49. This idea of a computer priesthood buds off from the notion of the technocratic elite as itself a priesthood, an idea brought home by the conveniently titled book by Ralph Lapp, *The New Priesthood* (New York: Harper and Row, 1965).

50. "The Cybernated Generation," *Time*, April 2, 1965, 84.

51. Ibid., 86.

52. Ibid., 86–87.

53. Roszak explains, "Until the mid-1970s, the prevailing public image of information technology was austere and exotic. It focused on a mysterious, highly expensive machinery that belonged in the exclusive care of trained technicians. . . . There was very little the public knew about computers that did not make the machines seem elite and intimidating" (*Cult of Information*, 135).

54. For a thorough account of gender in the configuring of technology, see Juliet Webster, *Shaping Women's Work: Gender, Employment and Information Technology* (London and New York: Addison Wesley Longman, 1996). In her discussion of the early days of women in computing, Webster quotes the following statement of women's obvious fitness for computer work: "It has been said that computer programming is the job for the future and the best programmers are intelligent girls who are good in embroidering because they have the patience and conscientiousness that is needed" (39). See also Ceruzzi, "When Computers Were Human," 237–44.

55. Florman, *Blaming Technology*, 87.

56. Jacques Vallee, *The Network Revolution: Confessions of a Computer Scientist* (Berkeley: And/Or Press, 1982), 174.

57. "Computers: The 'Software' Snarl," 76. This article also refers to programmers as "fractious fellows who delight in disdaining the button-down graces of corporate life such as wearing a necktie to work. . . . Clannish, often introverted, programmers labor over problems that demand logical thinking . . . yet defy solution by any standard of scientifically disciplined approach."

58. Jean Meynaud, *Technocracy*, trans. Paul Barnes (first published in French, 1964; New York: Free Press, 1969), 59.

59. Ibid., 295–96.
60. For a compelling history, see Colin Burke, *Information and Secrecy: Vannevar Bush, Ultra, and the Other Memex* (Metuchen, N.J.: Scarecrow Press, 1994). For a cyberpunk novel that intertwines the history of computing with secrecy, encryption, and conspiracy, see Neal Stephenson, *Cryptonomicon* (New York: Avon Books, 1999).
61. Vallee, *Network Revolution*, 17.
62. Describing the late 1960s emergence of the microcomputing subculture, Freiberger and Swaine write, "The movement was developing in the San Francisco Bay Area out of the general spirit of the times and out of an understanding by those . . . who knew something of the power of computers. They resented that such immense power rested in the hands of the few and was jealously guarded. These technological revolutionaries were actively working to overthrow the computer hegemony of IBM and the other computer companies, and to breach the 'computer priesthood' of programmers, engineers, and computer operators who controlled access to the machines" (*Fire in the Valley*, 100).
63. Nelson, *Computer Lib*, 3.
64. Brand, *Cybernetic Frontiers*, 77. See also Paul Ceruzzi, "Inventing the Personal Computer," in *The Social Shaping of Technology*, 2d ed., ed. Donald MacKenzie and Judy Wajcman (Buckingham, U.K., and Philadelphia: Open University Press, 1999), 64–86. In a thoughtful account of the calculator and electronic hobbyist subculture, Ceruzzi rejects Brand's emphasis on play (or, more precisely, on a Utopia of free information) to argue for the impact of the free market in bringing "computers to the people." I don't see these views as conflicting: play (and the Utopia of free information) opened up the ideological spaces within which personal computing came to be assembled as a general set of practices, technologies, ideals, and expectations. For a nuanced methodological account of ways of analyzing how computers and computing are "thought," how their terms of intelligibility are established, see Richard Hull, "Governing the Conduct of Computing: Computer Science, the Social Sciences and Frameworks of Computing," *Accounting, Management and Information Technology* 7, 4 (1997): 213–40.
65. "The Computer Moves In," *Time*, January 3, 1983, 16.
66. For an account of the hacker ethic, see Levy, *Hackers*.
67. Ibid., 246.
68. "The Seeds of Success," *Time*, February 15, 1982, 40.
69. "My IBM Baby," *Time*, November 19, 1965, 84–85.
70. Elizabeth Stone, "Getting Personal with Your Personal Computer," *Mademoiselle*, April 1984, 74ff.
71. "X-Rated: The Joys of CompuSex," *Time*, May 14, 1984, 83.
72. John Sculley, *Odyssey: Pepsi to Apple . . . A Journey of Adventure, Ideas, and the Future* (New York: Harper and Row, 1987), 58.
73. Ibid., 158.

74. Ibid., 178.
75. Ibid., 95 (the chart I've provided here is not exhaustive).
76. Dechert, "Development of Cybernetics," 18. For detailed analysis of the Macy conferences, see Steven Joshua Heims, *The Cybernetics Group* (Cambridge, Mass.: MIT Press, 1991); and Hayles, *How We Became Posthuman.*
77. Frank Webster and Kevin Robins, *Information Technology: A Luddite Analysis* (Norwood, N.J.: Ablex Publishing, 1986), 314.
78. Ibid., 8.
79. Stuart Ewen explains that the use of market surveys and public opinion research grew in America in the 1930s in response to the Great Depression. He cites a *New York Times* headline from April 5, 1931, "Stores Need Facts on Buying Habits." Further, he refers to an early analysis by Yale psychologist Henry Link that, well, links computers with the monitoring of public attitudes: "These ingenious devices have made it feasible to record and classify the behavior of the buying public as well as the behavior of those who serve that public on a scale heretofore impracticable"; Ewen, *PR! A Social History of Spin* (New York: Basic Books, 1996), 183–85.
80. On the spectralization of the fetish, see Slavoj Žižek, *The Plague of Fantasies* (London: Verso, 1997). Using "the making of" films that accompany big-budget motion pictures as paradigmatic cases, he writes that

> far from destroying the "fetishist" illusion, the insight into the production mechanism in fact even strengthens it, in so far as it renders palpable the gap between bodily causes and their surface-effect. . . . The same goes, more and more, for political campaign advertisements and publicity in general: where the stress was initially on the product (or candidate) itself, it then moved to the effect-image, and now shifts more and more to the making of the image (the strategy of making an advertisement is itself advertised, etc.). The paradox is—in a kind of reversal of the cliché according to which Western ideology dissimulates the production process at the expense of the final product—the production process, far from being the secret locus of the prohibited, of what cannot be shown, of what is concealed by the fetish, serves as the fetish which fascinates with its presence. (102)

81. See my argument in Dean, *Aliens in America*, chap. 2.
82. Herbert Marcuse, *One Dimensional Man: Studies in the Ideology of Advanced Industrial Society* (Boston: Beacon Press, 1964), x.
83. Ibid., 189.
84. Jürgen Habermas, *Toward a Rational Society*, trans. Jeremy J. Shapiro (Boston: Beacon Press, 1970), 111.
85. Ibid., 118.
86. Ibid., 89.
87. Marcuse, *One Dimensional Man*, 252.

88. Habermas, *Toward a Rational Society*, 113.

89. Ibid., 119.

90. See Žižek, *Ticklish Subject*, esp. chap. 6. Žižek writes, "The problem is that there is no objective scientific or other way to acquire certainty about existence and extent: it is not simply a matter of exploitative corporations or governmental agencies downplaying the dangers—there is in fact no way to establish the extent of the risk with certainty; scientists and speculators themselves are unable to provide the final answer; we are bombarded daily by new discoveries which reverse previously common sense views" (336).

91. See my discussion in Dean, *Aliens in America*.

92. Žižek, *Ticklish Subject*, 332.

4. Celebrity's Drive

1. See, for example, Allucquere Rosanne Stone, *The War of Desire and Technology at the Close of the Mechanical Age* (Cambridge, Mass.: MIT Press, 1995). Slavoj Žižek also makes this point in *The Ticklish Subject* (London: Verso, 1999).

2. For a strong collection of essays that move beyond this concern with identity, see Andrew Herman and Thomas Swiss, eds., *The World Wide Web and Contemporary Cultural Theory* (New York: Routledge, 2000).

3. Žižek, *Ticklish Subject*, 296.

4. Žižek makes this point with reference to "the well-known paradoxes of desire . . . from, 'I can't love you unless I give you up' to 'Don't give me what I ask for, because that's not *it*' " (ibid., 297).

5. Ibid.

6. Ibid., 304.

7. This discussion is informed by Slavoj Žižek's discussion of objects in *Looking Awry* (Cambridge, Mass.: MIT Press, 1991), 133–40.

8. "Surveying the Digital Future," UCLA Internet Report, www.ccp.ucla.edu.

9. My discussion here relies on Slavoj Žižek, *Tarrying with the Negative* (Durham, N.C.: Duke University Press, 1993), 196–99.

10. Ibid., 197.

11. See also Henry Krips, *Fetish: An Erotics of Culture* (Ithaca, N.Y.: Cornell University Press, 1999). Krips provides a persuasive critique of the notion of the gaze as developed in feminist film theory as well as an interesting comparison of the concept of the gaze in Barthes, Benjamin, and Lacan.

12. In her influential book, *Contested Culture: The Image, the Voice, and the Law* (Chapel Hill: University of North Caroline Press, 1991), Jane M. Gaines describes the legal development of "privacy" into "publicity" in the context of celebrities' rights "to circulate their images in public without fear of commercial piracy" (94). Moreover, she anchors her analysis of law in studies of mass culture that demonstrate how "both motion pictures and theater produced a new

kind of subject with a specially constructed public persona." Gaines describes "the developments in photographic technology and photo processing that transformed the ordinary person into a celebrity and in turn produced the celebrity as common" (184).

13. Daniel J. Boorstin, *The Image* (New York: Atheneum, 1962), 57 (italics in original). Boorstin's etymology indicates that "celebrity" was used originally to refer not to a person but to "the condition of being much talked about."

14. Žižek, *Tarrying with the Negative*, 73.

15. Consider the following statement from Kathleen Hughes: "Privacy now means that whole companies of strangers know that I, myself, am not apt to buy popcorn, although perhaps cheese and chocolate; they know if they really want to get me, offer the new Patty Griffin CD"; Hughes, "Surveillance Society," *Providence Phoenix*, January 10, 2001, available at www.alternet.org. Hughes's remark captures the proto-paranoiac dimension of being known to others.

16. Žižek locates the opposition between the subject of desire and the subject of drive in lack and surplus (*Ticklish Subject*, 304).

17. Žižek, *Tarrying with the Negative*, 197.

18. Marjorie Garber invokes a similar proto-paranoia as well as Lacan's *subject supposed to know* in her critical essay on greatness. She writes, "Greatness is an effect of decontextualization, of the decontextualizing of the sign—and of a fantasy of control, a fantasy of the *sujet supposé savoir*, of a powerful agency, divine or other. . . . Someone knows; someone—someone *else*—is in control"; Garber, *Symptoms of Culture* (New York: Routledge, 1998), 43.

19. See Žižek's discussion of the circulation of detailed databases in cyberspace (*Ticklish Subject*, 260). I rely here on his reading of Althusser: "Althusser's point is that my recognition in the interpellative call of the Other is performative in the sense that, in the very gesture of recognition, it *constitutes* (or 'posits') this big Other" (ibid.). Additionally, my account of celebrity as a technocultural mode of subjectivization responds to Žižek's claim that today's primary mode is proto-paranoiac. I'm trying to specify the sense in which we understand ourselves as "known."

20. See Slavoj Žižek's discussion of symbolic identification in "Class Struggle or Postmodernism? Yes, Please!" in *Contingency, Hegemony, Universality*, Judith Butler, Ernesto Laclau, and Slavoj Žižek (London: Verso: 2000), 116–17.

21. Joshua Gamson notes that "we live in a time when many people seem to worry that they are nobody . . . television has come to serve as a certification of somebodyness"; Gamson, *Freaks Talk Back* (Chicago: University of Chicago Press, 1998), 214.

22. Lauren Berlant, *The Queen of America Goes to Washington City* (Durham, N.C.: Duke University Press, 1997).

23. Wendy Brown, *States of Injury* (Princeton, N.J.: Princeton University Press, 1995).

24. Slavoj Žižek, *The Fragile Absolute* (London: Verso, 2000), 60.

25. See also Aida Hozic, "Making of the Unwanted Colonies: (Un)imagining Desire," in *Cultural Studies and Political Theory*, ed. Jodi Dean (Ithaca, N.Y.: Cornell University Press, 2000), 228–40.

26. The examples here come from Neal Gabler, *Life: The Movie* (New York: Vintage, 1998), 181–85.

27. Darian Leader and Judy Groves, *Introducing Lacan* (Cambridge: Icon Books, 2000), 11–13; David Macey, *Lacan in Contexts* (London: Verso, 1988), 70–71. Macey emphasizes the seminal role of the Aimee analysis for the subsequent development of Lacan's thought.

28. Boorstin touches on this point when he describes how Charles A. Lindbergh became "degraded into a celebrity" (*Image*, 66).

29. Gabler writes: "Traditionally fame had been tied, however loosely, to ability or accomplishment or office. Celebrity, on the other hand, seemed less a function of what one did than of how one was perceived" (*Life: The Movie*, 144).

30. Stuart Ewen writes, "The whole story of their success is that they come from the 'mass.' They were once unknown. In a society where conditions of anonymity fertilize the desire 'to be somebody,' the *dream of identity*, the *dream of wholeness*, is intimately woven together with the desire to be known; to be visible; to be documented, for all to see"; Ewen, *All Consuming Images* (New York: Basic Books, 1988), 94.

31. This helpful formulation comes from Krips, *Fetish*, 74. Krips's account of ideological interpellation emphasizes that "the effectiveness of the call depends not upon the precision of the terms in which it addresses individuals but rather upon the gaps in what it says. Individuals conceal from themselves the existence of such gaps by piecing out the content of the call, thus constituting for themselves a picture of what the caller wants of or for them." Moreover, Krips captures nicely the celebrity component of contemporary subjectivization when he writes: "Subjects are also led to misrecognize their active role in the production of such positions, thus preserving their sense that already before the call *they were someone in the eyes of the caller*" (74; my emphasis).

32. See also the discussion of mass publicity in terms of consumption and display, in Michael Warner, "The Mass Public and the Mass Subject," in *Habermas and the Public Sphere*, ed. Craig Calhoun (Cambridge, Mass.: MIT Press, 1997), 377–401.

33. P. David Marshall, *Celebrity and Power* (Minneapolis: University of Minnesota Press, 1997), 242. My argument is that contemporary technoculture involves a reflexivization and extension of this phenomenon. If, as Marshall argues, celebrities are complex systems of collectively held and negotiated identities and relations of power, then the increasing differentiations and demands of technoculture mean that individuals come to be subjectivized in terms of celebrity.

34. Gamson, *Freaks Talk Back*, 21.

35. Indeed, my emphasis on drive is perhaps the primary difference between my account and Warner's. Whereas Warner ("The Mass Public and the Mass Subject") is interested in the kinds of identification allowed or required by the discourse of publicity, I focus on the way in which the heterogeneous network of screens interpellates a celebrity subject. This form of subjectivization relies on neither imaginary nor symbolic identification. Instead, its entanglement in publicity is brought about through the circular movement of drive.

36. Žižek, *Ticklish Subject*, 326.

37. I make this argument in Jodi Dean, *Aliens in America: Conspiracy Culture from Outerspace to Cyberspace* (Ithaca, N.Y.: Cornell University Press, 1998).

38. Žižek writes, "[Donald] Davidson's Principle of Charity is therefore another name for the Lacanian 'big Other' as the ultimate guarantee of Truth to which we have to make reference even when we are lying or trying to deceive our partners in communication, precisely in order to be successful in our deceit" (*Fragile Absolute*, 114).

39. Žižek, *Looking Awry*, 73.

40. Alenka Zupancic considers this option in the course of her thorough analysis of Kant's discussion of the lie in its legal and ethical dimensions. She writes, "If we want to deceive another, the intention to do so is not sufficient. In other words—and this is what Kant is getting at—there is no *necessary* connection between my answer to the murderer's question and his subsequent actions. Thus, if I tell the truth, I cannot be held responsible for my friend's death. This is not only because I cannot know with absolute certainty where my friend is at the moment I am speaking, but also because I have no means of knowing how the murderer will take my answer of 'yes' or 'no,' whether he will believe me or whether he will assume I am attempting to protect my friend by lying"; Zupancic, *Ethics of the Real* (London: Verso, 2000), 47–48.

41. Žižek, *Looking Awry*, 73.

42. Ibid., 74–75.

43. Žižek, *Ticklish Subject*, 313–22.

44. Thomas Frank, *One Market under God: Extreme Capitalism, Market Populism, and the End of Economic Democracy* (New York: Doubleday, 2000), 260.

45. Žižek, *Ticklish Subject*, 368.

46. Gabler, *Life: The Movie*, 232.

47. The very phenomena of parallel universes is appearing with growing frequency: from theoretical physics to movies like *Groundhog Day*, television shows like *The X-Files*, and even some conspiracy theories, we find plots, story lines, and accounts of actions have become uncoupled from single timelines.

48. Žižek, *Ticklish Subject*, 337–38.

49. Ibid., 354.

50. I'm particularly struck by the parallel with global financial mar-

kets. Manuel Castells, *End of Millennium* (Oxford: Blackwell Publishers, 1998), describes the contemporary "global casino." He writes, "The programming and forecasting capabilities of financial management models makes it possible to colonize the future, and the interstices of the future (that is, possible alternative scenarios), selling this 'unreal estate' as property rights of the immaterial" (343). Indeed, as Castells points out, one of the more perverse effects of the emergence of forecasting technologies (especially when the speed of global telecommunications networks enables rapid dissemination of these predictions) is the way that the forecasts themselves reflexively figure into the very terrain they aim to describe.

51. Jürgen Habermas, *Between Facts and Norms*, trans. William Rehg (Cambridge, Mass.: MIT Press, 1996), 97.

52. Seyla Benhabib, "The Critique of Instrumental Reason," in *Mapping Ideology*, ed. Slavoj Žižek (London: Verso, 1994), 85.

53. Renata Salecl, "The Silence of Feminine Jouissance," in *Cogito and the Unconscious*, ed. Slavoj Žižek (Durham, N.C.: Duke University Press, 1998), 179.

54. Habermas describes popular sovereignty as "sublimated into the elusive interactions between culturally mobilized public spheres and a will-formation institutionalized according to the rule of law" (*Between Facts and Norms*, 486).

55. See William Rehg's fine introduction to Habermas, *Between Facts and Norms*. As Rehg suggests, Habermas's conception of modern law is usefully thought of as "between Rawls and Luhman" (xx).

56. Habermas, *Between Facts and Norms*, 360.

57. Ibid., 374.

58. Ibid.

59. William E. Scheuerman, "Between Radicalism and Resignation: Democratic Theory in Habermas's *Between Facts and Norms*," in *Habermas: A Critical Reader*, ed. Peter Dews (London: Blackwell, 1999), 153–77.

60. Ibid., 167.

61. Habermas, *Between Facts and Norms*, 487.

62. Ibid., 364.

63. Ibid., 375.

64. Marshall, *Celebrity and Power*, 244.

65. Habermas, *Between Facts and Norms*, 381.

66. Jürgen Habermas, *Postmetaphysical Thinking*, trans. William Mark Hohengarten (Cambridge, Mass.: MIT Press, 1992), 187.

67. Ibid., 186.

68. Žižek, *Ticklish Subject*, 373.

69. Ibid., 304.

70. Habermas, *Postmetaphysical Thinking*, 186.

71. Žižek, *Ticklish Subject*, 305.

72. Ibid., 248.

Conclusion

1. Slavoj Žižek writes, "a fantasy constitutes our desire, provides its co-ordinates; that is, it literally 'teaches us how to desire' "; Žižek, *The Plague of Fantasies* (London: Verso, 1997), 7.
2. Jürgen Habermas, *The Theory of Communicative Action*, trans. Thomas McCarthy, vols. 1 and 2 (Boston: Beacon Press, 1984, 1987). See also my discussion in Jodi Dean, *Solidarity of Strangers: Feminism after Identity Politics* (Berkeley: University of California Press, 1996).
3. Jürgen Habermas, *The Structural Transformation of the Public Sphere*, trans. Thomas Burger (Cambridge, Mass.: MIT Press, 1989), 106–7.
4. Jürgen Habermas, "Citizenship and National Identity," in *Between Facts and Norms*, trans. William Rehg (Cambridge, Mass.: MIT Press, 1996), 513.
5. Ibid., 502.
6. I should add that there are at least two complicating factors to be included here—Freemasonry and the market. Both asserted an abstract form of public that transcended national boundaries to the extent that it was based on laws of reason. As I discuss in chap. 1, in Freemasonry this version of a public was always bounded by the secret. The secret enabled Freemasonry to present itself as a public; it never claimed to be fully open in the sense of including everyone or in establishing itself as a framework for legal and political recognition. With respect to the market, as I argue throughout this book, the ideological presentation of the market in terms of the public is precisely the problem that the concept of publicity poses for democratic theory.
7. Habermas, "Citizenship and National Identity," 499.
8. Jürgen Habermas, "Popular Sovereignty as Procedure," in *Between Facts and Norms*, 475.
9. See Paul A. Passavant, *No Escape: Freedom of Speech and the Paradox of Rights* (New York: New York University Press, 2002).
10. Paul A. Passavant, "The Governmentality of Discussion," in *Cultural Studies and Political Theory*, ed. Jodi Dean (Ithaca, N.Y.: Cornell University Press, 2000), 119.
11. Ibid., 125.
12. See the account of the unfeasibility of national monetary policies by Manuel Castells, *The Information Age: Economy, Society, and Culture* (Oxford: Blackwell Publishers, 1996), 20. On interconnectivity issues challenging national boundaries, see Herbert Ungerer, "Access Issues under EU Regulation and Antitrust Law: The Case of Telecommunications and Internet Markets," *Harvard Journal of Convergence* 1 (winter 2001). Available at http://information. harvard.edu/journal/.
13. Habermas, "Citizenship and National Identity," 514.
14. Habermas, *Between Facts and Norms*, 361.
15. Ibid., 360.

16. Dan Schiller, *Digital Capitalism: Networking the Global Market System* (Cambridge, Mass.: MIT Press, 2000).

17. Perhaps the most thorough account of capitalism in its information mode of development comes from Manuel Castells, *The Rise of the Network Society* (Oxford, U.K.: Blackwell Publishers, 1996).

18. Robert W. McChesney, "So Much for the Magic of Technology and the Free Market," in *The World Wide Web and Contemporary Cultural Theory*, ed. Andrew Herman and Thomas Swiss (New York: Routledge, 2000), 7.

19. See also Robert W. McChesney, *Rich Media, Poor Democracy: Communication Politics in Dubious Times* (New York: New Press, 1999). McChesney's data are extremely helpful. His analysis, however, continues to rely on the opposition between publicity and secrecy that I'm calling into question. Thus, in his critique of the impact of the market on media, he argues: "the policies that put the system in place in our name and with our monies have been made in secret, without our informed consent" (xxiii). Still, he goes beyond most media analyses in his politicization of the market basis of contemporary communications.

20. See the testimony of Jerry Berman, Executive Director, and Alan B. Davidson, Associate Director, Center for Democracy and Technology, "ICANN: Towards Domain Name Administration in the Public Interest," before the House Committee on Energy and Commerce, Subcommittee on Telecommunications, February 8, 2001. Available at http://www.cdt.org/testimony/010208davidson.shtml.

21. See a discussion of psychosis and the inability to create new metaphors in Bruce Fink, *A Clinical Introduction to Lacanian Psychoanalysis* (Cambridge: Harvard University Press, 1997), 90–94.

22. See also Schiller's account of digital capital, the "march to the market," and the corresponding redistribution of wealth in the 1990s (*Digital Capitalism*).

23. This comes from Slavoj Žižek, "The Spectre of Ideology," in *Mapping Ideology*, ed. Slavoj Žižek (London: Verso, 1994), 1.

24. Kathy Foley, "Porn: Not What It Used to Be," *Nua Internet Surveys and Nua Knowledge News*, issue 1, no. 140 (August 21, 2000). Available at www.nua.ie.

25. Paul Passavant explained this point to me with reference to Justice Scalia's opinion in *Bush V. Gore*. Concurring with the majority decision to order a stay of the recounts of Florida ballots following the election of 2000, Scalia focuses on the question of irremediable harm should the recounts proceed. Granting the stay thus presumes harm. Presuming harm to Bush means presuming that he is president, but that is precisely what is in question. See *Bush V. Gore* U.S. Lexis 8277 (2000).

26. See Slavoj Žižek, "Class Struggle or Postmodernism? Yes, Please!" in *Contingency, Hegemony, Universality*, Judith Butler, Ernesto Laclau, and Slavoj Žižek (London: Verso, 2000). In his response to La-

clau, Žižek emphasizes the double impossibility at work in the notion of antagonism. Not only is Society impossible, but representing this impossibility is impossible. This is where ideological fantasy come in—as a representation both of the impossible fullness of society and of that which makes its fullness impossible. Žižek writes: "When this very *impossibility* is represented in a positive element, inherent impossibility is changed into an external obstacle. 'Ideology' is also the name for the guarantee that *the negativity which prevents Society from achieving its fullness does actually exist*, that it has a positive existence in the guise of a big Other who pulls the strings of social life. . . . In short, the basic operation of ideology is not only the dehistoricizing gesture of transforming an empirical obstacle into the eternal condition (women, Blacks . . . are by nature subordinated, etc.), but also the *opposite* gesture of transposing the a priori closure/impossibility of a field into an empirical obstacle" (100–101; italics in original).

27. Christopher Hitchens, "Just an Oversight," *The Nation*, March 30, 2000.

28. How exactly the dumping of information is deployed politically is contingent. That is to say, the injunction to know works in more than one direction. If voters are typically chastised for being uninformed, for not going out and doing their homework, then politicians or academics who aren't sufficiently succinct are scolded in the other direction—for giving too much information, for being too complicated, for wasting people's time by not properly summarizing the issues, and so forth. Invocations of the public-supposed-to-know, in other words, oscillate between a public that is supposed to know everything and a public that doesn't have time to know everything but needs to know some things—in fact, it needs "just enough" information. But, of course, this "just enough" is thoroughly ideological, a designator of its own impossibility.

29. Slavoj Žižek, *The Ticklish Subject* (London: Verso, 1999), 338.

30. William Connolly, *Why I'm Not a Secularist* (Minneapolis: University of Minnesota Press, 1999).

31. William Connolly, *The Ethos of Pluralization* (Minneapolis: University of Minnesota Press, 1995), xx.

32. Michael Hardt and Antonio Negri, *Empire* (Cambridge: Harvard University Press, 2000).

33. I am indebted to Paul Passavant for making this point clear to me. For a more developed account of the problem of representation in Hardt and Negri, *Empire*, see Paul A. Passavant and Jodi Dean, "Representation and the Event," *Theory and Event* (2001).

34. Slavoj Žižek, "The Matrix, or The Two Sides of Perversion," available at http://www.nettime.org/nettime.w3archive/199912/msg00019.html.

35. I was fortunate enough to be invited to their workshop "Competing Realities: The Social Lives of Issues on and off the Web," Budapest, July 23–28, 2001.

36. Richard Rogers, *Four Instruments for the Information Society*, manuscript.

37. Richard Rogers and Noortje Marres, "French Scandals on the Web, and on the Streets: A Small Experiment in Stretching the Limits of Reported Reality," manuscript.

38. See Noortje Marres and Richard Rogers, "Depluralising the Web, Repluralising Public Debate. The Case of the GM Food Debate on the Web," in *Preferred Placement: Knowledge Politics on the Web*, ed. Richard Rogers (Maastricht, The Netherlands: Jan van Eyck Editions, 2000), 113–36.

39. My thinking here is stimulated by Castells's observation that "*The most fundamental transformation of relationships of experience in the Information Age is their transition to a pattern of social interaction constructed, primarily, by the actual experience of the relationship*. Nowadays, people produce forms of sociability, rather than follow models of behavior"; Manuel Castells, *End of Millennium* (Oxford: Blackwell Publishers, 1998), 349 (italics in original). My appeal to democratic configurations, then, endeavors to highlight the way people produce democratic possibilities that may challenge communicative capitalism. I am not seeking to provide a model of democratic governance or behavior.

40. See Passavant's discussion of John Stuart Mill and the landscape of rights claiming in *No Escape*.

41. Castells designates these information age cleavages as: "first, the internal fragmentation of labor between informational producers and replaceable generic labor. Secondly, the social exclusion of a significant segment of society made up of discarded individuals whose value as workers/consumers is used up, and whose relevance as people is ignored. And, thirdly, the separation between the market logic of global networks of capital flows and the human experience of workers' lives" (*End of Millennium*, 346).

42. Aida Hozic, "Hollywood, Violence, and the Construction of War Zones," presented at the International Studies Association Annual Meeting, Los Angeles, March 14–18, 2000.

Index

absolutist state, 24–30, 44, 181n20
access, 2–3, 15, 40, 44, 85, 190n16;
    conspiracy theory and, 12, 72–73
action, 5–7, 25, 153, 163–65; audience
    and, 148–49; celebrity and, 124–25;
    communicative, 153; conspiracy
    theory and, 56–57; multitude and,
    165–66; purposive-rational, 107–8
activism, 144, 163, 168–69, 174
advertising, 3–4, 36–39, 100–102,
    110–11, 190–91n23
Alphaville (Godard), 91
Althusser, Louis, 197n19
American dream, 87–89, 190n22
appearances, 5, 132, 144
Apple 1984 commercial, 80, 83–86
audience, 33–34, 144, 145; postconven-
    tional ego and, 146–47, 148–49; pub-
    lic as, 138, 141, 144
authority, 23–24, 130, 133–38, 162–63

Bagehot, Walter, 156
Baillet, Adrien, 182n31
Bailyn, Bernard, 55
banality, 128–29
Bantam, Jeremy, 154
Baty, S. Paige, 188n63
belief, 5–7, 11, 52, 118, 131; material-
    ization of, 5–7, 38–40, 43–45, 69,
    166; technology's role, 39–40, 48, 69,
    115, 142, 149–50, 160. *See also* Pub-
    lic-supposed-to-believe
Bell, Daniel, 92
Benhabib, Seyla, 138, 184n54
Bentham, Jeremy, 11, 16–23, 25, 27,
    39–40, 43–44, 64, 117, 131, 180n8
Berlant, Lauren, 124, 183–84n47
Between Facts and Norms (Habermas),
    152, 154
Big Brother, 71, 80, 83–86, 131. *See
    also* Little Brothers

Big Brother (game show), 82, 127
Bok, Sisela, 9–10, 182n36
Boorstin, Daniel J., 122, 197n13
boundaries, 154, 159
bourgeoisie, 23, 28–29, 181n20
Boys Don't Cry, 50
Brand, Stewart, 88, 94, 98, 194n64
Brautigan, Richard, 89
Bremer, Arthur, 125
Brown, Wendy, 124
Buchstein, Hubertus, 2
Buckley, William F., 66
Buck-Morss, Susan, 177n5
Burn Rate (Wolff), 5–6
Bush, George W., 160–61

capitalism, 151; Other and, 137–38;
    power of, 142–44; resilience of,
    105–6. *See also* Communicative cap-
    italism
Castells, Manuel, 177n7, 200n50,
    204n39
causality, 60–61
celebrity, 12–13, 17, 135, 165, 197n13,
    198nn29, 31; action and, 124–25; as
    banality, 128–29; contingency and,
    126–29; desire to be known, 12–13,
    122–24, 127, 129, 142, 198n30; drive
    and, 121–26; hysteria/perversion
    and, 117–18; as mode of subjec-
    tivization, 114, 124, 128, 162,
    199n35; obscenity and, 119–21;
    127–28; personality, 125–26; post-
    conventional ego and, 146–47; World
    Wide Web and, 126–27
center-periphery model, 36, 141–42,
    152
certainty/uncertainty, 21, 44, 47, 117,
    131–32
Ceruzzi, Paul E., 190n15, 194n64
Chapman, Mark David, 125

citizens, 35–37, 69, 153. *See also* Identity; Subject
Clinton, Hillary Rodham, 64–69, 71–72
command to reveal, 24, 68–69
committees, ethical, 111–12
communication: capitalist technoculture and, 142–44; as fetish, 109–10; public as, 140–41, 157; reflexivization of, 111, 138–45, 147–50
communicative capitalism, 3–4, 79–80, 117–19, 148; communicative rationality and, 108–10; competing worldviews, 7–8; contestation of, 172–73; periods of consolidation, 168–69. *See also* Capitalism
communicative drive, 138–45, 149–50
communicative rationality, 107–11, 139, 159
communicative reflection, 110–12, 119
computer liberation, 80, 88–92
computers, 190n15; advertising focus, 80, 83–86, 100–102; as American dream, 87–89, 190n22; inescapability of, 92–93; play and, 95–100, 125, 194n64; programmers, 80–82, 95–98, 193nn49, 54, 57, 194n62; sexuality and, 99–100; as tool of democracy, 2, 100–102
Connolly, William, 58, 60, 165, 171
conscience, 25–26, 32
consensuality, 52–53
conspiracy theory, 48; academic accounts, 49–50; access and, 12, 72–73; American history of, 54–57; changes in meaning of, 70–71; command to reveal, 68–69; communicative drive and, 149–50; as critical theory, 51–53; criticism of, 61–62; Declaration of Independence as, 54–55, 71; exclusion, 58–64, 77–78; fears of obsession, 57–64; information and, 54, 70–72; judgment and, 63–64; literal interpretation of, 49–54; methodology, 52; outsider status, 51, 58, 61–62; as pathological, 49, 51–52, 60–61; plot, 49–51, 188n63; pluralism and, 58–61; power and, 50, 53–54, 58; public split and, 61–69, 73, 78; rationality and, 55–56, 62–63, 68, 70–71; style, 49–50, 64; World Wide Web and, 69–78. *See also* Suspicion
Constitution, U.S., 155
consumerism, 36–42, 88, 104
content, 85, 128–29, 142

contestation, 9–10, 18, 59, 162–63, 173–75; of communicative capitalism, 172–73; World Wide Web as site of, 166–72
contingency, 126–29, 165
corporations, 101–3
corruption, 55–56
criminality, 125–26
critical-rational judgment, 37
critical theory, 52, 152, 163; drive and, 138–39
criticism, 23, 28, 110–11; consumer-oriented, 36–42
Critique and Crisis (Koselleck), 24
Critique of Pure Reason (Kant), 33
cyberia, 158, 166–67
cybernetics, 94, 103
cyberspace, opacity of, 122–24. *See also* World Wide Web
cynicism, 4–5, 7, 38–39, 119

Dechert, Charles, 90
Declaration of Independence, 54–55, 71
democracy: computers as tool of, 2, 100–102; contestation and, 171–75; corporations as vehicles for, 102–3; deliberative, 3, 12, 81, 139, 153; fantasy of unity, 9–10, 34, 43, 48, 59, 77, 151; markets, equation with, 157–58; neo-democracies, 14, 170–75; potential, 10–12, 15, 17–18, 44, 151, 166, 183n41, 204n4; procedural components, 154–56; two-track model of, 141–42
depersonalization, 90–92
Descartes, René, 182n31
desire to be known, 122–24, 124, 127, 129, 198n30
desiring subject, 10–13, 48, 69, 115–17, 121
Disch, Lisa, 43
discourse, 74–77, 139, 155–56, 184n54
discovery, 126
domain names, 158–59
domestic sphere, 30–32, 145
drive, 12–13, 115–17; celebrity and, 121–26; communicative, 138–45, 149–50; critical theory and, 138–39
Dyson, Esther, 72–73

ECHELON, 161–62
economy, signifying, 116–17
economy of desire, 129–30
efficiency, 105–8; symbolic, 129–38, 146, 158, 161
ego, 133–38, 145–59

Empire, 166
ENIGMA, 97
enjoyment, 21–22, 40–41, 47, 49, 137;
    acceptance of capitalist exploitation,
    105–6; computers and, 95–100, 125;
    drive and, 116–17; father function
    and, 134–35
Enlightenment, 16, 24, 31, 55–56
entertainment, 4, 15, 20–21
entertainment culture, 12, 45, 118
Essay on Political Tactics (Bentham), 16
ethnocentrism, 154
Ewen, Stuart, 195n79, 198n30
exceptionality, 25–26, 28, 33
excess, 74, 123
exclusion, 45, 58–64, 77–78, 177n7,
    179n2, 204n41
experts, 40, 110–12, 163; technocracy
    and, 90–92, 94–95, 192n43

false consciousness, 4–5, 7
fantasy, 7–8, 17, 46, 178n14, 201n1; of
    unity, 9–10, 34, 43, 48, 59, 77, 151
father function, 133–38, 178n14
Ferkiss, Victor, 90
fetishism, 7, 11, 109–10, 172, 195n80
Fineman, Howard, 73–74, 187n61
First Amendment, 155, 184n54
Fischer, Frank, 191–92n35
Foucault, Michel, 178–79n18
Frank, Thomas, 135
Frankfurt school, 104, 138
Fraser, Nancy, 36, 183n38
freedom, 12, 25–26, 32–33, 110
Freemasonry, 17, 24–31, 44, 145,
    182n31, 201n6; judgment and,
    27–28; moral coercion, 26–27; ra-
    tionality and, 29–30
free speech, 155–56
French Revolution, 56, 180n15
Freud, Sigmund, 133–34, 178n14
Friedman, Thomas L., 189n7
Fuller, Buckminster, 89
Furet, François, 56–57, 180n15

Gabler, Neal, 135
Gaines, Jane M., 196–97n12
Gamson, Joshua, 198n21
Garber, Marjorie, 197n18
Garfinkel, Simson, 81–82
Gates, Bill, 82
gaze, 23, 121–24, 196n11
Genealogy of Morals, The (Nietzsche),
    116–17
globalization, 119, 151, 156–59, 161,
    199–200n50; impact on world's peo-
    ples, 3–4, 7–8, 80, 177n7

global top-level domains (gTLDs),
    158–59
Godard, Jean-Luc, 91
Gore, Al, 160
government, 18–20, 156, 165–66. *See
    also* Absolutist state; Nation-state;
    Sovereignty
Grossman, Wendy M., 187n59
guilt, 21–22, 42

Habermas, Jürgen, 2, 23–24, 40, 69, 81,
    183nn38, 41, 199n54; communica-
    tion, view of, 106–8, 110–11, 138,
    145; ego identity, view of, 145–59;
    Freemasonry, account of, 17, 31–34;
    publicity, view of, 23–24; universal-
    ity, view of, 152–59; versions of pub-
    lic sphere, 36–38
hackers, 81, 99
Hardt, Michael, 80, 165–66
Harmon, Amy, 74
Hayles, N. Katherine, 190n16
hegemony, 164, 172–73
Hitchens, Christopher, 161–62
Hobbes, Thomas, 24, 29
Hofstadter, Richard, 49, 61–62
Hollywood Stock Exchange, 126
Hozic, Aida, 172, 182–83n37
Hughes, Kathleen, 197n15
hysteria, 117–18, 126, 149–50

IBM, 98
ICANN (Internet Corporation for As-
    signed Names and Numbers), 158–59
identity, 114–15; national, 155–56;
    postconventional, 145–49
identity politics, 124, 128
ideology: publicity as, 4–8, 17, 34–42,
    114, 161; of technocracy, 103–6; of
    technoculture, 4–8, 81, 107–10
ideology critique, 4–9, 151
Illuminati, 26, 31
inclusion, 154, 173
independent media movement, 144
individuality, 92, 128
"Industrial Society and Its Future"
    (Kaczynski), 83
information, 88, 110, 130, 151; capital-
    ist technoculture and, 142–44; com-
    municative exchange as, 141; con-
    spiracy theory and, 54, 70–72;
    judgment and, 19–21; obligation to
    be informed, 12, 15–16, 34–36, 40,
    52, 69, 203n28; obscenity and,
    120–21; presumed value of, 34–35;
    suspicion and, 47–48. *See also* Ac-
    cess

information age, 34–35, 47–48
institutions, 167–68, 171. *See also*
 Zero institution
interest groups, 37, 58
interiority, 25, 32, 181n20
Internet. *See* World Wide Web
intersubjective network, 129–38
issue networks, 169–75, 172–73, 174–75

Jobs, Steve, 99, 100–102
Johnson, Stephen, 186n62
jouissance, 49, 117, 137, 184n48. *See
 also* Enjoyment
judgment, 25, 31; conspiracy theory
 and, 63–64; Freemasonry and, 27–28;
 three classes of public, 19–23

Kaczynski, Theodore, 83, 125
Kant, Immanuel, 32–33, 132–33,
 199n40
Kennedy, John F., 91
knowledge, 5–6, 35, 85, 110. *See also*
 Public-supposed-to-know
Koch, Hugo, 97
Koselleck, Reinhart, 17, 23–29, 31,
 181n20
Krips, Henry, 196n11, 198n31

Lacan, Jacques, 125–26, 132, 179n6,
 180n13, 198n27
Lacanian theory, 5, 115–16
Laclau, Ernesto, 178n13
law, 22–29, 44, 140, 180n8
legal system, 140–42
legitimation, 144, 152–53
Lévi-Strauss, Claude, 167
Lewis, Anthony, 193n45
Lipset, Seymour Martin, 59–60
literary public, 28–32
Little Brothers, 79, 82–83, 114, 119,
 148, 188n2, 189n7; attack on Big
 Brother, 83–86
Locke, John, 25, 28
Lola Rennt, 130, 135–38

Macey, David, 198n27
Maier, Pauline, 54–55
Marcuse, Herbert, 81, 104–10
marginalized people, 61–62, 152
market, 5, 110, 135, 157–58, 201n6
Marres, Noortje, 169–70
Marshall, P. David, 128, 144, 198n33
Marxism, 4, 105–6
MasterCard ad campaign, 119–21
materialization: of belief, 5–7, 38–40,
 43–45, 69, 166; of publicity, 2,
 11–12, 18, 151, 161, 165

Matrix, The, 164–65, 170
matrix of publicity and secrecy, 1, 4,
 16–17, 48, 151–52, 159–64, 170
McChesney, Robert, 157–58, 202n19
McLuhan, Marshall, 89
McNamara, Robert S., 91
McVeigh, Timothy, 125
media, 3, 34, 37, 45, 144; self-criticism, 38–40, 110–11
Meynaud, Jean, 97
moral law, 17, 24–28, 32, 44
Moses and Monotheism (Freud),
 133–34
Mouffe, Chantal, 178n13
multitude, 165–66

nation-state, 153–59, 171; national discourse, 155–56; as zero institution,
 167–68
Negri, Antonio, 80, 165–66
Nelson, Ted, 88, 91, 94, 98
neo-democracies, 14, 170–75
netlocator software, 169–70
Network Revolution, The (Vallee), 96
networks: issue networks, 169–75;
 public sphere as, 140–41. *See also*
 Communication; Communicative
 capitalism
"New World Dawns, A" (Rosenblatt),
 87
Nietzsche, Friedrich, 116–17
normativity, 2–3, 81, 139–40, 143–44,
 153
Nye, Joseph, 35

O'Brien, Cathy, 49
obscenity, 119–21, 127–28, 171–72
Oedipus complex, 133, 135
one-dimensional society, 104–5
Other, 33–34, 41–42, 124, 161, 180n13,
 197n19, 199n38, 203n26; capital as,
 137–38; drive and, 116–17; symbolic
 efficiency and, 132, 134, 136–37; validity of self and, 146–47
outsider status, 51, 58, 61–62
Owens, William, 35

Packard, Vance, 92
paranoia, 60–61, 186n40, 197nn15, 18,
 19
"Paranoid Style in American Politics,
 The" (Hofstadter), 49
Passavant, Paul, 155–56, 202n25
pathology, 49, 51–52
People's Computer Company, 88
perversion, 117–18, 126
Peters, Bernard, 141–42

Pipes, Daniel, 59, 62, 67
plot, 49–51, 188n63
pluralism, 55, 58–61, 63–64, 165, 186n33
political antagonism. *See* Contestation
politics, 3–4, 24, 48; impact of Web, 73–76; role of public, 140–42
Post, Jerold M., 49–50, 60–62, 186n40
postconventional identity, 145–49
postmodernity, 8–9
power, 10, 29, 35, 173–74; capitalist technoculture and, 142–44; conspiracy theory and, 50, 53–54, 58; obscenity as, 171–72; technoculture as formation, 80, 112–13
presidential election of 2000, 160–61, 202n25
"priceless" commercials, 119–22, 127
principle of charity, 132, 199n38
privacy, 45, 71–72, 145, 187n59, 196–97n12, 197n15
proceduralism, 59–60
programmers, 80–82, 95–98, 193n49, 193nn49, 54, 57, 194n62
public: as audience, 138, 141, 144; as conspiracy theorists, 48–49; contestability of, 162–63; legitimizing role, 152–53; literary, 28–32; as network, 140–41, 157; as nonexistent, 41–43, 46, 77, 122, 161; openness of, 162–63; political role of, 140–42; production of, 10–11, 22, 45, 122; three classes of, 19–23, 66. *See also* Right to know
publicity, 1–2; action and, 5–7; aspirational quality of, 152–59; conspiracy theory and, 53, 62, 68; constitutive dimension, 16–17, 24; consumer-oriented, 36–42; as desiring subject, 10–11; as form of control, 23–24; historical dimension of, 17, 23; ideals of, 2–4, 77–78, 81, 151; as ideology, 4–8, 17, 34–42, 114; law of, 22–23; limit of, 16, 42, 46, 117; materialization of, 2, 11–12, 18, 151, 161, 165; norms of, 2–3, 81; sovereign and, 30, 33; as system of distrust, 10–11, 17–23, 33, 44–45, 47, 53, 62, 68, 117, 131, 159
public opinion, 15, 19, 23, 25, 28–29, 33–34, 46, 141, 143, 180n8
public relations, 36–37
public sphere, 42, 153, 183n38; as cosmopolitan, 153–54; globalization and, 156–57; Habermas's view, 36–38; nation-state and, 153–54, 159; neo-democracies as, 170–75

public split, 11, 16–24, 39–40, 43–44, 117; conspiracy theory and, 48, 61–69, 73, 78; nation-state and, 154, 159
public-supposed-not-to-know, 41–42, 65–66
public-supposed-to-believe, 18–23, 31, 45, 117, 131, 160, 180n8; conspiracy theory and, 61, 65–66, 73, 78; critical/consumerist orientation, 39–40; World Wide Web and, 73–74, 78. *See also* Belief
public-supposed-to-know, 18–23, 31, 45, 123, 165, 179–80n6, 180n8, 203n28; conspiracy theory and, 61, 65–66, 68–69, 73; critical/consumerist orientation and, 39–40; drive and, 115, 117; World Wide Web and, 73–74, 78
public tribunal, 18, 20, 33–34, 37. *See also* Public-supposed-to-know
purposive-rational action, 107–8

Raab, Earl, 59–60
rationality, 12, 60, 174, 201n6; communicative, 107–11, 139, 159; conspiracy theory and, 55–56, 62–63, 68, 70–71; Freemasonry and, 29–30; instrumental, 109, 112; opinions of others and, 33–34; secrecy and, 17, 23–24, 28, 30–31; technocracy as, 105–7
realist political theory, 141–42
reality, 7–8, 82
recursive validation, 184n54
reflection, 32–34, 81; communicative, 110–12, 119
reflexivization, 142, 144, 198n33; of authority, 162–63; of communication, 111, 138–45, 147–50; of communicative drive, 149–50; of drive, 117; symbolic efficiency and, 138
Rehg, William, 200n55
representation, 166
Richtel, Matt, 189n6
Ricoeur, Paul, 52
rights, national discourse of, 155–56
right to know, 15, 18, 34, 41, 43, 68, 81, 118, 122, 151–52, 182n36; celebrity and, 122, 130
risk society theory, 111, 146
Robbins, Bruce, 183n38
Roberts, Ed, 189n12
Robins, Kevin, 104
Robins, Robert S., 49–50, 60–62, 186n40
Rogers, Richard, 169–70

Rogin, Michael, 59
Rosenblatt, Roger, 87, 109
Rosicrucians, 181–82n31
Roszak, Theodore, 88–89, 192n43, 193n53
Rousseau, Jean-Jacques, 180n8
R U HOT OR NOT, 125–26
runaway technology, 93–95, 102, 107
Rushkoff, Douglas, 38

Salecl, Renata, 139–40
Salvaggio, Jerry L., 190–91n23
Sassen, Saskia, 3
Scalia, Antonin, 202n25
Schattschneider, E. E., 186n33
Scheuerman, William, 141–42, 183n40
Schiller, Dan, 157
scoop, 12, 118–19, 129, 165
Sculley, John, 100–101
search for information, 12, 15–16, 34–36, 40, 52, 69, 115
secrecy, 1–2, 159, 202n19; command to reveal, 68–69; economies of, 117, 129; as form, 42–43, 48, 117; freedom as, 25–26; government by, 18–20; historical context, 23–24; political antagonism as, 9–10; programmers and, 96–98; public split and, 20–23; reason and, 17, 23–24, 28, 30–31; sovereignty and, 17, 26–31
secret societies, 181–82n31. See also Freemasonry; Illuminati
Sedgwick, Eve Kosofsky, 52
Segal, George, 86, 109
sexuality, 99–100, 156167–168
Shepard, Nolan E., 192n41
silence, 119, 149–50
Simmel, Georg, 10, 178n16, 179n2
Smith, Howard, 191n35
Smyth, William H., 191n35
Social Science Research Council, 92
Solomon, Lauren, 189n12
Solomon, Les, 189n12
sovereignty, 17, 24–25, 33, 44; popular, 154–55, 199n54; secrecy and, 17, 26–31. See also Absolutist state
Soviet Union, 103–4
Spacewar, 98
spatiality, 44–45, 141–42
Stewart, Kathleen, 47
Structural Transformation of the Public Sphere (Habermas), 24, 145, 152, 153, 183nn38, 41
style, 49–50, 64
subject: as content, 128–29; desiring, 10–13, 48, 69, 115–17, 121; Hobbes-

ian, 24–25; as object, 25, 114; orientation to audience, 33–34; postconventional ego, 149–50; self-recognition, 122–23; split, 24–25; suspicious, 33, 48–49, 57–58. See also Celebrity
subjectivity, 8–9, 147; celebrity as form of, 114, 124, 128, 162, 199n35; in cyberspace, 8, 122–23; economy of, 12–13; Other and, 41–42; silence and, 149–50
subject supposed to know, 179–80n6
surveillance, 13, 15, 45, 161–62, 189n6. See also Big Brother; Little Brothers
suspicion, 11, 12, 26, 52, 151–52, 159–60; guilt and, 21–22; information and, 47–48
suspicious subject, 33, 48–49, 57–58
symbolic efficiency, 129–38, 146, 158, 161; father function and, 133–38

technocracy, 80, 191n35, 192n37; experts, 90–92, 94–95, 192n43; failures, 93–95; as ideological, 103–6; as rational, 105–7; systemic analysis, 106–8
technoculture, 2–3; anxieties, 71–73, 76–77, 148; command to reveal and, 68–69; ideology of, 4–8, 81, 107–10; power and, 80, 112–13, 142–44; search for information, 12, 15–16, 34–36, 40, 52, 69. See also World Wide Web
technology: role in belief, 48, 69, 115, 142, 149–50, 160; runaway, 93–95, 102, 107
technopopulism, 89
totality, 7–8
Totem and Taboo (Freud), 133–34, 178n14
Toynbee, Arnold, 92–93
Trance Formation in America (O'Brien), 49
transparency, 32–34, 37, 106, 123, 158; of power, 173–74
trust, 18, 19, 111, 118, 131
truth, 132–33
Tumminia, Diana, 186–87n46
Turing, Alan, 97
Turner, Patricia, 186n40
Tykwer, Tom, 135–38

Unabomber, 83, 125
unity, fantasy of, 9–10, 34, 43, 48, 59, 77, 151
universality, 9, 29, 152–59

validity, 139–40, 146–47
Vallee, Jacques, 96
Veblen, Thorstein, 191n35
victimization, 124–25

Webster, Frank, 104
Webster, Juliet, 193n54
Whig theory, 55–56
will formation, 2, 154–56
Wolff, Michael, 5–6
Wood, Gordon, 55–56
World Trade Organization, 168
World Wide Web, 69–78, 156; celebrity and, 126–27; changes in discourse of, 74–77; identity and, 114–15; political impact of, 73–76; as site of contestation, 166–71; as threat to ideal of public, 77–78; users as vulnerable, 75–77; as zero institution, 167–68, 171
Wozniak, Steve, 99

Yates, Frances A., 181n31

zero institution, 167–68, 171
Žižek, Slavoj, 4–8, 11, 17, 38, 41–42, 49–50, 82, 85, 149, 171, 178n13, 179n1, 180n13, 184n48, 196n90, 199n38, 202–3n26; on decisions, 163–64; drive, view of, 115–17, 121–23; nation, view of, 167; reflexivity, view of, 147; symbolic efficiency, view of, 130–38; on trust, 111
Zupancic, Alenka, 199n40